C-4800   CAREER EXAMINATION SERIES

This is your
PASSBOOK for...

Promotion Opportunities in Transportation Management

Test Preparation Study Guide
Questions & Answers

COPYRIGHT NOTICE

This book is SOLELY intended for, is sold ONLY to, and its use is RESTRICTED to individual, bona fide applicants or candidates who qualify by virtue of having seriously filed applications for appropriate license, certificate, professional and/or promotional advancement, higher school matriculation, scholarship, or other legitimate requirements of education and/or governmental authorities.

This book is NOT intended for use, class instruction, tutoring, training, duplication, copying, reprinting, excerption, or adaptation, etc., by:

1) Other publishers
2) Proprietors and/or Instructors of "Coaching" and/or Preparatory Courses
3) Personnel and/or Training Divisions of commercial, industrial, and governmental organizations
4) Schools, colleges, or universities and/or their departments and staffs, including teachers and other personnel
5) Testing Agencies or Bureaus
6) Study groups which seek by the purchase of a single volume to copy and/or duplicate and/or adapt this material for use by the group as a whole without having purchased individual volumes for each of the members of the group
7) Et al.

Such persons would be in violation of appropriate Federal and State statutes.

PROVISION OF LICENSING AGREEMENTS – Recognized educational, commercial, industrial, and governmental institutions and organizations, and others legitimately engaged in educational pursuits, including training, testing, and measurement activities, may address request for a licensing agreement to the copyright owners, who will determine whether, and under what conditions, including fees and charges, the materials in this book may be used them. In other words, a licensing facility exists for the legitimate use of the material in this book on other than an individual basis. However, it is asseverated and affirmed here that the material in this book CANNOT be used without the receipt of the express permission of such a licensing agreement from the Publishers. Inquiries re licensing should be addressed to the company, attention rights and permissions department.

All rights reserved, including the right of reproduction in whole or in part, in any form or by any means, electronic or mechanical, including photocopying, recording, or by any information storage and retrieval system, without permission in writing from the Publisher.

Copyright © 2025 by
National Learning Corporation

212 Michael Drive, Syosset, NY 11791
(516) 921-8888 • www.passbooks.com
E-mail: info@passbooks.com

PASSBOOK® SERIES

THE *PASSBOOK® SERIES* has been created to prepare applicants and candidates for the ultimate academic battlefield – the examination room.

At some time in our lives, each and every one of us may be required to take an examination – for validation, matriculation, admission, qualification, registration, certification, or licensure.

Based on the assumption that every applicant or candidate has met the basic formal educational standards, has taken the required number of courses, and read the necessary texts, the *PASSBOOK® SERIES* furnishes the one special preparation which may assure passing with confidence, instead of failing with insecurity. Examination questions – together with answers – are furnished as the basic vehicle for study so that the mysteries of the examination and its compounding difficulties may be eliminated or diminished by a sure method.

This book is meant to help you pass your examination provided that you qualify and are serious in your objective.

The entire field is reviewed through the huge store of content information which is succinctly presented through a provocative and challenging approach – the question-and-answer method.

A climate of success is established by furnishing the correct answers at the end of each test.

You soon learn to recognize types of questions, forms of questions, and patterns of questioning. You may even begin to anticipate expected outcomes.

You perceive that many questions are repeated or adapted so that you can gain acute insights, which may enable you to score many sure points.

You learn how to confront new questions, or types of questions, and to attack them confidently and work out the correct answers.

You note objectives and emphases, and recognize pitfalls and dangers, so that you may make positive educational adjustments.

Moreover, you are kept fully informed in relation to new concepts, methods, practices, and directions in the field.

You discover that you are actually taking the examination all the time: you are preparing for the examination by "taking" an examination, not by reading extraneous and/or supererogatory textbooks.

In short, this PASSBOOK®, used directedly, should be an important factor in helping you to pass your test.

PROMOTION OPPORTUNITIES IN TRANSPORTATION MANAGEMENT

TEST

The written test is designed to test for knowledge, skills, and/or abilities in such areas as:

1. **Effectively interacting with others** - These questions test candidates' knowledge of techniques used to interact effectively with a variety of individuals, to provide information about topics of concern, to publicize or clarify agency programs or policies, and to negotiate conflicts or resolve complaints.
2. **Preparing reports and official documents** - These questions test for the ability to prepare reports and other official documents for use within and among governmental agencies, in legal or regulatory settings, or for dissemination to the public. Some questions test for a knowledge of correct grammar, usage, punctuation, and sentence structure. Others test for the ability to use the proper tone and to express information clearly and accurately.
3. **Administrative principles for managers** - These questions test for knowledge of the managerial functions involved in directing an organization or an organizational segment. These questions cover such areas as: developing objectives and formulating policies; making decisions based on the context of the administrator's position and authority; forecasting and planning; organizing; developing personnel; coordinating and informing; guiding and leading organizational units; as well as the delegation of authority and responsibility.
4. **Administrative supervision** - These questions test for knowledge of the principles and practices involved in directing the activities of a large subordinate staff, including subordinate supervisors. Questions relate to the personal interactions between an upper level supervisor and his/her subordinate supervisors in the accomplishment of objectives. These questions cover such areas as assigning work to and coordinating the activities of several units, establishing and guiding staff development programs, evaluating the performance of subordinate supervisors, and maintaining relationships with other organizational sections.
5. **Understanding and interpreting tabular material** - These questions test your ability to understand, analyze, and use the internal logic of data presented in tabular form. You may be asked to perform tasks such as completing tables, drawing conclusions from them, analyzing data trends or interrelationships, and revising or combining data sets. The concepts of rate, ratio, and proportion are tested. Mathematical operations are simple, and computational speed is not a major factor in the test.
6. **Evaluating conclusions based on factual information** - These questions test your ability to evaluate and draw conclusions from factual information presented. Each question consists of a set of factual statements and a conclusion. You will be asked to determine whether the conclusion can be proven to be true by the facts, proven to be false by the facts, or if the facts are inadequate to prove the conclusion.
7. **Analyzing and evaluating information** - These questions test for the ability to analyze, interpret, and draw reasonable conclusions from information presented in text, data, images or symbols. Analysis may involve identifying a significant problem or issue; focusing on relevant data and text; identifying trends, relationships, and significant features; assessing relevant alternatives; suggesting or evaluating possible conclusions; and applying logical principles to information provided.

HOW TO TAKE A TEST

I. YOU MUST PASS AN EXAMINATION

A. *WHAT EVERY CANDIDATE SHOULD KNOW*

Examination applicants often ask us for help in preparing for the written test. What can I study in advance? What kinds of questions will be asked? How will the test be given? How will the papers be graded?

As an applicant for a civil service examination, you may be wondering about some of these things. Our purpose here is to suggest effective methods of advance study and to describe civil service examinations.

Your chances for success on this examination can be increased if you know how to prepare. Those "pre-examination jitters" can be reduced if you know what to expect. You can even experience an adventure in good citizenship if you know why civil service exams are given.

B. *WHY ARE CIVIL SERVICE EXAMINATIONS GIVEN?*

Civil service examinations are important to you in two ways. As a citizen, you want public jobs filled by employees who know how to do their work. As a job seeker, you want a fair chance to compete for that job on an equal footing with other candidates. The best-known means of accomplishing this two-fold goal is the competitive examination.

Exams are widely publicized throughout the nation. They may be administered for jobs in federal, state, city, municipal, town or village governments or agencies.

Any citizen may apply, with some limitations, such as the age or residence of applicants. Your experience and education may be reviewed to see whether you meet the requirements for the particular examination. When these requirements exist, they are reasonable and applied consistently to all applicants. Thus, a competitive examination may cause you some uneasiness now, but it is your privilege and safeguard.

C. *HOW ARE CIVIL SERVICE EXAMS DEVELOPED?*

Examinations are carefully written by trained technicians who are specialists in the field known as "psychological measurement," in consultation with recognized authorities in the field of work that the test will cover. These experts recommend the subject matter areas or skills to be tested; only those knowledges or skills important to your success on the job are included. The most reliable books and source materials available are used as references. Together, the experts and technicians judge the difficulty level of the questions.

Test technicians know how to phrase questions so that the problem is clearly stated. Their ethics do not permit "trick" or "catch" questions. Questions may have been tried out on sample groups, or subjected to statistical analysis, to determine their usefulness.

Written tests are often used in combination with performance tests, ratings of training and experience, and oral interviews. All of these measures combine to form the best-known means of finding the right person for the right job.

II. HOW TO PASS THE WRITTEN TEST

A. NATURE OF THE EXAMINATION

To prepare intelligently for civil service examinations, you should know how they differ from school examinations you have taken. In school you were assigned certain definite pages to read or subjects to cover. The examination questions were quite detailed and usually emphasized memory. Civil service exams, on the other hand, try to discover your present ability to perform the duties of a position, plus your potentiality to learn these duties. In other words, a civil service exam attempts to predict how successful you will be. Questions cover such a broad area that they cannot be as minute and detailed as school exam questions.

In the public service similar kinds of work, or positions, are grouped together in one "class." This process is known as *position-classification*. All the positions in a class are paid according to the salary range for that class. One class title covers all of these positions, and they are all tested by the same examination.

B. FOUR BASIC STEPS

1) Study the announcement

How, then, can you know what subjects to study? Our best answer is: "Learn as much as possible about the class of positions for which you've applied." The exam will test the knowledge, skills and abilities needed to do the work.

Your most valuable source of information about the position you want is the official exam announcement. This announcement lists the training and experience qualifications. Check these standards and apply only if you come reasonably close to meeting them.

The brief description of the position in the examination announcement offers some clues to the subjects which will be tested. Think about the job itself. Review the duties in your mind. Can you perform them, or are there some in which you are rusty? Fill in the blank spots in your preparation.

Many jurisdictions preview the written test in the exam announcement by including a section called "Knowledge and Abilities Required," "Scope of the Examination," or some similar heading. Here you will find out specifically what fields will be tested.

2) Review your own background

Once you learn in general what the position is all about, and what you need to know to do the work, ask yourself which subjects you already know fairly well and which need improvement. You may wonder whether to concentrate on improving your strong areas or on building some background in your fields of weakness. When the announcement has specified "some knowledge" or "considerable knowledge," or has used adjectives like "beginning principles of..." or "advanced ... methods," you can get a clue as to the number and difficulty of questions to be asked in any given field. More questions, and hence broader coverage, would be included for those subjects which are more important in the work. Now weigh your strengths and weaknesses against the job requirements and prepare accordingly.

3) Determine the level of the position

Another way to tell how intensively you should prepare is to understand the level of the job for which you are applying. Is it the entering level? In other words, is this the position in which beginners in a field of work are hired? Or is it an intermediate or advanced level? Sometimes this is indicated by such words as "Junior" or "Senior" in the class title. Other jurisdictions use Roman numerals to designate the level – Clerk I, Clerk II, for example. The word "Supervisor" sometimes appears in the title. If the level is not indicated by the title, check the description of duties. Will you be working under very close supervision, or will you have responsibility for independent decisions in this work?

4) Choose appropriate study materials

Now that you know the subjects to be examined and the relative amount of each subject to be covered, you can choose suitable study materials. For beginning level jobs, or even advanced ones, if you have a pronounced weakness in some aspect of your training, read a modern, standard textbook in that field. Be sure it is up to date and has general coverage. Such books are normally available at your library, and the librarian will be glad to help you locate one. For entry-level positions, questions of appropriate difficulty are chosen – neither highly advanced questions, nor those too simple. Such questions require careful thought but not advanced training.

If the position for which you are applying is technical or advanced, you will read more advanced, specialized material. If you are already familiar with the basic principles of your field, elementary textbooks would waste your time. Concentrate on advanced textbooks and technical periodicals. Think through the concepts and review difficult problems in your field.

These are all general sources. You can get more ideas on your own initiative, following these leads. For example, training manuals and publications of the government agency which employs workers in your field can be useful, particularly for technical and professional positions. A letter or visit to the government department involved may result in more specific study suggestions, and certainly will provide you with a more definite idea of the exact nature of the position you are seeking.

III. KINDS OF TESTS

Tests are used for purposes other than measuring knowledge and ability to perform specified duties. For some positions, it is equally important to test ability to make adjustments to new situations or to profit from training. In others, basic mental abilities not dependent on information are essential. Questions which test these things may not appear as pertinent to the duties of the position as those which test for knowledge and information. Yet they are often highly important parts of a fair examination. For very general questions, it is almost impossible to help you direct your study efforts. What we can do is to point out some of the more common of these general abilities needed in public service positions and describe some typical questions.

1) General information

Broad, general information has been found useful for predicting job success in some kinds of work. This is tested in a variety of ways, from vocabulary lists to questions about current events. Basic background in some field of work, such as sociology or economics, may be sampled in a group of questions. Often these are principles which have become familiar to most persons through exposure rather than through formal training. It is difficult to advise you how to study for these questions; being alert to the world around you is our best suggestion.

2) Verbal ability

An example of an ability needed in many positions is verbal or language ability. Verbal ability is, in brief, the ability to use and understand words. Vocabulary and grammar tests are typical measures of this ability. Reading comprehension or paragraph interpretation questions are common in many kinds of civil service tests. You are given a paragraph of written material and asked to find its central meaning.

3) Numerical ability

Number skills can be tested by the familiar arithmetic problem, by checking paired lists of numbers to see which are alike and which are different, or by interpreting charts and graphs. In the latter test, a graph may be printed in the test booklet which you are asked to use as the basis for answering questions.

4) Observation

A popular test for law-enforcement positions is the observation test. A picture is shown to you for several minutes, then taken away. Questions about the picture test your ability to observe both details and larger elements.

5) Following directions

In many positions in the public service, the employee must be able to carry out written instructions dependably and accurately. You may be given a chart with several columns, each column listing a variety of information. The questions require you to carry out directions involving the information given in the chart.

6) Skills and aptitudes

Performance tests effectively measure some manual skills and aptitudes. When the skill is one in which you are trained, such as typing or shorthand, you can practice. These tests are often very much like those given in business school or high school courses. For many of the other skills and aptitudes, however, no short-time preparation can be made. Skills and abilities natural to you or that you have developed throughout your lifetime are being tested.

Many of the general questions just described provide all the data needed to answer the questions and ask you to use your reasoning ability to find the answers. Your best preparation for these tests, as well as for tests of facts and ideas, is to be at your physical and mental best. You, no doubt, have your own methods of getting into an exam-taking mood and keeping "in shape." The next section lists some ideas on this subject.

IV. KINDS OF QUESTIONS

Only rarely is the "essay" question, which you answer in narrative form, used in civil service tests. Civil service tests are usually of the short-answer type. Full instructions for answering these questions will be given to you at the examination. But in case this is your first experience with short-answer questions and separate answer sheets, here is what you need to know:

1) Multiple-choice Questions

Most popular of the short-answer questions is the "multiple choice" or "best answer" question. It can be used, for example, to test for factual knowledge, ability to solve problems or judgment in meeting situations found at work.

A multiple-choice question is normally one of three types—
- It can begin with an incomplete statement followed by several possible endings. You are to find the one ending which *best* completes the statement, although some of the others may not be entirely wrong.
- It can also be a complete statement in the form of a question which is answered by choosing one of the statements listed.

- It can be in the form of a problem – again you select the best answer.

Here is an example of a multiple-choice question with a discussion which should give you some clues as to the method for choosing the right answer:

When an employee has a complaint about his assignment, the action which will *best* help him overcome his difficulty is to
- A. discuss his difficulty with his coworkers
- B. take the problem to the head of the organization
- C. take the problem to the person who gave him the assignment
- D. say nothing to anyone about his complaint

In answering this question, you should study each of the choices to find which is best. Consider choice "A" – Certainly an employee may discuss his complaint with fellow employees, but no change or improvement can result, and the complaint remains unresolved. Choice "B" is a poor choice since the head of the organization probably does not know what assignment you have been given, and taking your problem to him is known as "going over the head" of the supervisor. The supervisor, or person who made the assignment, is the person who can clarify it or correct any injustice. Choice "C" is, therefore, correct. To say nothing, as in choice "D," is unwise. Supervisors have and interest in knowing the problems employees are facing, and the employee is seeking a solution to his problem.

2) True/False Questions

The "true/false" or "right/wrong" form of question is sometimes used. Here a complete statement is given. Your job is to decide whether the statement is right or wrong.

SAMPLE: A roaming cell-phone call to a nearby city costs less than a non-roaming call to a distant city.

This statement is wrong, or false, since roaming calls are more expensive.

This is not a complete list of all possible question forms, although most of the others are variations of these common types. You will always get complete directions for answering questions. Be sure you understand *how* to mark your answers – ask questions until you do.

V. RECORDING YOUR ANSWERS

Computer terminals are used more and more today for many different kinds of exams.
For an examination with very few applicants, you may be told to record your answers in the test booklet itself. Separate answer sheets are much more common. If this separate answer sheet is to be scored by machine – and this is often the case – it is highly important that you mark your answers correctly in order to get credit.

An electronic scoring machine is often used in civil service offices because of the speed with which papers can be scored. Machine-scored answer sheets must be marked with a pencil, which will be given to you. This pencil has a high graphite content which responds to the electronic scoring machine. As a matter of fact, stray dots may register as answers, so do not let your pencil rest on the answer sheet while you are pondering the correct answer. Also, if your pencil lead breaks or is otherwise defective, ask for another.

Since the answer sheet will be dropped in a slot in the scoring machine, be careful not to bend the corners or get the paper crumpled.

The answer sheet normally has five vertical columns of numbers, with 30 numbers to a column. These numbers correspond to the question numbers in your test booklet. After each number, going across the page are four or five pairs of dotted lines. These short dotted lines have small letters or numbers above them. The first two pairs may also have a "T" or "F" above the letters. This indicates that the first two pairs only are to be used if the questions are of the true-false type. If the questions are multiple choice, disregard the "T" and "F" and pay attention only to the small letters or numbers.

Answer your questions in the manner of the sample that follows:

32. The largest city in the United States is
    A. Washington, D.C.
    B. New York City
    C. Chicago
    D. Detroit
    E. San Francisco

1) Choose the answer you think is best. (New York City is the largest, so "B" is correct.)
2) Find the row of dotted lines numbered the same as the question you are answering. (Find row number 32)
3) Find the pair of dotted lines corresponding to the answer. (Find the pair of lines under the mark "B.")
4) Make a solid black mark between the dotted lines.

VI. BEFORE THE TEST

Common sense will help you find procedures to follow to get ready for an examination. Too many of us, however, overlook these sensible measures. Indeed, nervousness and fatigue have been found to be the most serious reasons why applicants fail to do their best on civil service tests. Here is a list of reminders:

- Begin your preparation early – Don't wait until the last minute to go scurrying around for books and materials or to find out what the position is all about.
- Prepare continuously – An hour a night for a week is better than an all-night cram session. This has been definitely established. What is more, a night a week for a month will return better dividends than crowding your study into a shorter period of time.
- Locate the place of the exam – You have been sent a notice telling you when and where to report for the examination. If the location is in a different town or otherwise unfamiliar to you, it would be well to inquire the best route and learn something about the building.
- Relax the night before the test – Allow your mind to rest. Do not study at all that night. Plan some mild recreation or diversion; then go to bed early and get a good night's sleep.
- Get up early enough to make a leisurely trip to the place for the test – This way unforeseen events, traffic snarls, unfamiliar buildings, etc. will not upset you.
- Dress comfortably – A written test is not a fashion show. You will be known by number and not by name, so wear something comfortable.

- Leave excess paraphernalia at home – Shopping bags and odd bundles will get in your way. You need bring only the items mentioned in the official notice you received; usually everything you need is provided. Do not bring reference books to the exam. They will only confuse those last minutes and be taken away from you when in the test room.
- Arrive somewhat ahead of time – If because of transportation schedules you must get there very early, bring a newspaper or magazine to take your mind off yourself while waiting.
- Locate the examination room – When you have found the proper room, you will be directed to the seat or part of the room where you will sit. Sometimes you are given a sheet of instructions to read while you are waiting. Do not fill out any forms until you are told to do so; just read them and be prepared.
- Relax and prepare to listen to the instructions
- If you have any physical problem that may keep you from doing your best, be sure to tell the test administrator. If you are sick or in poor health, you really cannot do your best on the exam. You can come back and take the test some other time.

VII. AT THE TEST

The day of the test is here and you have the test booklet in your hand. The temptation to get going is very strong. Caution! There is more to success than knowing the right answers. You must know how to identify your papers and understand variations in the type of short-answer question used in this particular examination. Follow these suggestions for maximum results from your efforts:

1) Cooperate with the monitor

The test administrator has a duty to create a situation in which you can be as much at ease as possible. He will give instructions, tell you when to begin, check to see that you are marking your answer sheet correctly, and so on. He is not there to guard you, although he will see that your competitors do not take unfair advantage. He wants to help you do your best.

2) Listen to all instructions

Don't jump the gun! Wait until you understand all directions. In most civil service tests you get more time than you need to answer the questions. So don't be in a hurry. Read each word of instructions until you clearly understand the meaning. Study the examples, listen to all announcements and follow directions. Ask questions if you do not understand what to do.

3) Identify your papers

Civil service exams are usually identified by number only. You will be assigned a number; you must not put your name on your test papers. Be sure to copy your number correctly. Since more than one exam may be given, copy your exact examination title.

4) Plan your time

Unless you are told that a test is a "speed" or "rate of work" test, speed itself is usually not important. Time enough to answer all the questions will be provided, but this does not mean that you have all day. An overall time limit has been set. Divide the total time (in minutes) by the number of questions to determine the approximate time you have for each question.

5) Do not linger over difficult questions

If you come across a difficult question, mark it with a paper clip (useful to have along) and come back to it when you have been through the booklet. One caution if you do this – be sure to skip a number on your answer sheet as well. Check often to be sure that you have not lost your place and that you are marking in the row numbered the same as the question you are answering.

6) Read the questions

Be sure you know what the question asks! Many capable people are unsuccessful because they failed to *read* the questions correctly.

7) Answer all questions

Unless you have been instructed that a penalty will be deducted for incorrect answers, it is better to guess than to omit a question.

8) Speed tests

It is often better NOT to guess on speed tests. It has been found that on timed tests people are tempted to spend the last few seconds before time is called in marking answers at random – without even reading them – in the hope of picking up a few extra points. To discourage this practice, the instructions may warn you that your score will be "corrected" for guessing. That is, a penalty will be applied. The incorrect answers will be deducted from the correct ones, or some other penalty formula will be used.

9) Review your answers

If you finish before time is called, go back to the questions you guessed or omitted to give them further thought. Review other answers if you have time.

10) Return your test materials

If you are ready to leave before others have finished or time is called, take ALL your materials to the monitor and leave quietly. Never take any test material with you. The monitor can discover whose papers are not complete, and taking a test booklet may be grounds for disqualification.

VIII. EXAMINATION TECHNIQUES

1) Read the general instructions carefully. These are usually printed on the first page of the exam booklet. As a rule, these instructions refer to the timing of the examination; the fact that you should not start work until the signal and must stop work at a signal, etc. If there are any *special* instructions, such as a choice of questions to be answered, make sure that you note this instruction carefully.

2) When you are ready to start work on the examination, that is as soon as the signal has been given, read the instructions to each question booklet, underline any key words or phrases, such as *least, best, outline, describe* and the like. In this way you will tend to answer as requested rather than discover on reviewing your paper that you *listed without describing*, that you selected the *worst* choice rather than the *best* choice, etc.

3) If the examination is of the objective or multiple-choice type – that is, each question will also give a series of possible answers: A, B, C or D, and you are called upon to select the best answer and write the letter next to that answer on your answer paper – it is advisable to start answering each question in turn. There may be anywhere from 50 to 100 such questions in the three or four hours allotted and you can see how much time would be taken if you read through all the questions before beginning to answer any. Furthermore, if you come across a question or group of questions which you know would be difficult to answer, it would undoubtedly affect your handling of all the other questions.

4) If the examination is of the essay type and contains but a few questions, it is a moot point as to whether you should read all the questions before starting to answer any one. Of course, if you are given a choice – say five out of seven and the like – then it is essential to read all the questions so you can eliminate the two that are most difficult. If, however, you are asked to answer all the questions, there may be danger in trying to answer the easiest one first because you may find that you will spend too much time on it. The best technique is to answer the first question, then proceed to the second, etc.

5) Time your answers. Before the exam begins, write down the time it started, then add the time allowed for the examination and write down the time it must be completed, then divide the time available somewhat as follows:
    - If 3-1/2 hours are allowed, that would be 210 minutes. If you have 80 objective-type questions, that would be an average of 2-1/2 minutes per question. Allow yourself no more than 2 minutes per question, or a total of 160 minutes, which will permit about 50 minutes to review.
    - If for the time allotment of 210 minutes there are 7 essay questions to answer, that would average about 30 minutes a question. Give yourself only 25 minutes per question so that you have about 35 minutes to review.

6) The most important instruction is to *read each question* and make sure you know what is wanted. The second most important instruction is to *time yourself properly* so that you answer every question. The third most important instruction is to *answer every question*. Guess if you have to but include something for each question. Remember that you will receive no credit for a blank and will probably receive some credit if you write something in answer to an essay question. If you guess a letter – say "B" for a multiple-choice question – you may have guessed right. If you leave a blank as an answer to a multiple-choice question, the examiners may respect your feelings but it will not add a point to your score. Some exams may penalize you for wrong answers, so in such cases *only*, you may not want to guess unless you have some basis for your answer.

7) Suggestions
    a. Objective-type questions
        1. Examine the question booklet for proper sequence of pages and questions
        2. Read all instructions carefully
        3. Skip any question which seems too difficult; return to it after all other questions have been answered
        4. Apportion your time properly; do not spend too much time on any single question or group of questions

5. Note and underline key words – *all, most, fewest, least, best, worst, same, opposite,* etc.
6. Pay particular attention to negatives
7. Note unusual option, e.g., unduly long, short, complex, different or similar in content to the body of the question
8. Observe the use of "hedging" words – *probably, may, most likely,* etc.
9. Make sure that your answer is put next to the same number as the question
10. Do not second-guess unless you have good reason to believe the second answer is definitely more correct
11. Cross out original answer if you decide another answer is more accurate; do not erase until you are ready to hand your paper in
12. Answer all questions; guess unless instructed otherwise
13. Leave time for review

  b. Essay questions
1. Read each question carefully
2. Determine exactly what is wanted. Underline key words or phrases.
3. Decide on outline or paragraph answer
4. Include many different points and elements unless asked to develop any one or two points or elements
5. Show impartiality by giving pros and cons unless directed to select one side only
6. Make and write down any assumptions you find necessary to answer the questions
7. Watch your English, grammar, punctuation and choice of words
8. Time your answers; don't crowd material

8) Answering the essay question

Most essay questions can be answered by framing the specific response around several key words or ideas. Here are a few such key words or ideas:

M's: manpower, materials, methods, money, management
P's: purpose, program, policy, plan, procedure, practice, problems, pitfalls, personnel, public relations

  a. Six basic steps in handling problems:
1. Preliminary plan and background development
2. Collect information, data and facts
3. Analyze and interpret information, data and facts
4. Analyze and develop solutions as well as make recommendations
5. Prepare report and sell recommendations
6. Install recommendations and follow up effectiveness

  b. Pitfalls to avoid
1. *Taking things for granted* – A statement of the situation does not necessarily imply that each of the elements is necessarily true; for example, a complaint may be invalid and biased so that all that can be taken for granted is that a complaint has been registered

2. *Considering only one side of a situation* – Wherever possible, indicate several alternatives and then point out the reasons you selected the best one
3. *Failing to indicate follow up* – Whenever your answer indicates action on your part, make certain that you will take proper follow-up action to see how successful your recommendations, procedures or actions turn out to be
4. *Taking too long in answering any single question* – Remember to time your answers properly

IX. AFTER THE TEST

Scoring procedures differ in detail among civil service jurisdictions although the general principles are the same. Whether the papers are hand-scored or graded by machine we have described, they are nearly always graded by number. That is, the person who marks the paper knows only the number – never the name – of the applicant. Not until all the papers have been graded will they be matched with names. If other tests, such as training and experience or oral interview ratings have been given, scores will be combined. Different parts of the examination usually have different weights. For example, the written test might count 60 percent of the final grade, and a rating of training and experience 40 percent. In many jurisdictions, veterans will have a certain number of points added to their grades.

After the final grade has been determined, the names are placed in grade order and an eligible list is established. There are various methods for resolving ties between those who get the same final grade – probably the most common is to place first the name of the person whose application was received first. Job offers are made from the eligible list in the order the names appear on it. You will be notified of your grade and your rank as soon as all these computations have been made. This will be done as rapidly as possible.

People who are found to meet the requirements in the announcement are called "eligibles." Their names are put on a list of eligible candidates. An eligible's chances of getting a job depend on how high he stands on this list and how fast agencies are filling jobs from the list.

When a job is to be filled from a list of eligibles, the agency asks for the names of people on the list of eligibles for that job. When the civil service commission receives this request, it sends to the agency the names of the three people highest on this list. Or, if the job to be filled has specialized requirements, the office sends the agency the names of the top three persons who meet these requirements from the general list.

The appointing officer makes a choice from among the three people whose names were sent to him. If the selected person accepts the appointment, the names of the others are put back on the list to be considered for future openings.

That is the rule in hiring from all kinds of eligible lists, whether they are for typist, carpenter, chemist, or something else. For every vacancy, the appointing officer has his choice of any one of the top three eligibles on the list. This explains why the person whose name is on top of the list sometimes does not get an appointment when some of the persons lower on the list do. If the appointing officer chooses the second or third eligible, the No. 1 eligible does not get a job at once, but stays on the list until he is appointed or the list is terminated.

X. HOW TO PASS THE INTERVIEW TEST

The examination for which you applied requires an oral interview test. You have already taken the written test and you are now being called for the interview test – the final part of the formal examination.

You may think that it is not possible to prepare for an interview test and that there are no procedures to follow during an interview. Our purpose is to point out some things you can do in advance that will help you and some good rules to follow and pitfalls to avoid while you are being interviewed.

What is an interview supposed to test?

The written examination is designed to test the technical knowledge and competence of the candidate; the oral is designed to evaluate intangible qualities, not readily measured otherwise, and to establish a list showing the relative fitness of each candidate – as measured against his competitors – for the position sought. Scoring is not on the basis of "right" and "wrong," but on a sliding scale of values ranging from "not passable" to "outstanding." As a matter of fact, it is possible to achieve a relatively low score without a single "incorrect" answer because of evident weakness in the qualities being measured.

Occasionally, an examination may consist entirely of an oral test – either an individual or a group oral. In such cases, information is sought concerning the technical knowledges and abilities of the candidate, since there has been no written examination for this purpose. More commonly, however, an oral test is used to supplement a written examination.

Who conducts interviews?

The composition of oral boards varies among different jurisdictions. In nearly all, a representative of the personnel department serves as chairman. One of the members of the board may be a representative of the department in which the candidate would work. In some cases, "outside experts" are used, and, frequently, a businessman or some other representative of the general public is asked to serve. Labor and management or other special groups may be represented. The aim is to secure the services of experts in the appropriate field.

However the board is composed, it is a good idea (and not at all improper or unethical) to ascertain in advance of the interview who the members are and what groups they represent. When you are introduced to them, you will have some idea of their backgrounds and interests, and at least you will not stutter and stammer over their names.

What should be done before the interview?

While knowledge about the board members is useful and takes some of the surprise element out of the interview, there is other preparation which is more substantive. It *is* possible to prepare for an oral interview – in several ways:

1) Keep a copy of your application and review it carefully before the interview

This may be the only document before the oral board, and the starting point of the interview. Know what education and experience you have listed there, and the sequence and dates of all of it. Sometimes the board will ask you to review the highlights of your experience for them; you should not have to hem and haw doing it.

2) Study the class specification and the examination announcement

Usually, the oral board has one or both of these to guide them. The qualities, characteristics or knowledges required by the position sought are stated in these documents. They offer valuable clues as to the nature of the oral interview. For example, if the job involves supervisory responsibilities, the announcement will usually indicate that knowledge of modern supervisory methods and the qualifications of the candidate as a supervisor will be tested. If so, you can expect such questions, frequently in the form of a hypothetical situation which you are expected to solve. NEVER go into an oral without knowledge of the duties and responsibilities of the job you seek.

3) Think through each qualification required

Try to visualize the kind of questions you would ask if you were a board member. How well could you answer them? Try especially to appraise your own knowledge and background in each area, *measured against the job sought*, and identify any areas in which you are weak. Be critical and realistic – do not flatter yourself.

4) Do some general reading in areas in which you feel you may be weak

For example, if the job involves supervision and your past experience has NOT, some general reading in supervisory methods and practices, particularly in the field of human relations, might be useful. Do NOT study agency procedures or detailed manuals. The oral board will be testing your understanding and capacity, not your memory.

5) Get a good night's sleep and watch your general health and mental attitude

You will want a clear head at the interview. Take care of a cold or any other minor ailment, and of course, no hangovers.

What should be done on the day of the interview?

Now comes the day of the interview itself. Give yourself plenty of time to get there. Plan to arrive somewhat ahead of the scheduled time, particularly if your appointment is in the fore part of the day. If a previous candidate fails to appear, the board might be ready for you a bit early. By early afternoon an oral board is almost invariably behind schedule if there are many candidates, and you may have to wait. Take along a book or magazine to read, or your application to review, but leave any extraneous material in the waiting room when you go in for your interview. In any event, relax and compose yourself.

The matter of dress is important. The board is forming impressions about you – from your experience, your manners, your attitude, and your appearance. Give your personal appearance careful attention. Dress your best, but not your flashiest. Choose conservative, appropriate clothing, and be sure it is immaculate. This is a business interview, and your appearance should indicate that you regard it as such. Besides, being well groomed and properly dressed will help boost your confidence.

Sooner or later, someone will call your name and escort you into the interview room. *This is it.* From here on you are on your own. It is too late for any more preparation. But remember, you asked for this opportunity to prove your fitness, and you are here because your request was granted.

What happens when you go in?

The usual sequence of events will be as follows: The clerk (who is often the board stenographer) will introduce you to the chairman of the oral board, who will introduce you to the other members of the board. Acknowledge the introductions before you sit down. Do not be surprised if you find a microphone facing you or a stenotypist sitting by. Oral interviews are usually recorded in the event of an appeal or other review.

Usually the chairman of the board will open the interview by reviewing the highlights of your education and work experience from your application – primarily for the benefit of the other members of the board, as well as to get the material into the record. Do not interrupt or comment unless there is an error or significant misinterpretation; if that is the case, do not hesitate. But do not quibble about insignificant matters. Also, he will usually ask you some question about your education, experience or your present job – partly to get you to start talking and to establish the interviewing "rapport." He may start the actual questioning, or turn it over to one of the other members. Frequently, each member undertakes the questioning on a particular area, one in which he is perhaps most competent, so you can expect each member to participate in the examination. Because time is limited, you may also expect some rather abrupt switches in the direction the questioning takes, so do not be upset by it. Normally, a board member will not pursue a single line of questioning unless he discovers a particular strength or weakness.

After each member has participated, the chairman will usually ask whether any member has any further questions, then will ask you if you have anything you wish to add. Unless you are expecting this question, it may floor you. Worse, it may start you off on an extended, extemporaneous speech. The board is not usually seeking more information. The question is principally to offer you a last opportunity to present further qualifications or to indicate that you have nothing to add. So, if you feel that a significant qualification or characteristic has been overlooked, it is proper to point it out in a sentence or so. Do not compliment the board on the thoroughness of their examination – they have been sketchy, and you know it. If you wish, merely say, "No thank you, I have nothing further to add." This is a point where you can "talk yourself out" of a good impression or fail to present an important bit of information. Remember, *you close the interview yourself.*

The chairman will then say, "That is all, Mr. _____, thank you." Do not be startled; the interview is over, and quicker than you think. Thank him, gather your belongings and take your leave. Save your sigh of relief for the other side of the door.

How to put your best foot forward

Throughout this entire process, you may feel that the board individually and collectively is trying to pierce your defenses, seek out your hidden weaknesses and embarrass and confuse you. Actually, this is not true. They are obliged to make an appraisal of your qualifications for the job you are seeking, and they want to see you in your best light. Remember, they must interview all candidates and a non-cooperative candidate may become a failure in spite of their best efforts to bring out his qualifications. Here are 15 suggestions that will help you:

1) Be natural – Keep your attitude confident, not cocky

If you are not confident that you can do the job, do not expect the board to be. Do not apologize for your weaknesses, try to bring out your strong points. The board is interested in a positive, not negative, presentation. Cockiness will antagonize any board member and make him wonder if you are covering up a weakness by a false show of strength.

2) Get comfortable, but don't lounge or sprawl

Sit erectly but not stiffly. A careless posture may lead the board to conclude that you are careless in other things, or at least that you are not impressed by the importance of the occasion. Either conclusion is natural, even if incorrect. Do not fuss with your clothing, a pencil or an ashtray. Your hands may occasionally be useful to emphasize a point; do not let them become a point of distraction.

3) Do not wisecrack or make small talk

This is a serious situation, and your attitude should show that you consider it as such. Further, the time of the board is limited – they do not want to waste it, and neither should you.

4) Do not exaggerate your experience or abilities

In the first place, from information in the application or other interviews and sources, the board may know more about you than you think. Secondly, you probably will not get away with it. An experienced board is rather adept at spotting such a situation, so do not take the chance.

5) If you know a board member, do not make a point of it, yet do not hide it

Certainly you are not fooling him, and probably not the other members of the board. Do not try to take advantage of your acquaintanceship – it will probably do you little good.

6) Do not dominate the interview

Let the board do that. They will give you the clues – do not assume that you have to do all the talking. Realize that the board has a number of questions to ask you, and do not try to take up all the interview time by showing off your extensive knowledge of the answer to the first one.

7) Be attentive

You only have 20 minutes or so, and you should keep your attention at its sharpest throughout. When a member is addressing a problem or question to you, give him your undivided attention. Address your reply principally to him, but do not exclude the other board members.

8) Do not interrupt

A board member may be stating a problem for you to analyze. He will ask you a question when the time comes. Let him state the problem, and wait for the question.

9) Make sure you understand the question

Do not try to answer until you are sure what the question is. If it is not clear, restate it in your own words or ask the board member to clarify it for you. However, do not haggle about minor elements.

10) Reply promptly but not hastily

A common entry on oral board rating sheets is "candidate responded readily," or "candidate hesitated in replies." Respond as promptly and quickly as you can, but do not jump to a hasty, ill-considered answer.

11) Do not be peremptory in your answers

A brief answer is proper – but do not fire your answer back. That is a losing game from your point of view. The board member can probably ask questions much faster than you can answer them.

12) Do not try to create the answer you think the board member wants

He is interested in what kind of mind you have and how it works – not in playing games. Furthermore, he can usually spot this practice and will actually grade you down on it.

13) Do not switch sides in your reply merely to agree with a board member

Frequently, a member will take a contrary position merely to draw you out and to see if you are willing and able to defend your point of view. Do not start a debate, yet do not surrender a good position. If a position is worth taking, it is worth defending.

14) Do not be afraid to admit an error in judgment if you are shown to be wrong

The board knows that you are forced to reply without any opportunity for careful consideration. Your answer may be demonstrably wrong. If so, admit it and get on with the interview.

15) Do not dwell at length on your present job

The opening question may relate to your present assignment. Answer the question but do not go into an extended discussion. You are being examined for a *new* job, not your present one. As a matter of fact, try to phrase ALL your answers in terms of the job for which you are being examined.

Basis of Rating

Probably you will forget most of these "do's" and "don'ts" when you walk into the oral interview room. Even remembering them all will not ensure you a passing grade. Perhaps you did not have the qualifications in the first place. But remembering them will help you to put your best foot forward, without treading on the toes of the board members.

Rumor and popular opinion to the contrary notwithstanding, an oral board wants you to make the best appearance possible. They know you are under pressure – but they also want to see how you respond to it as a guide to what your reaction would be under the pressures of the job you seek. They will be influenced by the degree of poise you display, the personal traits you show and the manner in which you respond.

ABOUT THIS BOOK

This book contains tests divided into Examination Sections. Go through each test, answering every question in the margin. We have also attached a sample answer sheet at the back of the book that can be removed and used. At the end of each test look at the answer key and check your answers. On the ones you got wrong, look at the right answer choice and learn. Do not fill in the answers first. Do not memorize the questions and answers, but understand the answer and principles involved. On your test, the questions will likely be different from the samples. Questions are changed and new ones added. If you understand these past questions you should have success with any changes that arise. Tests may consist of several types of questions. We have additional books on each subject should more study be advisable or necessary for you. Finally, the more you study, the better prepared you will be. This book is intended to be the last thing you study before you walk into the examination room. Prior study of relevant texts is also recommended. NLC publishes some of these in our Fundamental Series. Knowledge and good sense are important factors in passing your exam. Good luck also helps. So now study this Passbook, absorb the material contained within and take that knowledge into the examination. Then do your best to pass that exam.

EXAMINATION SECTION

EXAMINATION SECTION
TEST 1

DIRECTIONS: Each question or incomplete statement is followed by several suggested answers or completions. Select the one that BEST answers the question or completes the statement. *PRINT THE LETTER OF THE CORRECT ANSWER IN THE SPACE AT THE RIGHT.*

1. Which of the following are covered under the definition of customer service?
    A. A positive environment set up to efficiently handle customer requests
    B. Infrastructure designed to distribute merchandise in a timely fashion
    C. Employees filling distinct roles to meet customer needs
    D. All of the above

    1.____

2. An organization that has a clearly established customer service approach can distinguish itself from competitors. This is referred to as the organization's
    A. customer prioritization   B. service culture
    C. imagineering   D. none of the above

    2.____

3. The physical space of a hospitality setting is MOST commonly referred to as the
    A. customer landscape   B. business policy
    C. servicescape   D. arena of service

    3.____

4. When dealing with a customer, one must be knowledgeable, capable and enthusiastic when delivering products and/or services and it must be done in a manner that satisfies
    A. both identified and unidentified needs
    B. local and global competition
    C. quality and quantity of goods/services
    D. all demands of the customer

    4.____

5. Employees at the center learn at their orientation that services are inseparable because service quality and customer satisfaction are largely dependent on which of the following?
    A. Interactions between employees and customers
    B. Uniform offerings for individuals
    C. Establishing patents for individual services
    D. All of the above

    5.____

6. An organization with a strong customer service culture
    A. allows employees to use their own initiative to solve customer problems
    B. has policies that allow employees to easily please customers
    C. provides extensive customer service training for employees
    D. all of the above

    6.____

1

7. Which of the following is TRUE of customer contact through electronic mail?
   A. Be sure to use all caps for important aspects of the e-mail
   B. State the purpose of the message clearly
   C. Do not feel the need to respond immediately
   D. Include lengthy descriptions in the body of the e-mail

8. A clerk is speaking to residents at a zoning committee meeting and uses the word "coulda" instead of "could have" in his presentation.
   This is an example of
   A. good enunciation
   B. poor tone
   C. poor enunciation
   D. proper pitch

9. An employee is delivering a presentation to parents about the benefits of children joining summer camps when someone complains that the employee's changing pitch makes it hard to hear what he is saying and that he needs to fix it.
   What does the parent mean by fixing his pitch?
   The employee needs to
   A. keep his voice from going too high or too low
   B. keep his voice from getting too soft or too loud
   C. keep his attitude towards certain subjects in check
   D. make sure his words are clearly spoken and not garbled

10. A clerk recently moved from answering phone calls every day to working face-to-face with residents.
    Which of the following will help her be most successful when transferring from phone to personal communication?
    A. Focus on sharing only positive information
    B. Speak more authoritatively
    C. Maintain a more casual tone and familiarity with residents
    D. Positive communication through eye contact and body language

11. Talking via telephone
    A. is less personal than sending an e-mail message
    B. is a poor way to reach most residents
    C. can allow residents to receive instant feedback
    D. is not popular within public services

12. An employee is in charge of calling local homeowners to tell them about upcoming activities, and more often than not she needs to leave a voicemail.
    Which of the following is the MOST effective way to leave voicemails?
    A. Be courteous
    B. Provide the appropriate information
    C. Contain lengthy details
    D. Both A and B

13. You are dealing with a parent who is upset about a miscommunication related to her child's application for an activity. Which of the following would be LEAST frustrating for the parent to hear from you?
    A. "I don't know. I will do my best."
    B. "Let me see what I can do for you."
    C. "I apologize, but you will have to…"
    D. "Oh, my manager should be able to help you, but he's not in right now."

    13.____

14. If a part-time assistant employee should need to apologize to customers, which of the following should he NOT do when apologizing?
    A. Apologize right away
    B. Be sincere in his apology
    C. Make the apology personal
    D. Offer an official apology from the department

    14.____

15. If a clerk's office is looking to improve its processes to increase community satisfaction, feedback received should be each of the following EXCEPT
    A. centered on internal customers
    B. ongoing
    C. available internally to everyone from employees to supervisors
    D. focused on a limited number of indicators

    15.____

16. A member of the community has identified a flaw in one of the policies regarding town hall meetings. Now that the problem has been identified, all of the following should be steps toward resolving the issue EXCEPT
    A. following up on the problem resolution
    B. making whatever promises are necessary
    C. listening and responding to all complaints
    D. providing the resident with whatever was originally requested

    16.____

17. When looking to achieve the best results as someone who interacts with the public, one should always strive to represent
    A. the entire organization   B. the customer
    C. the department   D. their direct supervisor

    17.____

18. Approximately how long does it take a person on hold to become annoyed?
    A. 1 minute   B. 40 seconds   C. 20 seconds   D. 2 minutes

    18.____

19. If an employee answers the phone and is asked to transfer the call to a co-worker, which of the following would be the MOST appropriate response?
    A. "She isn't in right now, so I'll have to take a message."
    B. "She's still at lunch. Can I take a message?"
    C. "She should be back soon. Could you call back in 15 minutes?"
    D. "Let me transfer you. If she's not in, please leave a message and she will return your call."

    19.____

20. A public employee has been specifically assigned to deal with public complaints because he is remarkably skilled at dealing with residents. Which of the following mentalities would explain why the employee is so effective at dealing with residents?
    A. They always cave in to whatever demands the residents make
    B. They effectively manage residents' expectations
    C. They always sincerely apologize no matter who is at fault
    D. Both A and C

20.____

21. When dealing with a frustrated customer, which of the following practices should an employee avoid?
    A. Immediately offer a solution to their problem
    B. Soothe the customer's frustration first
    C. Remain positive and non-confrontational with the customer
    D. Let the customer vent and feel like they've shared their feelings accurately

21.____

22. The town clerk's office in Avondale is highly rated by town residents. When surveyed, residents of Avondale claim that their town clerks always have such great customer service.
    Of the customer service techniques listed below, which one is MOST likely the reason for such high ratings?
    A. When dealing with abusive residents, Avondale clerks always hang up on them
    B. Clerks in Avondale have a readied list of solutions to resident problems, so they are able to offer personalized solutions right away
    C. Avondale clerks always follow up with residents who call or come in
    D. Clerks always look customers in the eye even when they are frustrated and upset

22.____

23. If a parent was told there would be space in a day camp for all of her children, and only two of them ended up being placed together, which of the following actions would be PROPER for a parks employee to take?
    A. Offer a sincere apology and attempt to fix the problem
    B. Promise the parent that all her children will be together even if it means dropping other children from the camp
    C. Explain the Parks Department policy regarding camp sign-up and tell the parent to contact a manager for further explanation
    D. Tell the parent she needs to speak to someone with more authority

23.____

24. If a person has a hearing impairment, which of the following practical solutions could a clerk have in place to help them?
    A. Reading a description of policy to the person
    B. Write a note to answer a question they have
    C. Read the words communicated by the person's "communication board"
    D. Assist the person in maneuvering through the physical space of the office

24.____

25. When dealing with a call, who should end the phone call first? 25.____
    A. The person who answered B. The person who called
    C. Either one – it doesn't matter D. A manager

KEY (CORRECT ANSWERS)

1.	D		11.	C
2.	B		12.	D
3.	C		13.	B
4.	A		14.	D
5.	A		15.	A
6.	D		16.	B
7.	B		17.	A
8.	C		18.	C
9.	A		19.	D
10.	D		20.	B

21. A
22. C
23. A
24. B
25. B

TEST 2

DIRECTIONS: Each question or incomplete statement is followed by several suggested answers or completions. Select the one that BEST answers the question or completes the statement. *PRINT THE LETTER OF THE CORRECT ANSWER IN THE SPACE AT THE RIGHT.*

1. Which of the following would be considered acceptable for an office clerk when answering the phone?
    A. Chewing gum
    B. Listening to music
    C. Eating a snack while on mute
    D. Wearing a headset

    1.____

2. Why would asking a caller for their phone number be important?
    A. In case they get disconnected
    B. To show them you are polite and considerate
    C. In case the caller is rude, this way you can call them back
    D. For future instances where calling residents back might make sense

    2.____

3. When rolling out a new program to help train employees in better customer service, the manager starts off by talking about the importance of telephone greetings.
    Why is this so important?
    A. It is the first impression the customer has of the department
    B. It shows the customer that employees are happy
    C. It shows that you are polite
    D. It isn't that important, but the manager thinks it is

    3.____

4. Which of the following is the MOST important aspect of an employee's voice in a telephone call?
    A. Their volume
    B. Their speed
    C. Their tone
    D. All of these aspects are equally important

    4.____

5. A clerk is on the phone with a customer when another customer walks into the building.
    If the clerk must put the caller on hold, what do they need to say or ask?
    A. "Would you like to be put on hold?"
    B. "I apologize for the inconvenience, but please hold."
    C. "Would it be OK if I put you on hold for a moment?"
    D. "I have to let you go. Please call back later."

    5.____

6. When a resident comes into your office for a face-to-face meeting, it is of increased importance that you communicate positively with your
    A. words
    B. body language
    C. tone
    D. none of the above

    6.____

6

7. A customer calls when employees are at an all-staff meeting. When calling the customer back, a clerk reaches their voicemail.
Which of the following information is the MOST important to leave?
    A. The date and time
    B. Ask them to call back
    C. The employee's telephone number
    D. Apologize repeatedly for missing their call

8. If an employee is in the middle of a conversation about town hall policy with a co-worker and the phone rings, what should the employee do?
    A. Get caller's information and call back after the conversation is finished
    B. Tell the co-worker to wait until finished with the phone call
    C. Answer the call and put caller on hold until conversation is finished
    D. Answer the call and transfer it to another employee who is not currently busy

9. When dealing with a resident who casually uses vulgar language, it is MOST appropriate for a town employee to
    A. tell the resident to come back when he learns how to speak
    B. converse with the resident using equally coarse language
    C. politely ask the resident to refrain from using vulgar language
    D. make the resident wait longer so he knows it won't be tolerated

10. The mayor's office has recently come under fire for a variety of perceived scandals.
In this emergency situation, which of the following would NOT be a recommended step in handling the crisis?
    A. Minimizing damage to the office's reputation through whatever means necessary
    B. Taking responsibility and apologizing
    C. Providing constant updates on the situation
    D. Designating one spokesperson to handle the relaying of updates

11. A resident complains that recreation center employees are using bureaucratic or overly technical communication. This type of language is often referred to as
    A. clichés   B. jargon   C. euphemisms   D. legalese

12. Which of the following strategies does an employee need to utilize to convince the public to believe a message that is contrary to their beliefs?
    A. Cognitive dissonance
    B. Uses and gratification
    C. Sleeper effect
    D. Source credibility

13. When communicating with parents of a summer camp run by the district, which of the following should NOT be a goal of the process?
    A. Motivation
    B. Persuasion
    C. Mutual understanding
    D. Isolation of the conflict

14. A manager comes up with a new procedure that he believes would improve the claims process that residents need to go through. Some employees agree that the procedure would make sense and others do not. One employee openly criticizes the idea to the manager.
Which of the following actions should the manager take?
He should
    A. meet with the employee for a talk and explain why bypassing his authority is unacceptable
    B. not respond to the critics in order to avoid unnecessary risks
    C. reprimand the employee who went over his head
    D. only implement the procedures that all agreed were good in order to satisfy employees

14.____

15. The county clerk's office is working on improving its employees' professionalism.
If employees are attempting to maintain a professional demeanor, what should they NOT do after making a mistake?
    A. Work to do better at the next opportunity
    B. Move on
    C. Accept responsibility
    D. Explain or rationalize the error

15.____

16. According to most recent surveys, data reveals that most white-collar workers
    A. have about a 25 percent efficiency rate when listening
    B. lose only about 25 percent efficiency when listening
    C. never take listening for granted
    D. learn to listen effectively since hearing is the important active learned process

16.____

17. Which of the following are NOT one of the four phases of listening to a customer?
    A. Hearing   B. Translating   C. Responding   D. Comprehending

17.____

18. Which of the following societal factors might impact a resident/employee interaction?
    A. Increased efficiency in technology
    B. Globalization of the economy
    C. More people between the ages of 16-24 entering the workplace
    D. Geopolitical changes

18.____

19. If a resident comes in confused about a policy change, which of the following approaches should an employee take to handle the situation?
    A. Communicate negatively when they need to
    B. Avoid gestures such as smiling or looking at customers when speaking to them
    C. Recognize how they tend to communicate and adjust accordingly if the customer is still showing signs of confusion
    D. Understand that many people are doubtful of good customer service

19.____

20. In order to avoid negative public perception, which of the following "finger pointing" words/phrases should be avoided when interacting with the public?
    A. Let me   B. You   C. Why   D. Yes

21. In an effort to improve government/resident relations, the mayor wants to roll out a new PR format that stresses public communication.
    Which of the following strategies should NOT be suggested as part of the PR campaign?
    A. Plan the message
    B. Greet residents warmly
    C. Listen carefully and respond appropriately
    D. Let the residents initiate conversations

22. A resident complains that the department does not always treat the local residents as people.
    Of the following, which would be the BEST strategy for resolving this issue?
    A. Accept responsibility and offer specific assistance
    B. Blame the customer when necessary
    C. Provide policies as reasons for actions
    D. None of the above

23. When providing feedback to residents, which of the following strategies is NOT effective?
    A. Remain emotional when providing feedback
    B. Confirm residents' meaning before offering feedback
    C. Ensure the feedback is appropriate to the original message
    D. Avoid extreme criticism or negative language

24. An employee at City Hall receives special treatment from his manager. This causes the employee to feel empowered, which then leads to him abusing authority and power.
    Which of the following would MOST likely happen if this behavior is allowed to continue?
    A. Other employees would begin to feel empowered
    B. Co-workers would work harder to demonstrate their commitment
    C. Residents would begin to work with the empowered employee because he would be able to get things done
    D. The rest of the department would start to feel resentment and frustration, and might potentially retaliate

25. If a town clerk works well with customers on the phone but struggles with face-to-face interactions, which of the following might BEST explain the problem?
    A. The actual words the clerk uses   B. Facial and other body cues
    C. Vocal cues   D. Both A and C

KEY (CORRECT ANSWERS)

1.	D		11.	B
2.	A		12.	A
3.	A		13.	D
4.	D		14.	A
5.	C		15.	D
6.	B		16.	A
7.	C		17.	B
8.	B		18.	C
9.	C		19.	C
10.	A		20.	B

21.	D
22.	A
23.	A
24.	D
25.	B

TEST 3

DIRECTIONS: Each question or incomplete statement is followed by several suggested answers or completions. Select the one that BEST answers the question or completes the statement. *PRINT THE LETTER OF THE CORRECT ANSWER IN THE SPACE AT THE RIGHT.*

1. If an employee's body position is causing customers to feel she is projecting a mood/attitude that she isn't actually expressing, what does the employee need to work on improving?
    A. Pitch   B. Articulation   C. Posture   D. Inflection

    1.____

2. A newly hired assistant notices that everyone in his department has received a new computer system except for him.
   What should he do?
    A. Assume this is a mistake and speak to his manager
    B. Complain to H.R.
    C. Quit
    D. Confront his manager regarding his unfair treatment

    2.____

3. A team leader in your department notices that ample amounts of department-labeled property have come up missing in recent weeks. The leader notices a fellow supervisor putting stationery and other equipment into a personal bag on a few different occasions and believes this person is responsible.
   What is the LEAST effective response to the situation?
    A. Gather more evidence to catch the person in the act
    B. Do nothing – if guilty, someone else will likely catch the colleague
    C. Privately ask other colleagues if they've noticed anything suspicious recently
    D. Inform a supervisor higher up in the organization that this person is a potential suspect

    3.____

4. Near the end of the work day, an official advisor accidentally sends an e-mail containing confidential information to the wrong person.
   Which of the following would be the BEST thing for the advisor to do?
    A. Overlook the error. Send the e-mail to the correct person and leave things as they are.
    B. Find a senior advisor and explain the mistake and have them deal with the problem
    C. Leave the office and deal with any fallout tomorrow
    D. Immediately send a follow-up e-mail to the "wrong" person explaining the mistake. Then send the e-mail to the correct person.

    4.____

5. If an employee is engaged with a customer and no one else is around when the phone rings, what is the PROPER step to take in this situation?
    A. Let the phone ring and continue to work with the customer in person
    B. Take the call and address the caller's issue, then hang up and come back to the customer
    C. Ask the customer to answer the phone while trying to resolve their issue.
    D. Tell the customer "excuse me" while answering the phone, then put the caller on hold while going back to the customer

6. According to many national retailer surveys, what do consumers remember the MOST about their customer service experience?
    A. The cost of the merchandise/experience
    B. The demeanor of the employee who engaged them
    C. The cleanliness of the office/area
    D. How nice the employees were

7. When attempting to help a resident make a decision about programs offered by your agency, it is important to remember that the majority of purchasing decisions consumers make are based upon
    A. what they think
    B. a potential free gift
    C. how they feel
    D. all of the above

8. In an effort to improve procedures in your department, a memo has been sent to employees. In it, one highlighted section focuses on the importance of avoiding closed-ended questions/comments.
    Following the advice of the memo, which question/comment should an employee avoid stating to a resident?
    A. "Can I help you?"
    B. "What is it you would like to see accomplished?"
    C. "So the challenges you've faced so far are..."
    D. "How would you like to see that improved?"

9. Numerous surveys indicate that consumers would actually pay more for
    A. self-checkout machines
    B. free product/demonstration giveaways
    C. more streamlined customer service
    D. apps using customer-service bots

10. Which of the following is an example of a proper "Activation Greeting"?
    A. "My name is _____. Let me tell you about our programs."
    B. "How many are there in your group?"
    C. "Hi! Welcome to _____."
    D. Both A and C

11. When interacting with members of the public, which of the following is the MOST important thing to do?   11.____
    A. Ask them to pay for services up front
    B. Smile at them
    C. Learn their name and call them by it
    D. Ask questions

12. Which of the following pieces of advice would help a clerk the MOST when working with the public?   12.____
    A. Pay attention to needs of others and offer only general solutions
    B. Hear what others are saying but do not take their comments to heart
    C. Focus on efficiency of service over quality of service
    D. Clearly understand the motives and needs of others

13. A member of the community complains that counselors at her child's camp do not listen to what she is telling them.   13.____
    Which technique listed below would improve understanding between the two parties?
    A. Reflective listening   B. Narrow selections
    C. Reflective thinking   D. Valid suggestions

14. When dealing with elderly residents, which of the following facts should be considered by a public official?   14.____
    A. They expect to be treated with courtesy and respect
    B. Expect them to avoid eye contact
    C. They prefer the telephone to personal contact
    D. They expect text and e-mail over face-to-face communication

15. If you are hired as a camp counselor for younger residents, it is important to remember all of the following about their behavior EXCEPT that they   15.____
    A. value technology
    B. are used to multitasking and access to instant information
    C. make less eye contact
    D. prefer more formal interactions

16. If one is trying to improve morale regarding customer/worker relations, which of the following is NOT a recommended thing to do?   16.____
    A. Publicly embarrass customers who are rude to the office employees
    B. Greet the customer with "Good Morning"
    C. Politely ask customers who cut in line to wait until it is their turn
    D. Thank customers for doing business with you

17. When hired by a public office, which of the following would be part of the newly hired employee's performance code?   17.____
    A. Report on time in a calm and controlled manner
    B. Present oneself in a neat and clean way
    C. Treat co-workers and residents with dignity and respect
    D. All of the above

18. If an employee sometimes "bends the rules" to honor a request from a customer, what service concept would explain this action?
    A. Motivated marketing strategy
    B. Power selling philosophy
    C. Employee empowerment
    D. Selling out for the customer

19. A Parks and Recreation worker is attempting to improve relations with the groups who sign up for his arts and crafts program.
    He should remember all of the following "Customer Service Rules" EXCEPT
    A. Customer service has a large effect on customer satisfaction
    B. Modern consumers are already more satisfied with customer service today than ever before
    C. Modern consumers have many different mechanisms by which to complain
    D. Feeling empowered as an employee usually leads to higher customer satisfaction

20. A marketing executive employee wishes to emphasize customer loyalty. Which of the following marketing strategies should the employee focus on when working with customers?
    A. Relationship marketing
    B. Undercover marketing
    C. Diversity marketing
    D. Transactional marketing

21. Why would a campaign manager for an elected official be interested in conducting a mail survey over other methods of surveying?
    It would
    A. avoid non-response problems
    B. speed up the process by which surveys are returned to them
    C. avoid participation by incorrect respondents
    D. enable the completion of the survey at a convenient time

22. At the end of each session, a counselor takes it upon herself to conduct research on the effectiveness of the program. She is worried that respondents won't be truthful, so she decides that the BEST way to avoid bias would be to conduct a(n) _____ survey.
    A. personal   B. telephone   C. internet   D. observational

23. A resident walks into the office and submits an application. When she is given additional forms to complete, she grumbles about "bureaucratic red tape" and how it's slowing down her application approval.
    How should an employee handle this situation?
    A. Be patient with the resident but do not explain the reason for the forms
    B. Tell the resident why the additional forms are necessary
    C. Suggest that the resident take it up with the manager if she wants the policy changed
    D. Say that the application will not be processed until ALL forms are completed

24. An employee's next-door neighbor has been hired as summer help, which the employee knows about because he has to type a confidential letter from the director to human resources about the hire. The neighbor does not yet know of the hiring decision, and the employee will see the neighbor later that day. Which one of the following should the employee do?
    A. Say nothing and wait for the offer to become official
    B. Congratulate the neighbor confidentially
    C. Inform a handful of people including the neighbor's close friends
    D. None of the above

25. A child with vision impairment wants to join a summer day camp and is denied access because the camp focuses on games and activities in which sight is required. If the parent comes in and complains to you, which of the following actions should you take and why?
    A. Modify the camp so the child can join because it is bad publicity to deny a child with a disability
    B. Offer another camp that does not focus on so many "sight-based" activities at a reduced rate so the parent and child do not feel left out
    C. Enroll the child and ensure they are allowed to participate in a meaningful way, because it's against the law to prevent the child from signing up
    D. Tell the parent they can talk to a supervisor because you have no authority to change the decision

KEY (CORRECT ANSWERS)

1.	C		11.	B
2.	A		12.	D
3.	B		13.	A
4.	D		14.	A
5.	D		15.	D
6.	B		16.	A
7.	C		17.	D
8.	A		18.	C
9.	C		19.	B
10.	C		20.	A

21.	D
22.	C
23.	B
24.	A
25.	C

TEST 4

DIRECTIONS: Each question or incomplete statement is followed by several suggested answers or completions. Select the one that BEST answers the question or completes the statement. *PRINT THE LETTER OF THE CORRECT ANSWER IN THE SPACE AT THE RIGHT.*

1. If a customer tells an employee they need to work on having open body language, which of the following would be an example?
    A. Fiddling
    B. Minimal eye contact
    C. Folded arms
    D. Frequent hand gestures

2. As a phone operator for the bureau director's office, it is important that you make the constituents feel as though you are actively listening to their concerns.
What is the MOST effective way to demonstrate this?
    A. Use affirmation with words like "ok", "yes" and "I understand"
    B. Interrupt with your own thoughts
    C. Ask numerous closed questions
    D. Talk over the constituent

3. When a resident walks up to a clerk's desk, which of the following is the BEST way to greet them?
    A. Wave
    B. Ask them what they need
    C. Welcome them and ask how they can be helped
    D. Ignore them until finished with the current task

4. When a customer complains through e-mail, an office clerk should
    A. forward the e-mail to a supervisor
    B. reply right away with a potential solution
    C. share the complaint via the office's official Twitter handle
    D. reply right away with a hurried answer

5. Interacting with the public is a constant back and forth where feedback is essential to improving service.
Which of the following methods would be BEST to obtain feedback from the public?
    A. Cold calling
    B. Tweeting
    C. Survey via website
    D. Ask the staff what they think

6. If residents continually complain that clerks do not truly understand what they are trying to tell them, which of the following practices might help improve this communication barrier?
    A. Paraphrasing
    B. Encoding
    C. Rapport building
    D. Decoding

2 (#4)

7. A customer complains to an employee and demands to see a supervisor. The employee is not sure to who to direct this angry customer. Which of the following methods of illustrating hierarchy of the company would help the employee out?
   A. Diagramming
   B. Negotiation
   C. Brainstorming
   D. Organizational charts

7.____

8. A village clerk and a resident have a strong disagreement about how an office policy applies to their situation. A co-worker is asked to weigh in on the situation. How should the co-worker handle the situation?
   A. Take the employee's side since they have to work side by side
   B. Try to help both parties walk away feeling like they got what they wanted
   C. Take the resident's side since the office cannot afford bad publicity
   D. Have a supervisor intervene – it's better to pass responsibility onto someone in power

8.____

9. A parent accuses your department of making generalizations about their child based on the group to which they belong. Which of the following unfair, but common, ideas is the department being accused of?
   A. Racism
   B. Stereotyping
   C. Confirmation bias
   D. Rationale judgment

9.____

10. When a resident calls a government office, they expect the phone to be picked up by the _____ ring otherwise they feel as though their call is unimportant.
    A. 1st   B. 4th   C. 3rd   D. 7th

10.____

11. When working directly with a consumer on the phone or in person, which of the following would be considered inappropriate?
    A. Eating, drinking or chewing gum
    B. Speaking slowly and enunciating clearly
    C. Asking permission to put someone on hold
    D. Wearing a headset

11.____

12. Someone calls village hall and is extremely upset by a policy change enacted in the last board meeting. They demand an explanation that the clerk does not have. As the clerk tries to find the answer, how often should she update the angry caller on the status of the complaint (even if the clerk has no answer)?
    A. 2-3 minutes
    B. 35 seconds
    C. 1 minute
    D. Do not update them until an answer has been found

12.____

13. A resident is irate over how a co-worker of yours handled his claim process and now you have to handle his appeal. Throughout the process of filling out the necessary paperwork, this resident continues to not only berate the co-worker, but also starts complaining about how slow you are.
In this stressful situation, why is it important to stay calm and not let the resident get to you?
    A. They could be having a bad day and your anger may make the situation worse
    B. You need to show the resident you are willing to take the time necessary to resolve his or her problem
    C. They might be violent and could end up hurting you
    D. Both A and B

13._____

14. An employee is calling residents to thank them for volunteering for a food drive. As the employee moves through his list, he accidentally dials the wrong number, and a person on the other line answers.
What should the employee do?
    A. Apologize to the person for calling the wrong number
    B. Thank the person anyway
    C. Hang up before the person says anything else
    D. Try to sign the person up for the next food drive

14._____

15. Which of the following questions tell the customer that the employee wants to ensure that every need has been met before the interaction is over?
    A. "You've said everything you need to say, right?"
    B. "Is there anything else I can help you with?"
    C. "How can I help you today?"
    D. "Would you like me to transfer you to someone else?"

15._____

16. An elderly resident calls your department, but was trying to reach the Health and Sanitation Department. What should you do?
    A. Be polite
    B. Hastily transfer the person to the correct department
    C. Try to determine who they need to speak to and transfer them to that person directly if possible
    D. Both A and C

16._____

17. Which of the following would NOT be considered an example of good customer service?
    A. A parent waits three minutes to pick up their child from an after-school activity
    B. A clearly defined resolution process is in place for residents who have disagreements with public officials
    C. There is no line at the DMV, and a person waits 10 minutes before being serviced
    D. The park's pools briefly close at noon and 4 p.m. so they can be skimmed and checked for debris

17._____

18. A resident is angry about a zoning issue that prevents him from adding on to his garage.
    When dealing with this customer, which of the following should an employee NOT do?
    A. Acknowledge their emotion
    B. Ask questions
    C. Avoid escalating the argument
    D. Agree that the code is silly

    18.____

19. A resident comes into the office where you work and complains that he was screened out of a job because of a vision impairment. He asks if this is legal and what he should do.
    You tell him it is not against the Americans With Disabilities Act if the employer screens him because
    A. clients prefer not to be served by the disabled
    B. a business cannot make a reasonable accommodation to work tasks for a specific disability
    C. co-workers dislike working with the disabled
    D. none of the above; ADA prevents any kind of "screening out" of disabled persons

    19.____

20. During holidays and special events, the school office can sometimes be short-staffed, which requires all employees to know the different roles within the office. Some parents do not like when certain staff members act as the receptionist and those staff members do not like being the receptionist.
    Since both sides do not like the employees in that role, the employees should
    A. learn the receptionist's job and fill in when needed, but tell the principal that they, and parents, would prefer that they work in a different area
    B. tell the principal they don't want to work as a receptionist and ask to be excused from that role
    C. learn the receptionist's job, but when asked to fill in ask someone else to do it
    D. ask the principal to excuse then from the training, and explain that other employees who the parents like more could fill in for them

    20.____

21. In an attempt to promote the recreation center in a positive light, which of the following advertising strategies would be MOST credible to town residents?
    A. Employees telling people how great the recreation center environment is
    B. Have local celebrities endorse the recreation center as the place to be
    C. Use current satisfied customers by having them "spread the word" about the recreation center
    D. Offer incredible discounts to the first 25 new customers to sign up

    21.____

22. When a clerk is tasked with setting up a Town Hall meeting, all of the following are important EXCEPT
    A. spreading the word
    B. having an audience-selected moderator
    C. setting and following a schedule
    D. keeping things moving

    22.____

23. A librarian works in the computer lab and a patron comes to her and says, "My flash drive is full. I need to save the document I just created. Where can I get a new flash drive?"
How should the librarian respond?
   A. Offer to help the patron e-mail the document to himself and then show him how to do it
   B. Ask the patron what he needs to save and then save it to a "Google Document" for them
   C. Offer him the use of a library-owned flash drive on the promise that he will bring it back
   D. Direct him to the nearest computer/retail store to purchase the flash drive

24. If people call for a Town Hall meeting, which of the following would NOT be a good reason to hold one?
   A. To voice a common concern shared by members of the community
   B. To present a new proposal that impacts the public
   C. To settle a dispute between rival advisors at City Hall
   D. To collect feedback in response to a new rule or policy implementation

25. Of the following Town Hall meeting pitfalls, which would MOST leave residents feeling as though they wasted their time?
   A. Not participative or interactive
   B. Poorly designed PowerPoint or on-screen presentation
   C. Poor time management
   D. Meaningless or irrelevant content

KEY (CORRECT ANSWERS)

1.	D	11.	A
2.	A	12.	C
3.	C	13.	D
4.	B	14.	A
5.	C	15.	B
6.	A	16.	D
7.	D	17.	C
8.	B	18.	D
9.	B	19.	B
10.	C	20.	A

21.	C
22.	B
23.	A
24.	C
25.	D

EXAMINATION SECTION
TEST 1

DIRECTIONS: Each question or incomplete statement is followed by several suggested answers or completions. Select the one that BEST answers the question or completes the statement. *PRINT THE LETTER OF THE CORRECT ANSWER IN THE SPACE AT THE RIGHT.*

1. When conducting a needs assessment for the purpose of education planning, an agency's FIRST step is to identify or provide
    A. a profile of population characteristics
    B. barriers to participation
    C. existing resources
    D. profiles of competing resources

2. Research has demonstrated that of the following, the MOST effective medium for communicating with external publics is(are)
    A. video news releases
    B. television
    C. radio
    D. newspapers

3. Basic ideas behind the effort to influence the attitudes and behaviors of a constituency include each of the following EXCEPT the idea that
    A. words, rather than actions or events, are most likely to motivate
    B. demands for action are a usual response
    C. self-interest usually figures heavily into public involvement
    D. the reliability of change programs is difficult to assess

4. An agency representative is trying to craft a pithy message to constituents in order to encourage the use of agency program resources.
Choosing an audience for such messages is easiest when the message
    A. is project- or behavior-based
    B. is combined with other messages
    C. is abstract
    D. has a broad appeal

5. Of the following factors, the MOST important to the success of an agency's external education or communication programs is the
    A. amount of resources used to implement them
    B. public's prior experiences with the agency
    C. real value of the program to the public
    D. commitment of the internal audience

6. A representative for a state agency is being interviewed by a reporter from a local news network. The representative is being asked to defend a program that is extremely unpopular in certain parts of the municipality.
When a constituency is known to be opposed to a position, the MOST useful communication strategy is to present

A. only the arguments that are consistent with constituents' views
B. only the agency's side of the issue
C. both sides of the argument as clearly as possible
D. both sides of the argument, omitting key information about the opposing position

7. The MOST significant barriers to effective agency community relations include
   I. widespread distrust of communication strategies
   II. the media's "watchdog" stance
   III. public apathy
   IV. statutory opposition

   The CORRECT answer is:
   A. I only   B. I and II   C. II and III   D. III and IV

8. In conducting an education program, many agencies use workshops and seminars in a classroom setting.
   Advantages of classroom-style teaching over other means of educating the public include each of the following, EXCEPT
   A. enabling an instructor to verify learning through testing and interaction with the target audience
   B. enabling hands-on practice and other participatory learning techniques
   C. ability to reach an unlimited number of participants in a given length of time
   D. ability to convey the latest, most up-to-date information

9. The _____ model of community relations is characterized by an attempt to persuade the public to adopt the agency's point of view.
   A. two-way symmetric   B. two-way asymmetric
   C. public information   D. press agency/publicity

10. Important elements of an internal situation analysis include the
    I. list of agency opponents   II. communication audit
    III. updated organizational almanac   IV. stakeholder analysis

    The CORRECT answer is:
    A. I and II   B. I, II, and III   C. II and III   D. I, II, III and IV

11. Government agency information efforts typically involve each of the following objectives, EXCEPT to
    A. implement changes in the policies of government agencies to align with public opinion
    B. communicate the work of agencies
    C. explain agency techniques in a way that invites input from citizens
    D. provide citizen feedback to government administrators

12. Factors that are likely to influence the effectiveness of an educational campaign include the
    I. level of homogeneity among intended participants
    II. number and types of media used
    III. receptivity of the intended participants
    IV. level of specificity in the message or behavior to be taught

    The CORRECT answer is:
    A. I and II   B. I, II, and III   C. II and III   D. I, II, III, and IV

13. An agency representative is writing instructional objectives that will later help to measure the effectiveness of an educational program.
    Which of the following verbs, included in an objective, would be MOST helpful for the purpose of measuring effectiveness?
    A. Know   B. Identify   C. Learn   D. Comprehend

14. A state education agency wants to encourage participation in a program that has just received a boost through new federal legislation. The program is intended to include participants from a wide variety of socioeconomic and other demographic characteristics. The agency wants to launch a broad-based program that will inform virtually every interested party in the state about the program's new circumstances.
    In attempting to deliver this message to such a wide-ranging constituency, the agency's BEST practice would be to
    A. broadcast the same message through as many different media channels as possible
    B. focus on one discrete segment of the public at a time
    C. craft a message whose appeal is as broad as the public itself
    D. let the program's achievements speak for themselves and rely on word-of-mouth

15. Advantages associated with using the World Wide Web as an educational tool include
    I. an appeal to younger generations of the public
    II. visually-oriented, interactive learning
    III. learning that is not confined by space, time, or institutional association
    IV. a variety of methods for verifying use and learning

    The CORRECT answer is:
    A. I only   B. I and II   C. I, II, and III   D. I, II, II, and IV

16. In agencies involved in health care, community relations is a critical function because it
    A. serves as an intermediary between the agency and consumers
    B. generates a clear mission statement for agency goals and priorities
    C. ensures patient privacy while satisfying the media's right to information
    D. helps marketing professionals determine the wants and needs of agency constituents

17. After an extensive campaign to promote its newest program to constituents, an agency learns that most of the audience did not understand the intended message.
MOST likely, the agency has
   A. chosen words that were intended to inform, rather than persuade
   B. not accurately interpreted what the audience really needed to know
   C. overestimated the ability of the audience to receive and process the message
   D. compensated for noise that may have interrupted the message

17.____

18. The necessary elements that lead to conviction and motivation in the minds of participants in an educational or information program include each of the following, EXCEPT the _____ of the message.
   A. acceptability   B. intensity
   C. single-channel appeal D. pervasiveness

18.____

19. Printed materials are often at the core of educational programs provided by public agencies.
The PRIMARY disadvantage associated with print is that it
   A. does not enable comprehensive treatment of a topic
   B. is generally unreliable in term of assessing results
   C. is often the most expensive medium available
   D. is constrained by time

19.____

20. Traditional thinking on public opinion holds that there is about _____ percent of the public who are pivotal to shifting the balance and momentum of opinion—they are concerned about an issue, but not fanatical, and interested enough to pay attention to a reasoned discussion.
   A. 2   B. 10   C. 33   D. 51

20.____

21. One of the most useful guidelines for influencing attitude change among people is to
   A. invite the target audience to come to you, rather than approaching them
   B. use moral appeals as the primary approach
   C. use concrete images to enable people to see the results of behaviors or indifference
   D. offer tangible rewards to people for changes in behavior

21.____

22. An agency is attempting to evaluate the effectiveness of its educational program. For this purpose, it wants to observe several focus groups discussing the same program.
Which of the following would NOT be a guideline for the use of focus groups?
   A. Focus groups should only include those who have participated in the program.
   B. Be sure to accurately record the discussion.
   C. The same questions should be asked at each focus group meeting.
   D. It is often helpful to have a neutral, non-agency employee facilitate discussions.

22.____

23. Research consistently shows that _____ is the determinant most likely to make a newspaper editor run a news release.
    A. novelty   B. prominence   C. proximity   D. conflict

24. Which of the following is NOT one of the major variables to take into account when considering a population-needs assessment?
    A. State of program development   B. Resources available
    C. Demographics   D. Community attitudes

25. The FIRST step in any communications audit is to
    A. develop a research instrument
    B. determine how the organization currently communicates
    C. hire a contractor
    D. determine which audience to assess

KEY (CORRECT ANSWERS)

1.	A		11.	A
2.	D		12.	D
3.	A		13.	B
4.	A		14.	B
5.	D		15.	C
6.	C		16.	A
7.	D		17.	B
8.	C		18.	C
9.	B		19.	B
10.	C		20.	B

21. C
22. A
23. C
24. C
25. D

TEST 2

DIRECTIONS: Each question or incomplete statement is followed by several suggested answers or completions. Select the one that BEST answers the question or completes the statement. *PRINT THE LETTER OF THE CORRECT ANSWER IN THE SPACE AT THE RIGHT.*

1. A public relations practitioner at an agency has just composed a press release highlighting a program's recent accomplishments and success stories.
   In pitching such releases to print outlets, the practitioner should
   I. e-mail, mail, or send them by messenger
   II. address them to "editor" or "news director"
   III. have an assistant call all media contacts by telephone
   IV. ask reporters or editors how they prefer to receive them

   The CORRECT answer is:
   A. I and II   B. I and IV   C. II, III, and IV   D. III only

   1.____

2. The "output goals" of an educational program are MOST likely to include
   A. specified ratings of services by participants on a standardized scale
   B. observable effects on a given community or clientele
   C. the number of instructional hours provided
   D. the number of participants served

   2.____

3. An agency wants to evaluate satisfaction levels among program participants, and mails out questionnaires to everyone who has been enrolled in the last year.
   The PRIMARY problem associated with this method of evaluative research is that it
   A. poses a significant inconvenience for respondents
   B. is inordinately expensive
   C. does not allow for follow-up or clarification questions
   D. usually involves a low response rate

   3.____

4. A communications audit is an important tool for measuring
   A. the depth of penetration of a particular message or program
   B. the cost of the organization's information campaigns
   C. how key audiences perceive an organization
   D. the commitment of internal stakeholders

   4.____

5. The "ABCs" of written learning objectives include each of the following, EXCEPT
   A. Audience   B. Behavior   C. Conditions   D. Delineation

   5.____

6. When attempting to change the behaviors of constituents, it is important to keep in mind that
   I. most people are skeptical of communications that try to get them to change their behaviors
   II. in most cases, a person selects the media to which he exposes himself
   III. people tend to react defensively to messages or programs that rely on fear as a motivating factor
   IV. programs should aim for the broadest appeal possible in order to include as many participants as possible

   The CORRECT answer is:
   A. I and II B. I, II and III C. II and III D. I, II, III, and IV

   6._____

7. The "laws" of public opinion include the idea that it is
   A. useful for anticipating emergencies
   B. not sensitive to important events
   C. basically determined by self-interest
   D. sustainable through persistent appeals

   7._____

8. Which of the following types of evaluations is used to measure public attitudes before and after an information/educational program?
   A. Retrieval study   B. Copy test
   C. Quota sampling   D. Benchmark study

   8._____

9. The PRIMARY source for internal communications is(are) usually
   A. flow charts   B. meetings
   C. voice mail   D. printed publications

   9._____

10. An agency representative is putting together informational materials—brochures and a newsletter—outlining changes in one of the state's biggest benefits programs.
    In assembling print materials as a medium for delivering information to the public, the representative should keep in mind each of the following trends:
    I. For various reasons, the reading capabilities of the public are in general decline
    II. Without tables and graphs to help illustrate the changes, it is unlikely that the message will be delivered effectively
    III. Professionals and career-oriented people are highly receptive to information written in the form of a journal article or empirical study
    IV. People tend to be put off by print materials that use itemized and bulleted (●) lists

    The CORRECT answer is:
    A. I and II B. I, II and III C. II and III D. I, II, III, and IV

    10._____

11. Which of the following steps in a problem-oriented information campaign would typically be implemented FIRST?
    A. Deciding on tactics
    B. Determining a communications strategy
    C. Evaluating the problem's impact
    D. Developing an organizational strategy

12. A common pitfall in conducting an educational program is to
    A. aim it at the wrong target audience
    B. overfund it
    C. leave it in the hands of people who are in the business of education, rather than those with expertise in the business of the organization
    D. ignore the possibility that some other organization is meeting the same educational need for the target audience

13. The key factors that affect the credibility of an agency's educational program include
    A. organization   B. scope
    C. sophistication   D. penetration

14. Research on public opinion consistently demonstrates that it is
    A. easy to move people toward a strong opinion on anything, as long as they are approached directly through their emotions
    B. easier to move people away from an opinion they currently hold than to have them form an opinion about something they have not previously cared about
    C. easy to move people toward a strong opinion on anything, as long as the message appeals to their reason and intellect
    D. difficult to move people toward a strong opinion on anything, no matter what the approach

15. In conducting an education program, many agencies use meetings and conferences to educate an audience about the organization and its programs. Advantages associated with this approach include
    I. a captive audience that is known to be interested in the topic
    II. ample opportunities for verifying learning
    III. cost-efficient meeting space
    IV. the ability to provide information on a wider variety of subjects

    The CORRECT answer is:
    A. I and II   B. I, III and IV   C. II and III   D. I, II, III and IV

16. An agency is attempting to evaluate the effectiveness of its educational programs. For this purpose, it wants to observe several focus groups discussing particular programs.
    For this purpose, a focus group should never number more than _____ participants.
    A. 5   B. 10   C. 15   D. 20

17. A _____ speech is written so that several agency members can deliver it to different audiences with only minor variations.
    A. basic   B. printed   C. quota   D. pattern

18. Which of the following statements about public opinion is generally considered to be FALSE?
    A. Opinion is primarily reactive rather than proactive.
    B. People have more opinions about goals than about the means by which to achieve them.
    C. Facts tend to shift opinion in the accepted direction when opinion is not solidly structured.
    D. Public opinion is based more on information than desire.

19. An agency is trying to promote its educational program.
    As a general rule, the agency should NOT assume that
    A. people will only participate if they perceive an individual benefit
    B. promotions need to be aimed at small, discrete groups
    C. if the program is good, the audience will find out about it
    D. a variety of methods, including advertising, special events, and direct mail, should be considered

20. In planning a successful educational program, probably the first and most important question for an agency to ask is:
    A. What will be the content of the program?
    B. Who will be served by the program?
    C. When is the best time to schedule the program?
    D. Why is the program necessary?

21. Media kits are LEAST likely to contain
    A. fact sheets   B. memoranda
    C. photographs with captions D. news releases

22. The use of pamphlets and booklets as media for communication with the public often involves the disadvantage that
    A. the messages contained within them are frequently nonspecific
    B. it is difficult to measure their effectiveness in delivering the message
    C. there are few opportunities for people to refer to them
    D. color reproduction is poor

23. The MOST important prerequisite of a good educational program is an
    A. abundance of resources to implement it
    B. individual staff unit formed for the purpose of program delivery
    C. accurate needs assessment
    D. uneducated constituency

24. After an education program has been delivered, an agency conducts a program evaluation to determine whether its objectives have been met.
General rules about how to conduct such an education program valuation include each of the following, EXCEPT that it
   A. must be done immediately after the program has been implemented
   B. should be simple and easy to use
   C. should be designed so that tabulation of responses can take place quickly and inexpensively
   D. should solicit mostly subjective, open-ended responses if the audience was large

25. Using electronic media such as television as means of educating the public is typically recommended ONLY for agencies that
   I. have a fairly simple message to begin with
   II. want to reach the masses, rather than a targeted audience
   III. have substantial financial resources
   IV. accept that they will not be able to measure the results of the campaign with much precision

   The CORRECT answer is:
   A. I and II   B. I, II and III   C. II and IV   D. I, II, III and IV

KEY (CORRECT ANSWERS)

1.	B		11.	C
2.	C		12.	D
3.	D		13.	A
4.	C		14.	D
5.	D		15.	B
6.	B		16.	B
7.	C		17.	D
8.	D		18.	D
9.	D		19.	C
10.	A		20.	D

21.	B
22.	B
23.	C
24.	D
25.	D

COMMUNICATION

EXAMINATION SECTION
TEST 1

DIRECTIONS: Each question or incomplete statement is followed by several suggested answers or completions. Select the one that BEST answers the question or completes the statement. *PRINT THE LETTER OF THE CORRECT ANSWER IN THE SPACE AT THE RIGHT.*

1. In some agencies the counsel to the agency head is given the right to bypass the chain of command and issue orders directly to the staff concerning matters that involve certain specific processes and practices.
 This situation MOST nearly illustrates the principle of _____ authority.
    A. the acceptance theory of
    B. multiple-linear
    C. splintered
    D. functional

    1.____

2. It is commonly understood that communication is an important part of the administrative process.
 Which of the following is NOT a valid principle of the communication process in administration?
    A. The channels of communication should be spontaneous.
    B. The lines of communication should be as direct and as short as possible.
    C. Communications should be authenticated.
    D. The persons serving in communications centers should be competent.

    2.____

3. Of the following, the one factor which is generally considered LEAST essential to successful committee operations is
    A. stating a clear definition of the authority and scope of the committee
    B. selecting the committee chairman carefully
    C. limiting the size of the committee to four persons
    D. limiting the subject matter to that which can be handled in group discussion

    3.____

4. Of the following, the failure by line managers to accept and appreciate the benefits and limitations of a new program or system VERY FREQUENTLY can be traced to the
    A. budgetary problems involved
    B. resultant need to reduce staff
    C. lack of controls it engenders
    D. failure of top management to support its implementation

    4.____

5. If a manager were thinking about using a committee of subordinates to solve an operating problem, which of the following would generally NOT be an advantage of such use of the committee approach?
    A. Improved coordination
    B. Low cost
    C. Increased motivation
    D. Integrated judgment

    5.____

33

6. Every supervisor has many occasions to lead a conference or participate in a conference of some sort.
   Of the following statements that pertain to conferences and conference leadership, which is generally considered to be MOST valid?
   A. Since World War II, the trend has been toward fewer shared decisions and more conferences.
   B. The most important part of a conference leader's job is to direct discussion.
   C. In providing opportunities for group interaction, management should avoid consideration of its past management philosophy.
   D. A good administrator cannot lead a good conference if he is a poor public speaker.

7. Of the following, it is usually LEAST desirable for a conference leader to
   A. call the name of a person after asking a question
   B. summarize proceedings periodically
   C. make a practice of repeating questions
   D. ask a question without indicating who is to reply

8. Assume that, in a certain organization, a situation has developed in which there is little difference in status or authority between individuals.
   Which of the following would be the MOST likely result with regard to communication in this organization?
   A. Both the accuracy and flow of communication will be improved.
   B. Both the accuracy and flow of communication will substantially decrease.
   C. Employees will seek more formal lines of communication.
   D. Neither the flow nor the accuracy of communication will be improved over the former hierarchical structure.

9. The main function of many agency administrative officers is "information management." Information that is received by an administrative officer may be classified as active or passive, depending upon whether or not it requires the recipient to take some action.
   Of the following, the item received which is clearly the MOST active information is
   A. an appointment of a new staff member
   B. a payment voucher for a new desk
   C. a press release concerning a past event
   D. the minutes of a staff meeting

10. Of the following, the one LEAST considered to be a communication barrier is
    A. group feedback   B. charged words
    C. selective perception   D. symbolic meanings

11. Management studies support the hypothesis that, in spite of the tendency of employees to censor the information communicated to their supervisor, subordinates are more likely to communicate problem-oriented information UPWARD when they have a
    A. long period of service in the organization
    B. high degree of trust in the supervisor
    C. high educational level
    D. low status on the organizational ladder

12. Electronic data processing equipment can produce more information faster than can be generated by any other means.
    In view of this, the MOST important problem faced by management at present is to
    A. keep computers fully occupied
    B. find enough computer personnel
    C. assimilate and properly evaluate the information
    D. obtain funds to establish appropriate information systems

13. A well-designed management information system essentially provides each executive and manager the information he needs for
    A. determining computer time requirements
    B. planning and measuring results
    C. drawing a new organization chart
    D. developing a new office layout

14. It is generally agreed that management policies should be periodically reappraised and restated in accordance with current conditions.
    Of the following, the approach which would be MOST effective in determining whether a policy should be revised is to
    A. conduct interviews with staff members at all levels in order to ascertain the relationship between the policy and actual practice
    B. make proposed revisions in the policy and apply it to current problems
    C. make up hypothetical situations using both the old policy and a revised version in order to make comparisons
    D. call a meeting of top level staff in order to discuss ways of revising the policy

15. Your superior has asked you to notify division employees of an important change in one of the operating procedures described in the division manual. Every employee presently has a copy of this manual.
    Which of the following is normally the MOST practical way to get the employees to understand such a change?
    A. Notify each employee individually of the change and answer any questions he might have
    B. Send a written notice to key personnel, directing them to inform the people under them

C. Call a general meeting, distribute a corrected page for the manual, and discuss the change
D. Send a memo to employees describing the change in general terms and asking them to make the necessary corrections in their copies of the manual

16. Assume that the work in your department involves the use of any technical terms.
    In such a situation, when you are answering inquiries from the general public, it would usually be BEST to
    A. use simple language and avoid the technical terms
    B. employ the technical terms whenever possible
    C. bandy technical terms freely, but explain each term in parentheses
    D. apologize if you are forced to use a technical term

16._____

17. Suppose that you receive a telephone call from someone identifying himself as an employee in another city department who asks to be given information which your own department regards as confidential.
    Which of the following is the BEST way of handling such a request?
    A. Give the information requested, since your caller as official standing
    B. Grant the request, provided the caller gives you a signed receipt
    C. Refuse the request, because you have no way of knowing whether the caller is really who he claims to be
    D. Explain that the information is confidential and inform the caller of the channels he must go through to have the information released to him

17._____

18. Studies show that office employees place high importance on the social and human aspects of the organization. What office employees like best about their jobs is the kind of people with whom they work. So strive hard to group people who are most likely to get along well together.
    Based on this information, it is MOST reasonable to assume that office workers are most pleased to work in a group which
    A. is congenial   B. has high productivity
    C. allows individual creativity D. is unlike other groups

18._____

19. A certain supervisor does not compliment members of his staff when they come up with good ideas. He feels that coming up with good ideas is part of the job and does not merit special attention.
    This supervisor's practice is
    A. *poor*, because recognition for good ideas is a good motivator
    B. *poor*, because the staff will suspect that the supervisor has no good ideas of his own
    C. *good*, because it is reasonable to assume that employees will tell their supervisor of ways to improve office practice
    D. *good*, because the other members of the staff are not made to seem inferior by comparison

19._____

20. Some employees of a department have sent an anonymous letter containing many complaints to the department head.
    Of the following, what is this MOST likely to show about the department?
    A. It is probably a good place to work.
    B. Communications are probably poor.
    C. The complaints are probably unjustified.
    D. These employees are probably untrustworthy.

    20.____

21. Which of the following actions would usually be MOST appropriate for a supervisor to take after receiving an instruction sheet from his superior explaining a new procedure which is to be followed?
    A. Put the instruction sheet aside temporarily until he determines what is wrong with the old procedure.
    B. Call his superior and ask whether the procedure is one he must implement immediately.
    C. Write a memorandum to the superior asking for more details.
    D. Try the new procedure and advise the superior of any problems or possible improvements.

    21.____

22. Of the following, which one is considered the PRIMARY advantage of using a committee to resolved a problem in an organization?
    A. No one person will be held accountable for the decision since a group of people was involved.
    B. People with different backgrounds give attention to the problem.
    C. The decision will take considerable time so there is unlikely to be a decision that will later be regretted.
    D. One person cannot dominate the decision-making process.

    22.____

23. Employees in a certain office come to their supervisor with all their complaints about the office and the work. Almost every employee has had at least one minor complaint at some time.
    The situation with respect to complaints in this office may BEST be described as probably
    A. *good*; employees who complain care about their jobs and work hard
    B. *good*; grievances brought out into the open can be corrected
    C. *bad*; only serious complaints should be discussed
    D. *bad*; it indicates the staff does not have confidence in the administration

    23.____

24. The administrator who allows his staff to suggest ways to do their work will usually find that
    A. this practice contributes to high productivity
    B. the administrator's ideas produce greater output
    C. clerical employees suggest inefficient work methods
    D. subordinate employees resent performing a management function

    24.____

25. The MAIN purpose for a supervisor's questioning the employees at a conference he is holding is to
    A. stress those areas of information covered but not understood by the participants
    B. encourage participants to think through the problem under discussion
    C. catch those subordinates who are not paying attention
    D. permit the more knowledgeable participants to display their grasp of the problems being discussed

KEY (CORRECT ANSWERS)

1.	D		11.	B
2.	A		12.	C
3.	C		13.	B
4.	D		14.	A
5.	B		15.	C
6.	B		16.	A
7.	C		17.	D
8.	D		18.	A
9.	A		19.	A
10.	A		20.	B

21.	D
22.	B
23.	B
24.	A
25.	B

TEST 2

DIRECTIONS: Each question or incomplete statement is followed by several suggested answers or completions. Select the one that BEST answers the question or completes the statement. *PRINT THE LETTER OF THE CORRECT ANSWER IN THE SPACE AT THE RIGHT.*

1. For a superior to use *consultative supervision* with his subordinates effectively, it is ESSENTIAL that he
    A. accept the fact that his formal authority will be weakened by the procedure
    B. admit that he does not know more than all his men together and that his ideas are not always best
    C. utilize a committee system so that the procedure is orderly
    D. make sure that all subordinates are consulted so that no one feels left out

1.____

2. The *grapevine* is an informal means of communication in an organization. The attitude of a supervisor with respect to the grapevine should be to
    A. ignore it since it deals mainly with rumors and sensational information
    B. regard it as a serious danger which should be eliminated
    C. accept it as a real line of communication which should be listened to
    D. utilize it for most purposes instead of the official line of communication

2.____

3. The supervisor of an office that must deal with the public should realize that planning in this type of work situation
    A. is useless because he does not know how many people will request service or what service they will request
    B. must be done at a higher level but that he should be ready to implement the results of such planning
    C. is useful primarily for those activities that are not concerned with public contact
    D. is useful for all the activities of the office, including those that relate to public contact

3.____

4. Assume that it is your job to receive incoming telephone calls. Those calls which you cannot handle yourself have to be transferred to the appropriate office.
If you receive an outside call for an extension line which is busy, the one of the following which you should do FIRST is to
    A. interrupt the person speaking on the extension and tell him a call is waiting
    B. tell the caller the line is busy and let him know every thirty seconds whether or not it is free
    C. leave the caller on "hold" until the extension is free
    D. tell the caller the line is busy and ask him if he wishes to wait

4.____

5. Your superior has subscribed to several publications directly related to your division's work, and he has asked you to see to it that the publications are circulated among the supervisory personnel in the division. There are eight supervisors involved.
The BEST method of insuring that all eight see these publications is to
   A. place the publication in the division's general reference library as soon as it arrives
   B. inform each supervisor whenever a publication arrives and remind all of them that they are responsible for reading it
   C. prepare a standard slip that can be stapled to each publication, listing the eight supervisors and saying, "Please read, initial your name, and pass along"
   D. send a memo to the eight supervisors saying that they may wish to purchase individual subscriptions in their own names if they are interested in seeing each issue

6. Your superior has telephoned a number of key officials in your agency to ask whether they can meet at a certain time next month. He has found that they can all make it, and he has asked you to confirm the meeting.
Which of the following is the BEST way to confirm such a meeting?
   A. Note the meeting on your superior's calendar.
   B. Post a notice of the meeting on the agency bulletin board.
   C. Call the officials on the day of the meeting to remind them of the meeting.
   D. Write a memo to each official involved, repeating the time and place of the meeting.

7. Assume that a new city regulation requires that certain kinds of private organizations file information forms with your department. You have been asked to write the short explanatory message that will be printed on the front cover of the pamphlet containing the forms and instructions.
Which of the following would be the MOST appropriate way of beginning this message?
   A. Get the readers' attention by emphasizing immediately that there are legal penalties for organizations that fail to file before a certain date.
   B. Briefly state the nature of the enclosed forms and the types of organizations that must file.
   C. Say that your department is very sorry to have to put organizations to such an inconvenience.
   D. Quote the entire regulation adopted by the city, even if it is quite long and is expressed din complicated legal language.

8. Suppose that you have been told to make up the vacation schedule for the 18 employees in a particular unit. In order for the unit to operate effectively, only a few employees can be on vacation at the same time.
Which of the following is the MOST advisable approach in making up the schedule?
   A. Draw up a schedule assigning vacations in alphabetical order
   B. Find out when the supervisors want to take their vacations, and randomly assign whatever periods are left to the non-supervisory personnel

C. Assign the most desirable times to employees of longest standing and the least desirable times to the newest employees
D. Have all employees state their own preference, and then work out any conflicts in consultation with the people involved

9. Assume that you have been asked to prepare job descriptions for various positions in your department.
Which of the following are the basic points that should be covered in a *job description*?
   A. General duties and responsibilities of the position, with examples of day-to-day tasks
   B. Comments on the performances of present employees
   C. Estimates of the number of openings that may be available in each category during the coming year
   D. Instructions for carrying out the specific tasks assigned to your department

9.____

10. Of the following, the biggest DISADVANTAGE in allowing a free flow of communications in an agency is that such a free flow
    A. decreases creativity
    B. increases the use of the *grapevine*
    C. lengthens the chain of command
    D. reduces the executive's power to direct the flow of information

10.____

11. A downward flow of authority in an organization is one example of _____ communication.
    A. horizontal   B. informal   C. circular   D. vertical

11.____

12. Of the following, the one that would MOST likely block effective communication is
    A. concentration only on the issues at hand
    B. lack of interest or commitment
    C. use of written reports
    D. use of charts and graphs

12.____

13. An ADVANTAGE of the *lecture* as a teaching tool is that it
    A. enables a person to present his ideas to a large number of people
    B. allows the audience to retain a maximum of the information given
    C. holds the attention of the audience for the longest time
    D. enables the audience member to easily recall the main points

13.____

14. An ADVANTAGE of the *small-group* discussion as a teaching tool is that
    A. it always focuses attention on one person as the leader
    B. it places collective responsibility on the group as a whole
    C. its members gain experience by summarizing the ideas of others
    D. each member of the group acts as a member of a team

14.____

15. The one of the following that is an ADVANTAGE of a *large-group* discussion, when compared to a small-group discussion, is that the large-group discussion
    A. moves along more quickly than a small-group discussion
    B. allows its participants to feel more at ease, and speak out more freely
    C. gives the whole group a chance to exchange ideas on a certain subject at the same occasion
    D. allows its members to feel a greater sense of personal responsibility

15.____

KEY (CORRECT ANSWERS)

1.	D	6.	D	11.	D
2.	C	7.	B	12.	B
3.	D	8.	D	13.	A
4.	D	9.	A	14.	D
5.	C	10.	D	15.	C

EXAMINATION SECTION
TEST 1

DIRECTIONS: Each question or incomplete statement is followed by several suggested answers or completions. Select the one that BEST answers the question or completes the statement. *PRINT THE LETTER OF THE CORRECT ANSWER IN THE SPACE AT THE RIGHT.*

1. People will generally produce the most if
   A. management exercises close supervision over the work
   B. there is strict discipline in the group
   C. they are happy in their work
   D. they feel involved in their work
   E. they follow "the one best way"

   1.____

2. Which method would MOST likely be used to get first-hand information on complaints from the public?
   A. Study of correspondence
   B. Study of work volume
   C. Tracing specific transactions through a series of steps
   D. Tracing use of forms
   E. Worker desk audit

   2.____

3. An analysis of the flow of work in a department should begin with the _____ work.
   A. major routine   B. minor routine   C. supervisory
   D. technical   E. unusual

   3.____

4. Which one of the following may be defined as "a regulatory recurring appraisal of the manner in which all elements of agency management are being carried out?
   A. Functional survey   B. Operations audit
   C. Organization survey   D. Overall survey
   E. Reconnaissance survey

   4.____

5. Which one of the following is NOT an advantage of the interview method of collecting data?
   A. It enables interviewer to judge the person interviewed on such matters as general attitude, knowledge, etc.
   B. It helps build up personal relations for later installation of changes.
   C. It is a flexible method that can be adjusted to changing circumstances.
   D. It permits the obtaining of "off the record" information.
   E. It produces more accurate information than other methods.

   5.____

6. Which of the following seems LEAST useful as a guide in interviewing an employee in a procedures and methods survey?
    A. Explaining who you are and the purpose of your visit
    B. Having a general plan of what you intend to get from the interview
    C. Listening carefully and not interrupting
    D. Trying out his reactions to your ideas for improvements
    E. Trying to analyze his reasons for saying what he says

7. Which one of the following is an advantage of the questionnaire method of gathering facts as compared with the interview method?
    A. Different people may interpret the questions differently.
    B. Less "off the record" information is given.
    C. More time may be taken in order to give exact answers.
    D. Personal relationships with the people involved are not established.
    E. There is less need for follow-up.

8. Which one of the following is generally NOT an advantage of the personal observation method of gathering facts?
    A. It enables staff to use "off the record" information if personally observed.
    B. It helps in developing valid recommendations.
    C. It helps the person making the observation acquire "know how" valuable for later installation and follow-up.
    D. It is economical in time and money.
    E. It may turn up other problems in need of solution.

9. Which of the following would most often be the BEST way to minimize resistance to change?
    A. Break the news about the change gently to the people affected.
    B. Increase the salary of the people affected by the change.
    C. Let the people concerned participate in arriving at the decision to change.
    D. Notify all people concerned with the change, both orally and in writing.
    E. Stress the advantages of the new system.

10. The functional organization chart
    A. does not require periodic revision
    B. includes a description of the duties of each organization segment
    C. includes positions and titles for each organization segment
    D. is the simplest type of organization chart
    E. is used primarily by newly established agencies

11. The principle of span of control has frequently been said to be in conflict with the
    A. principle of unity of command
    B. principle that authority should be commensurate with responsibility
    C. principle that like functions should be grouped into one unit
    D. principle that the number of levels between the top of an organization and the bottom should be small
    E. scalar principle

12. If an executive delegates to his subordinates authority to handle problems of a routine nature for which standard solutions have been established, he may expect that
    A. fewer complaints will be received
    B. he has made it more difficult for his subordinates to solve these problems
    C. he has opened the way for confusion in his organization
    D. there will be a lack of consistency in the methods applied to the solution of these problems
    E. these routine problems will be handled efficiently and he will have more time for other non-routine work

12._____

13. Decentralization of the authority to make decisions is a necessary result of increased complexity in an organization, but for the sake of efficiency and coordination of operations, such decentralization must be planned carefully.
    A good general rule is that
    A. any decision should be made at the lowest possible point in the organization where all the information and competence necessary for a sound decision are available
    B. any decision should be made at the highest possible point in the organization, thus guaranteeing the best decision
    C. any decision should be made at the lowest possible point in the organization, but always approved by management
    D. any decision should be made by management and referred to the proper subordinate for comment
    E. no decision should be made by any individual in the organization without approval by a superior

13._____

14. Functional foremanship differs most markedly from generally accepted principles of administration in that it advocates
    A. an unlimited span of control
    B. less delegation of responsibility
    C. more than one supervisor for an employee
    D. nonfunctional organization
    E. substitution of execution for planning

14._____

15. In determining the type of organization structure of an enterprise, the one factor that might be given relatively greater weight in a small organization than in a larger organization of the same nature is the
    A. geographical location of the enterprise
    B. individual capabilities of incumbents
    C. method of financing to be employed
    D. size of the area served
    E. type of activity engaged in

15._____

16. Which of the following statements MOST accurately describes the work of the chiefs of most staff divisions in departments?   16.____
    A. Chiefs focus more on getting the job done than on how it is done.
    B. Chiefs are mostly interested in short range results.
    C. Chiefs nearly always advise but rarely if ever command or control.
    D. Chiefs usually command or control but rarely advise.
    E. Chiefs provide service to the rest of the organization and/or assist the chief executive in planning and controlling operations.

17. Usually the most difficult problem in connection with a major reorganization is   17.____
    A. adopting a pay plan to fit the new structure
    B. bringing the organization manual up-to-date
    C. determining the new organization structure
    D. gaining acceptance of the new plan by the higher level employees
    E. gaining acceptance of the new plan by the lower level employees

18. Which of the following would MOST likely be achieved by a change in the basic organization structure from the "process" or "functional" type to the "purpose" or "product" type?   18.____
    A. Easier recruitment of personnel in a tight labor market
    B. Fixing responsibility at a lower level in the organization
    C. Greater centralization
    D. Greater economy
    E. Greater professional development

19. In which of the following fields could two or more groups duplicating each other's work usually be BEST justified?   19.____
    A. Accounting   B. Personnel
    C. Public relations   D. Research and development
    E. Systems and procedures

20. Which of the following statements is MOST nearly accurate?   20.____
    A. A span of control of 5 people is better than that of 10 people.
    B. A span of control of 5 people may be better or worse than that of 10 people.
    C. A span of control of 5 people is worse than that of 10 people.
    D. The span of control is rarely over 20 minutes at any one time.
    E. The span of control means the same as the scalar system.

21. A linear responsibility chart is   21.____
    A. a graphical method of showing each sub-project making up a total project with the time it takes to complete each
    B. a graphical method of showing jobs, functions, and, by the use of appropriate symbols, the relationship of each job to each function
    C. a graphical method of solving linear equations used in doing operations research
    D. a new method of procedures analysis which makes it possible to focus on both the employees and the equipment they use
    E. another name for a special organization chart

22. An administrator of a public agency is faced with the problem of deciding   22.____
which of two divisions should be responsible for the statistical reporting of the
agency. This work is now located in one of them but each of the two division
chiefs believes that the work should be located within his division because of its
relationship to other activities under his supervision. The Organization
Planning Section is located in one of the two divisions.
Assuming that in this situation the administrator can select any one of the
following courses of action, the BEST for him to take would be to
    A. assign a staff member from the Organization Planning Section to study
       the problem, who for the duration of the assignment would report directly
       to the administrator
    B. assign staff from the Organization Planning Section to study the problem
    C. assign the statistical work to the other division for a trial period because of
       the problems which exist under the present arrangement
    D. call in an outside consultant or refer it to a competent staff employee not
       assigned to the divisions involved
    E. leave the organization as it is because the advantages of a change are
       not entirely clear to all concerned

23. The problem of whether office services such as filing, duplicating, and   23.____
stenography should be centralized or decentralized arises in every business
organization.
One advantage of decentralizing these services is that
    A. greater facility exists in such matters as finding correspondence
    B. greater flexibility exists in rotating workers during vacations
    C. higher production is attained at a lower cost per unit
    D. knowledge of the purpose and use of work acts as an incentive for
       production
    E. reduction in investment results from the use of less machinery

24. Research to date on the relationship between productivity and morale shows   24.____
that
    A. high productivity and high morale nearly always go together
    B. high productivity and low morale nearly always go together
    C. low productivity and high morale nearly always go together
    D. low productivity and low morale nearly always go together
    E. there is no clear relationship between productivity and morale

25. Which one of the following statements BEST describes "work measurement"   25.____
as commonly used in government?
It is
    A. a method of establishing an equitable relationship between volume of
       work performed and manpower utilized
    B. a new technique which may be substituted for traditional accounting
       methods
    C. the amount of work turned out by an organization in a given time period
    D. the same as the work count, as used in Work Simplification
    E. the same as time-motion study

26. Critics of work measurement have contended that any increase in production is more than offset by deterioration in standards of quality or service.
    The BEST answer to this charge is to
    A. argue that increases in production have not been offset by decreased quality
    B. define work units in terms of both quality and quantity
    C. ignore it
    D. point out that statistical quality control can be used to control quality
    E. point out that work measurement is not concerned with quality, and hence that the argument is irrelevant

26.____

27. When it is determined that a given activity or process is so intangible that it cannot be reflected adequately by a work unit, it is BEST for a work measurement system to
    A. combine that activity with others that are measurable
    B. discuss the activity only in narrative reports
    C. exclude it from the work measurement system
    D. include only the time devoted to that activity or process
    E. select the best available work unit, as better than none

27.____

28. Which one of the following is frequently referred to as the father of Statistical Quality Control?
    A. Ralph M. Barnes   B. John M. Pfiffner   C. Benjamin Selekman
    D. Walter A. Shewart   E. Donald C. Stone

28.____

29. Which one of the following BEST explains the use and value of the "upper control limit" (and "lower control limit" where applicable) in Statistical Quality Control?
    A. It automatically keeps production under control.
    B. It indicates that unit costs are too high or too low.
    C. It is useful as a training device for new workers.
    D. It tells what pieces to discard or errors to correct.
    E. It tells when assignable causes as distinguished from chance causes are at work.

29.____

30. The value of statistical records is MAINLY dependent upon the
    A. method of presenting the material
    B. number of items used
    C. range of cases sampled
    D. reliability of the information used
    E. time devoted to compiling the material

30.____

31. Which one of the following factors has the MOST bearing on the frequency with which a control report should be made?
    A. Degree of specialization of the work
    B. Degree of variability in activities
    C. Expense of the report
    D. Number of levels of supervision
    E. Number of personnel involved

31.____

32. The term "management control" is MOST frequently used to mean
    A. an objective and unemotional approach by management
    B. coordinating the efforts of all parts of the organization
    C. evaluation of results in relation to plan
    D. giving clear, precise orders to subordinates
    E. keeping unions from making managerial decisions

33. The PERT system is a
    A. method for laying out office space on a modular basis utilizing prefabricated partitions
    B. method of motivating personnel to be continuously alert and to improve their appearance
    C. method of program planning and control using a network or flow plan
    D. plan for expanding reporting techniques
    E. simplified method of cost accounting

34. Which of the following would MOST often not result from a highly efficient management control system?
    A. Facilitation of delegation
    B. Highlighting of problem areas
    C. Increase in willingness of people to experiment or to take calculated risks
    D. Provision of an objective test of new ideas or new methods and procedures
    E. Provision of information useful for revising objectives, programs, and operations

35. Which of the following statements BEST explains the significance of the famed Hawthorne Plant experiments?
    They showed that
    A. a large span of control leads to more production than a small span of control
    B. morale has no relationship to production
    C. personnel counseling is of relatively little importance in a going organization
    D. the special attention received by a group in an experimental situation has a greater impact on production than changes in working conditions
    E. there is a direct relationship between the amount of illumination and production

36. When deciding whether or not to approve a request for a new form, which reference is normally MOST pertinent?
    A. Alphabetical Forms File   B. Functional Forms File
    C. Numerical Forms File   D. Project Completion Report
    E. Records Retention Data

37. A two-part snapout form would be MOST properly justified if it   37.____
    A. is a cleaner operation
    B. is prepared ten times a week
    C. saves time in preparation
    D. is to be filled out by hand rather than by typewriter
    E. proper registration is critical

38. With a box design of a form, the caption title or question to be answered   38.____
    should be located in the _____ of the box.
    A. center at the bottom   B. center at the top
    C. lower left corner   D. lower right corner
    E. upper left corner

39. The MOST important reason for control of "bootleg" forms is that   39.____
    A. they are more expensive than authorized forms
    B. they are usually poorly designed
    C. they can lead to unnecessary procedures
    D. they cannot be re-ordered as easily as authorized forms
    E. violation of rules and regulations should not be allowed

40. In examining a number of different forms to see whether any could be   40.____
    combined or eliminated, which of the following would one be MOST likely to
    use?
    A. Forms analysis sheet of recurring data
    B. Forms control log
    C. Forms design and approval request
    D. Forms design and guide sheet
    E. Numerical file

41. A records center is of benefit in a records management program PRIMARILY 41.____
    because
    A. all the records of the organization are kept in one place
    B. inactive records can be stored economically in less expensive storage
       area
    C. it provides a place where useless records can be housed at little or no
       cost to the organization
    D. obsolete filing and storage equipment can be utilized out of view of the
       public
    E. records analysts can examine an organization's files without affecting the
       unit's operation or upsetting the supervisors

42. The basis filing system that would ordinarily be employed in a large   42.____
    administrative headquarters unit is the _____ file system.
    A. alphabetic   B. chronological
    C. mnemonic   D. retention
    E. subject classification

43. One drawback of converting a conventional consecutive filing system to a terminal digit filing system for a large installation is that
    A. conversion would be expensive in time and manpower
    B. conversion would prevent the proper use of recognized numeric classification systems, such as the Dewey Decimal, in classifying files material
    C. responsibility for proper filing cannot be pinpointed in the terminal digit system
    D. the terminal digit system requires considerably more space than a normal filing system
    E. the terminal digit system requires long, specialized training on the part of files personnel

43._____

44. The MOST effective leader would most likely be one who
    A. is able to use a variety of leadership styles depending on the circumstances
    B. issues clear, forceful directives
    C. knows the substance of the work better than any of his subordinates
    D. supervises his subordinates closely
    E. uses democratic methods

44._____

45. "One large office is a more efficient operating unit than the same number of square feet split into smaller offices."
    Of the following, the one that does NOT support this statement is:
    A. Better light and ventilation are possible.
    B. Changes in layout are less apt to be made, thus avoiding disruption of work flow.
    C. Communication between individual employees is more direct.
    D. Space is more fully utilized.
    E. Supervision and control are more easily maintained.

45._____

46. The MAJOR purpose for adopting specific space standards is to
    A. allocate equal space to employees doing the same kind of work
    B. cut costs
    C. keep space from becoming a status symbol
    D. prevent empire-building
    E. provide an accurate basis for charging for space allocated to each organization unit

46._____

47. The modular concept in office space planning is
    A. a method of pre-planning office space for economical use
    B. expensive because it complicates the air conditioning and electrical systems
    C. outdated because it lacks flexibility
    D. used as a basis for planning future space requirements
    E. used primarily for executive offices

47._____

48. Which one of the following statements is NOT correct?
    A. A general conference or committee room may eliminate the need for a number of private offices.
    B. In designing office space, the general trend is toward the use of a standard color scheme.
    C. Private offices should be constructed in such a way as to avoid cutting off natural light and ventilation.
    D. Private offices result in a larger investment in equipment and furnishings.
    E. Transparent or translucent glass can be used in the upper portion of the partition for private offices.

49. Which one of the following is NOT a good general rule of communications in an organization?
    A. All supervisors should know the importance of communications.
    B. Oral communications are better than written where persuasion is needed.
    C. People should be told facts that make them feel they "belong".
    D. The grapevine should be eliminated.
    E. The supervisor should hear information before his subordinates

50. In the communications process, the word "noise" is used to refer to
    A. anything that interferes with the message between transmitter and receiver
    B. meaningless communications
    C. the amplitude of verbal communications
    D. the level of general office and environmental sounds other than specific verbal communications
    E. the product of the grapevine

KEY (CORRECT ANSWERS)

1.	D	11.	D	21.	B	31.	B	41.	B
2.	A	12.	E	22.	D	32.	C	42.	E
3.	A	13.	A	23.	D	33.	C	43.	A
4.	B	14.	C	24.	E	34.	C	44.	A
5.	E	15.	B	25.	A	35.	D	45.	B
6.	D	16.	E	26.	B	36.	B	46.	A
7.	C	17.	D	27.	D	37.	E	47.	A
8.	D	18.	B	28.	D	38.	E	48.	B
9.	C	19.	D	29.	E	39.	C	49.	D
10.	B	20.	B	30.	D	40.	A	50.	A

TEST 2

DIRECTIONS: Each question or incomplete statement is followed by several suggested answers or completions. Select the one that BEST answers the question or completes the statement. *PRINT THE LETTER OF THE CORRECT ANSWER IN THE SPACE AT THE RIGHT.*

Questions 1-6.

DIRECTIONS: Questions 1 through 6 are to be answered solely on the basis of the following paragraphs.

Plan 1: "Hire broadly qualified people, work out their assignments from time to time to suit the needs of the enterprise and aptitudes of individuals. Let their progress and recognition be based on the length and overall quality of the service, regardless of the significance of individual assignments which they periodically assume."

Plan 2: "Hire experts and assign them well-defined duties. Their compensation, for the most part, should be dependent on the duties performed."

1. For Plan 1 to be successful, there must be assured, to a much greater extent than for Plan 2, the existence of
    A. a well-developed training program
    B. a widely publicized recruitment program
    C. in general, better working conditions
    D. more skilled administrators
    E. a greater willingness to work together toward a common goal

1.____

2. Plan 1 would tend to develop employees who were
    A. dissatisfied because of the impossibility of advancing rapidly to positions of importance
    B. conversant only with problems in the particular field in which they were employed
    C. in general, not satisfied with the work they perform
    D. intensely competitive
    E. able to perform a variety of functions

2.____

3. Large governmental organizations in the United States tend, in general, to use
    A. Plan 1
    B. Plan 2
    C. Plan 1 for technical positions and Plan 2 for clerical positions
    D. Plan 2 for administrative positions and Plan 1 for clerical and technical positions
    E. Plan 1 for office machine operations and Plan 2 for technical positions

3.____

53

4. "In organizations which operate on the basis of Plan 1, placement of a man in the proper job after selection is much more difficult than in those which operate on the basis of Plan 2."
This statement is, in general,
   A. *correct*; the organization would have only specific positions open and generalists would be forced into technical positions
   B. *not correct*; specific aptitudes and abilities would tend to be determined in advance as would be the case with Plan 2
   C. *correct*; it is much more difficult to determine specific aptitudes and abilities than general qualifications
   D. *not correct*; placement would be based on the needs of the organization; consequently only a limited number of positions would be available
   E. *correct*; the selection is not on the basis of specific aptitudes and abilities

4.____

5. "Administration in an organization operating on the basis of Plan 1 would tend to be less flexible than one operating on the basis of Plan 2."
This statement is, in general,
   A. *correct*; recruitment of experts permit rapid expansion
   B. *not correct*; the absence of well-defined positions permits wide and rapid recruitment without an extensive selection period
   C. *correct*; well-defined positions allow for replacement on an assembly-line basis without an extensive breaking in period and thus permits greater flexibility
   D. *not correct*; Plan 1 presents greater freedom in movement of individuals from one position to another and in redefining positions according to capabilities of employees and the needs of the moment
   E. *correct*; Plan 1 presents greater freedom in adjusting an organizational structure to unexpected stresses since the clear definition of duties shows where the danger points are

5.____

6. "To a greater extent than Plan 2, Plan 1 leads to conflict and overlapping in administrative operations."
In general, this is the case because
   A. employees paid on the basis of duties performed tend to be more conscious of overlapping operations and tend to limit their activities
   B. experts refuse to accept responsibilities in fields other than their own
   C. the lack of carefully defined positions may conceal many points at which coordination and reconciliation are necessary
   D. there tends to be more pressure for "empire building" where prestige is measured solely in terms of assignment
   E. there is less need, under Plan 1, to define lines of responsibility and authority and consequently conflict will arise

6.____

7. "The pay plan is a vital aspect of a duties classification. In fact, in most areas of personnel administration pay plan and classification are synonymous." This statement is
    A. *correct in general*; while the two are not, in general, synonymous, the pay plan is such a vital aspect that without it the classification plan is meaningless and useless
    B. *not correct*; while the pay plan is a vital aspect of a classification plan, it is not the only one
    C. *correct in general*; pay plan and duties classification are simply two different aspects of the same problem – "equal pay for equal work"
    D. *not correct*; although classification is usually a vital element of a pay plan, a pay plan is not essential to the preparation of a duties classification
    E. *meaningless* unless the specific nature of the classification plan and the pay plan are set forth

8. The one of the following objectives which is MOST characteristic of intelligent personnel management is the desire to
    A. obtain competent employees, and having them, to provide the climate which will be most conducive to superior performance, proper attitudes, and harmonious adjustments
    B. coordinate the activities of the workers in an organization so that the output will be maximized and cost minimized
    C. reduce the dependence of an organization on the sentiments, ambitions, and idiosyncrasies of individual employees and thus advance the overall aims of the organization
    D. recruit employees who can be trained to subordinate their interests to the interests of the organization and to rain them to do so
    E. mechanize the procedures involved so that problems of replacement and training are reduced to a minimum

9. Some organizations interview employees who resign or are discharged. This procedure is usually
    A. of great value in reducing labor turnover and creating good will toward the organization
    B. of little or no value as the views of incompetent or disgruntled employees are of questionable validity
    C. dangerous; it gives employees who are leaving an organization the opportunity to pay off old scores
    D. of great value in showing the way to more efficient methods of production and the establishment of higher work norms
    E. dangerous; it may lead to internal friction as operating departments believe that it is not the function of the personnel office to check on operations

10. The one of the following which is the MOST common flaw in the administration of an employee performance rating system is the
    A. failure to explain the objectives of the system to employees
    B. lack of safeguards to prevent supervisors from rating employees down for personal reasons
    C. tendency for rating supervisors to rate their employees much too leniently
    D. fact that employees are aware of the existence of the system
    E. increasing number of committees and boards required

11. As a result of its study of the operations of the Federal government, the Hoover Commission recommended that, for purposes of reduction in force, employees be ranked from the standpoint of their overall usefulness to the agency in question.
    The one of the following which is a MAJOR disadvantage of this proposal is that it would probably result in
    A. efficient employees becoming indifferent to the social problems posed
    B. a sense of insecurity on the part of employees which might tend to lower efficiency
    C. the retention of employees who are at or just past their peak performance
    D. the retention of generalists rather than specialists
    E. the loss of experience in the agency, as ability rather than knowledge will be the criteria

12. A personnel officer checking the turnover rate in his department found that, over a period of five years, the rate at which engineers left the organization was exactly the same as the rate at which junior clerks left the department.
    This information tends to indicate
    A. that something may be amiss with the organization; the rate for engineers under ordinary circumstances should be higher than for clerks
    B. that the organization is in good shape; neither the technical nor clerical aspects are being over-emphasized
    C. nothing which would be of value in determining the state of the organization
    D. that the organization is in good shape; working conditions, in general, are equivalent for all employees
    E. that something may be amiss with the organization; the turnover rate for engineers under ordinary circumstances should be lower than for clerks

13. Of the following, the MOST essential feature of a grievance procedure is that
    A. those who appeal be assured of expert counsel
    B. the administration have opportunity to review cases early in the procedure
    C. it affords assurance that those who use it will not be discriminated against
    D. general grievances be publicized
    E. it be simple to administer

5 (#2)

14. The one of the following which is a major objective expected to be gained by setting up a personnel council composed of representatives of the central personnel agency and departmental personnel officers is to
    A. provide an appeal board to which employees who feel aggrieved can appeal
    B. allow the departments to participate in making the day-to-day decisions faced by the central personnel agency
    C. prevent the departments from participating in making the day-to-day decisions faced by the central personnel agency
    D. establish good communications between the central personnel agency and the departments
    E. develop a broad base of responsibility for the actions of the central personnel agency

14.____

15. The BEST of the following ways to reduce the errors in supervisors' ratings of employee performance caused by variations in the application of the rating standards is to
    A. construct a method for translating each rating into a standard score
    B. inform each supervisor of the distribution of ratings expected in his unit
    C. review and change any rating which does not seem justified by the data presented by the rating supervisor
    D. arrange for practice sessions for supervisors at which rating standards will be applied and discussed
    E. confer with the supervisor when a case of disagreement is discovered between supervisor and review board

15.____

16. Of the following, the MOST accurate statement of current theory concerning the ultimate responsibility for employee training is that
    A. ultimate responsibility for training is best separated from responsibility for production and administration
    B. ultimate responsibility for training should be in the hands of a training specialist in the central personnel agency
    C. a committee of employees selected from the trainees should be given ultimate responsibility for the training program
    D. a departmental training specialist should be assigned ultimate responsibility for employee training
    E. each official should be ultimately responsible for the training of all employees under his direction

16.____

17. "An organizational structure which brings together, in a single work unit, work divisions which are non-homogeneous in work, in technology, or in purpose will tend to decrease the danger of friction."
    This opinion is, in general,
    A. *correct*; invidious comparisons tend to be made when everyone is doing the same thing
    B. *not correct*; a homogeneous organization tends to develop a strong competitive spirit among its employees
    C. *correct*; work which is non-homogeneous tends to be of greater interest to the employee, resulting in less friction

17.____

6 (#2)

   D. *not correct*; persons performing the same type of work tend to work together more efficiently
   E. *correct*; the presence of different kinds of work permits better placement of employees, resulting in better morale

18. You have been asked by the head of the bureau to recommend whether or not the work of the bureau requires an increase in the permanent staff of the bureau.
   Of the following questions, the one whose answer would MOST likely assist you in making your recommendation is:
   A. Are some permanent employees working irregular hours because they occasionally work overtime?
   B. Are the present permanent employees satisfied with their work assignments?
   C. Are temporary employees hired to handle seasonal fluctuations in work load?
   D. Are the current permanent employees keeping the work of the bureau current?
   E. Are the present temporary employees keeping the work of the bureau current?

18.____

19. In making job assignments to his subordinates, a supervisor should follow the principle that each individual generally is capable of
   A. performing one type of work well and less capable of performing other types well
   B. learning to perform a wide variety of different types of work
   C. performing best the type of work in which he has had experience
   D. learning to perform any type of work in which he is given training
   E. specializing only in his major interest areas

19.____

20. Assume that you are a supervisor of a large number of clerks in a unit in a public agency. Your unit has just been given an important assignment which must be completed a week from now. You know that, henceforth, your unit will be given this assignment every six months. You or any one of your subordinates who has been properly instructed can complete this assignment in one day. This assignment is of a routine type which is ordinarily handled by clerks. There is enough time for you to train one of your subordinates to handle the assignment and then have him do it. However, it would take twice as much time for you to take this course of action as it would for you to do the assignment yourself.
   The one of the following courses of action which you should take in this situation is to
   A. do the assignment yourself as soon as possible without discussing it with any of your subordinates at this time
   B. do the assignment yourself and then train one of your subordinates to handle it in the future
   C. give the assignment to one of your subordinates after training him to handle it

20.____

D. train each of your subordinates to do the assignment on a rotating basis after you have done it yourself the first time
E. let your subordinates "choose up" as to who shall take on the assignment

21. You are in charge of an office in which each member of the staff has a different set of duties, although each has the same title. No member of the staff can perform the duties of any other member of the staff without first receiving extensive training. Assume that it is necessary for one member of the staff to take on, in addition to his regular work, an assignment which any member of the staff is capable of carrying out.
The one of the following considerations which would have the MOST weight in determining which staff member is to be given the additional assignment is the
    A. quality of the work performed by the individual members of the staff
    B. time consumed by individual members of the staff in performing their work
    C. level of difficulty of the duties being performed by individual members of the staff
    D. relative importance of the duties being performed by individual members of the staff
    E. background of education and experience of the individual members

21._____

22. The one of the following causes of clerical error which is usually considered to be LEAST attributable to faulty supervision or inefficient management is
    A. inability to carry out instructions
    B. too much work to do
    C. an inappropriate record-keeping system
    D. continual interruptions
    E. lack of interest

22._____

23. Suppose you are in charge of a large unit in which all of the clerical staff perform similar tasks.
In evaluating the relative accuracy of the clerks, the clerk who should be considered to be the LEAST accurate is the one
    A. whose errors result in the greatest financial loss
    B. whose errors cost the most to locate
    C. who makes the greatest percentage of errors in his work
    D. who makes the greatest number of errors in the unit
    E. who makes the most basic type of errors

23._____

24. Assume that under a proposed procedure for handling employee grievances in a public agency, the first step to be taken is for the aggrieved employee to submit his grievance as soon as it arises to a grievance board set up to hear all employee grievances in the agency. The board, which is to consist of representatives of management and of rank and file employees, is to consider the grievance, obtain all necessary pertinent information, and then render a decision on the matter. Thus, the first-line supervisor would not be involved in the settlement of any of his subordinates' grievances except when asked by the board to submit information.
This proposed procedure would be generally undesirable CHIEFLY because

24._____

A. the board may become a bottleneck to delay the prompt disposition of grievances
B. the aggrieved employees and their supervisors have not been first given the opportunity to resolve the grievances themselves
C. employees would be likely to submit imaginary, as well as real, grievances to the board
D. the board will lack first-hand, personal knowledge of the factors involved in grievances
E. the board will be giving up its major responsibilities for handling employee grievances

25. "Sometimes jobs in private organizations and public agencies are broken down so as to permit a high degree of job specialization."
Of the following, an IMPORTANT effect of a high degree of job specialization in a public agency is that employees performing
    A. highly specialized jobs may not be readily transferable to other jobs in the agency
    B. similar duties may require closer supervision than employees performing unrelated functions
    C. specialized duties can be held responsible for their work to a greater extent than can employees performing a wide variety of functions
    D. specialized duties will tend to cooperate readily with employees performing other types of specialized duties
    E. employees will lose interest in their work

26. Assume that you are the supervisor of a clerical unit in a public agency. One of your subordinates violates a rule of the agency, a violation which requires that the employee be suspended from his work for one day. The violated rule is one that you have found to be unduly strict and you have recommended to the management of the agency that the rule be changed or abolished. The management has been considering your recommendation but has not yet reached a decision on the matter.
In these circumstances, you should
    A. not initiate disciplinary action, but instead explain to the employee that the rule may be changed shortly
    B. delay disciplinary action on the violation until the management has reached a decision on changing the rule
    C. modify the disciplinary action by reprimanding the employee and informing him that further action may be taken when the management has reached a decision on changing the rule
    D. initiate the prescribed disciplinary action without commenting on the strictness of the rule or on your recommendation
    E. inform the subordinate that disciplinary action is pending

27. Assume that a supervisor praises his subordinates for satisfactory aspects of their work only when he is about to criticize them for unsatisfactory aspects of their work.
Such a practice is undesirable PRIMARILY because
   A. his subordinates may expect to be praised for their work even if it is unsatisfactory
   B. praising his subordinates for some aspects of their work while criticizing other aspects will weaken the effects of the criticisms
   C. his subordinates would be more receptive to criticism if it were followed by praise
   D. his subordinates may come to disregard praise and wait for criticism to be given
   E. his subordinates may come to regard him as lacking in forthrightness

28. The one of the following which would be the BEST reason for an agency to eliminate a procedure for obtaining and recording certain information is that
   A. it is no longer legally required to obtain the information
   B. there is no advantage in obtaining the information
   C. the information could be compiled on the basis of other information available
   D. the information obtained is sometimes incorrect
   E. the information is too difficult to acquire

29. The MOST effective basis for an analysis of the flow of work in a large governmental agency is the
   A. analysis of descriptions written by employees
   B. discussion of operations with supervisors
   C. discussion of routines with selected employees
   D. initiation of a series of general staff meetings to discuss operational procedures
   E. observation of actual operations

30. The BEST reason for prescribing definite procedures for certain work in an organization is to
   A. enable supervisor to keep "on top of" details of work
   B. enable work to be processed speedily and consistently
   C. facilitate incorporation of new policies
   D. prevent individual discretion
   E. reduce training periods

31. In the course of a survey, a disgruntled employee of Unit A comes to your office with an offer to "tell all" about Unit B, where he used to work.
You should
   A. listen to him but ignore any statements he makes
   B. listen to him carefully, but verify his assertions before acting on them
   C. make him speak to you in the presence of the persons he is criticizing
   D. reprimand him for not minding his own business
   E. report him to the security officer

32. Combining several different procedures into a single flow of work would MOST likely achieve which of the following advantages?
    A. Better teamwork
    B. Higher quality decisions
    C. Improved morale
    D. Reduced fluctuations in workload
    E. Reduced problems of control

32.____

33. After conducting a systems survey in the Personnel Division you find that there is not sufficient work in the Division to keep a recently hired employee gainfully employed.
    The BEST solution to this problem is usually to
    A. lay off the employee with a full month's salary
    B. leave the employee in the Division because the workload may increase
    C. leave the employee in the Personnel Division, but assign him overflow work from other divisions
    D. reassign the employee when an appropriate opening occurs elsewhere in the organization
    E. request the employee to resign so that no unfavorable references will appear on his personnel record

33.____

34. You are making a study of a central headquarters office which processes claims received from a number of regional offices. You notice the following problems: some employees are usually busy while others assigned to the same kind of work in the same grade have little to do; high-level professional people frequently spend considerable time searching for files in the file room. Which of the following charts would be MOST useful to record and analyze the data needed to help solve these problems?
    A. Forms distribution chart
    B. Layout chart
    C. Operation chart
    D. Process chart
    E. Work distribution chart

34.____

35. A "therblig" is BEST defined as a
    A. follower of Frederick W. Taylor
    B. small element or task of an operation used in time-motion study
    C. special type of accounting machine used to sort punch cards
    D. type of curve used in charting certain mathematical relationships
    E. unit for measuring the effectiveness of air conditioning

35.____

36. One of the following advantages which is LEAST likely to accrue to a large organization as a result of establishing a centralized typing and stenographic unit is that
    A. less time is wasted
    B. morale of the stenographers increases
    C. the stenographers receive better training
    D. wages are more consistent
    E. work is more equally distributed

36.____

37. Which one of the following is the MOST important difference between clerks in small offices and those in large offices? Clerks in
    A. large offices are less closely supervised
    B. large offices have more freedom to exercise originality in their work
    C. small offices are more restricted by standardized procedure
    D. small offices are more specialized in their duties
    E. small offices need a greater variety of clerical skills

37.____

38. After taking the necessary steps to analyze a situation, an employee reaches a decision which is reviewed by his supervisor and found to be incorrect. Of the following possible methods of dealing with this incident, the MOST constructive for the employee would be for the supervisor to
    A. correct the decision and give the employee an explanation
    B. correct the decision and suggest more detailed analysis in the future
    C. help the employee discover what is wrong with the basis for decision
    D. set up a temporary control on this type of decision until the employee demonstrates he can handle it
    E. suggest that the employee review future cases of this type with him before reaching a decision

38.____

39. Which one of the following is NOT a purpose ordinarily served by charts?
    A. Aid in training employees
    B. Assist in presenting and selling recommendations
    C. Detect gaps or discrepancies in data collected
    D. Put facts in proper relationships to each other
    E. Show up problems of human relationships

39.____

40. Which of the following descriptive statements does NOT constitute a desirable standard in evaluating an administrative sequence or series of tasks having a definite objective?
    A. All material should be routed as directly as possible to reduce the cost of time and motion.
    B. Each form must clear the section chief before going to another section.
    C. Each task should be assigned to the lowest-ranking employee who can perform it adequately.
    D. Each task should contribute positively to the basic purpose of the sequence.
    E. Similar tasks should be combined.

40.____

41. Which one of the following is NOT a principle of motion economy?
    A. Continuous curved motions are preferable to straightline motions involving sudden and sharp changes in direction.
    B. Motions of the arms should be made in the same direction and should be made simultaneously.
    C. The hands should be relieved of all work that can be performed more advantageously by the feet.
    D. The two hands should begin and complete their motions at the same time.
    E. Two or more tools should be combined whenever possible.

41.____

42. Generally, the FIRST step in the measurement of relative efficiency of office employees engaged in machine operation is the
    A. analysis of the class of positions involved to determine the duties and responsibilities and minimum qualifications necessary for successful job performance
    B. analysis of those skills which make for difference in the production of various employees
    C. development of a service rating scale which can be scored accurately
    D. development of a standard unit of production that can be widely applied and that will give comparable data
    E. selection of an appropriate sampling of employees whose duties involve the specific factors to be measured

42.____

43. An executive assigns A, the head of a staff unit, to devise plans for reducing the delay in submittal of reports by a local agency headed by C. The reports are under the supervision of C's subordinate line official B with whom A is to deal directly. In his investigation, A finds: (1) the reasons for the delay; and (2) poor practices which have either been overlooked or condoned by line official B.
    Of the following courses of action A could take, the BEST one would be to
    A. develop recommendations with line official B with regard to reducing the delay and correcting the poor practices and then report fully to his own executive
    B. discuss the findings with C in an attempt to correct the situation before making any formal report on the poor practices
    C. report both findings to his executive, attaching the explanation offered by C
    D. report to his executive on the first finding and discuss the second in a friendly way with line official B
    E. report the first finding to his executive, ignoring the second until his opinion is requested

43.____

44. Drafts if a proposed policy, prepared by a staff committee, are circulated to ten members of the field staff of the organization by route slips with a request for comments within two weeks. Two members of the field staff make extensive comments, four offer editorial suggestions, and the remainder make minor favorable comments. Shortly after, it is found that the statement needs considerable revision by the field staff.
    Of the following possible reasons for the original failure of the field staff to identify difficulties, the MOST likely is that the
    A. field staff did not take sufficient time to review the material
    B. field staff had not been advised of the type of contribution expected
    C. low morale of the field staff prevented their showing interest
    D. policy statement was too advanced for the staff
    E. staff committee was not sufficiently representative

44.____

45. Operator participation in management improvement work is LEAST likely to 45.____
    A. assure the use of best available management technique
    B. overcome the stigma of the outside expert
    C. place responsibility for improvement in the person who knows the job best
    D. simplify installation
    E. take advantage of the desire of most operators to seek self-improvement

46. In general, the morale of workers in an agency is MOST frequently and MOST 46.____
    significantly affected by the
    A. agency policies of organizational structure and operational procedures
    B. distance of the employee's job from his home community
    C. fringe benefits
    D. number of opportunities for advancement
    E. relationship with supervisors

47. Of the following, the PRIMARY function of a work distribution chart is to 47.____
    A. analyze the soundness of existing divisions of labor
    B. eliminate unnecessary clerical detail
    C. establish better supervisory techniques
    D. simplify work methods
    E. weed out core functions

48. In analyzing a process chart, which one of the following should be asked 48.____
    FIRST?
    A. How   B. When   C. Where   D. Who   E. Why

49. The work count would be LEAST helpful in accomplishing which one of 49.____
    the following?
    A. Demonstrating personnel needs
    B. Improving the sequence of steps
    C. Measuring the value of a step
    D. Spotting bottlenecks
    E. Stimulating interest in work

50. The normal analysis of which chart listed below is MOST closely related 50.____
    to organizational analysis?
    A. Layout chart   B. Operation chart
    C. Process chart   D. Work count chart
    E. Work distribution chart

KEY (CORRECT ANSWERS)

1. A	11. B	21. B	31. B	41. B
2. E	12. E	22. A	32. D	42. D
3. B	13. C	23. E	33. D	43. A
4. E	14. D	24. B	34. E	44. B
5. D	15. D	25. A	35. B	45. A
6. C	16. E	26. D	36. B	46. E
7. D	17. D	27. D	37. E	47. A
8. A	18. D	28. E	38. C	48. E
9. A	19. B	29. E	39. E	49. B
10. C	20. C	30. B	40. B	50. E

TEST 3

DIRECTIONS: Each question or incomplete statement is followed by several suggested answers or completions. Select the one that BEST answers the question or completes the statement. *PRINT THE LETTER OF THE CORRECT ANSWER IN THE SPACE AT THE RIGHT.*

1. Which of the following is NOT an advantage of oral instructions as compared with written instructions when dealing with a small group?
   A. Oral instructions are more adaptable to complex orders.
   B. Oral instructions can be changed more easily and quickly.
   C. Oral instructions facilitate exchange of information between the order giver and order receiver.
   D. Oral instructions make it easier for order giver to ascertain whether the order is understood.
   E. The oral medium is suitable for instructions that will be temporary.

   1._____

2. "The employee opinion or attitude survey has for some time been accepted as a valuable communications device."
   Of the following, the benefit which is LEAST likely to occur from the use of such a survey is:
   A. A clearer view of employee understanding of management policies is obtained.
   B. Improved morale may result.
   C. Information useful for supervisory and executive development is obtained.
   D. The reasons why management policies were adopted are clarified.
   E. Useful comparisons can be made between organization units.

   2._____

3. Which of the following is the MOST important principle to remember in preparing written reports that are to be submitted to a superior?
   A. Avoid mentioning in writing errors or mistakes.
   B. Include human interest anecdotes.
   C. Put all information into graphical or tabular form.
   D. Report everything that has happened.
   E. Report results in relation to plan.

   3._____

4. In conducting an electronic data processing study, with which one of the following should you be LEAST concerned?
   A. Computer characteristics, i.e., word length requirements, type storage characteristics, etc.
   B. Data collection requirements
   C. Methods used by other governmental jurisdictions
   D. System input/output requirements and volume
   E. System integration and flow of work

   4._____

5. The MOST significant difference between a random access and a sequential type data processing computer system is:
   A. Generally, a random access system has lower "locating" or access times
   B. Random access provides the potential for processing data on a "first come-first serve" basis without the necessity of batching or pre-arranging the data in some sequence
   C. Random access systems are more often disk type storage systems
   D. Random access systems can operate more easily in conjunction with sequential tape or card oriented computer systems
   E. Random access systems have larger storage capacities

5.____

6. An electronic computer performs various arithmetic operations by
   A. adding and subtracting
   B. adding, subtracting, dividing, and multiplying
   C. Boolean algebra
   D. multiplying and dividing
   E. all operations listed in B and C above

6.____

7. The binary numbering system used in computers is one which
   A. is much more complicated than the usual decimal numbering system
   B. uses a radix or base of 8
   C. uses letters of the alphabet rather than numerical digits
   D. uses only two digits, 0 and 1
   E. uses the customary ten digits, 0 through 9

7.____

8. An analog computer is one which
   A. is classified as "medium" size
   B. is used primarily for solving scientific and engineering problems rather than for data processing
   C. operates on the principle of creating a physical, often electrical, analogy of the mathematical problem to be solved
   D. uses transistors rather than vacuum tubes
   E. works on the basis of logarithms

8.____

9. The PRINCIPAL justification for using office machines to replace hand labor is to
   A. achieve automation   B. eliminate errors
   C. increase productivity   D. make work easier
   E. reduce labor problems

9.____

10. Assume that an electric typewriter costs $400 and a manual typewriter costs $200. Except for speed of production, assume that in all other pertinent respects they are the same, including a life expectancy of 10 years each. What is the approximate amount of time a $1.85 per hour typist must save and re-invest in work to have her electric typewriter recoup the difference in purchase price?
    A. 11 hours annually   B. 110 hours annually
    C. 550 hours annually   D. 1100 hours annually
    E. One hour a day

10.____

11. Which of the following characteristics of a system would MOST likely lead to the conclusion that manual methods should be used rather than punch card equipment?
    A. High volume
    B. Low volume but complex computations
    C. Operations of a fixed sequence
    D. Relatively simple work
    E. Repetitive work

11.____

12. Which of the following statements MOST accurately defines "Operations Research"?
    A. A highly sophisticated reporting system used in the analysis of management problems
    B. A specialized application of electronic data processing in the analysis of management problems
    C. Research on operating problems
    D. Research on technological problems
    E. The application of sophisticated mathematical tools to the analysis of management problems

12.____

13. A "performance budget" puts emphasis on
    A. achieving greatest economy
    B. expenditures for salaries, travel, rent, supplies, etc.
    C. revenues rather than on expenditures
    D. tables of organization or staffing patterns
    E. what is accomplished, e.g., number of applications processed, trees planted, buildings inspected, etc.

13.____

14. Which of the following organizations is MOST noted for its training courses in various management subjects?
    A. American Management Association
    B. American Political Science Association
    C. American Society for Public Administration
    D. Society for the Advancement of Management
    E. Systems and Procedures Association

14.____

15. In which of the following professional journals would you be MOST apt to find articles on organization theory?
    A. Administrative Science Quarterly
    B. Factory Management and Maintenance
    C. Harvard Business Review
    D. O and M
    E. Public Administration Review

15.____

16. The composition of the workforce in American government and industry is changing. There has been an increase in the proportion of white collar to blue collar employees and an increase in the proportion of higher educated to lower educated employees.
    This change will MOST likely result in
    A. a more simplified forms control system
    B. closer supervision of employees
    C. further decentralization of decision making
    D. more employee grievances
    E. organization by process instead of purpose

16.____

17. The BEST way to secure efficient management is to
    A. allow staff agencies to solve administrative problems
    B. equip line management to solve its own problems
    C. get employees properly classified and trained
    D. prescribe standard operating procedures
    E. set up a board of control

17.____

18. A manager skilled in human relations can BEST be defined as one who
    A. can identify interpersonal problems and work out solutions to them
    B. can persuade people to do things his way
    C. gets along well with people and has many friends
    D. plays one role with his boss, another with his subordinates, and a third with this peers
    E. treats everyone fairly

18.____

19. The statement has been made that personnel administration is the most fundamental and important task of the head of any organization.
    This statement is based, for the most part, on the fact that
    A. success or failure of an organization to reach its objectives depends on the attitudes and abilities of the people in the organization
    B. the influence of personnel administration on organization success varies in proportion to the number, the complexity and the rarity of the virtues and qualities that are requisite to superior performance of the tasks involved
    C. a sound philosophy of personnel administration emphasizes the basic objective of superior service over any other consideration
    D. relative autonomy is permitted each department, particularly with respect to the handling of personnel
    E. diversity of personnel practices as to salaries, hours, etc., leads to poor morale

19.____

20. The requirement imposed by most civil service laws in the United States that tests shall be "practical in character and deal insofar as possible with the actual duties of the position," has led to a wide use of
    A. tests of social outlook   B. aptitude tests
    C. achievement tests   D. objective tests
    E. oral tests

20.____

21. In general, the one of the following which is the FIRST step in the construction of a test for the selection of personnel is to
    A. determine what the duties of the position to be filled are
    B. investigate the relationships among abilities and capacities required for success in the position to be filled
    C. study examinations which have been given in the past for similar positions
    D. evaluate existing examining instruments to determine their adequacy for making the desired selection
    E. set up the outline and start preliminary preparation of the examining instruments

21.____

22. The one of the following which in most cases is the BEST practical measure of the merits of the overall personnel policies of one organization as compared to the policies of similar organizations in the same area is the
    A. extent to which higher positions in the hierarchy are filled by career employees
    B. degree of loyalty and enthusiasm manifested by the workforce
    C. rate at which replacements must be made in order to maintain the workforce
    D. percentage of employees who have joined labor unions and the militancy of these unions
    E. scale of salaries

22.____

23. "Classification may most properly be viewed as the building of a structure." The fundamental unit in the classification structure is the
    A. assignment   B. position   C. service
    D. rank   E. grade

23.____

24. The one of the following which is NOT usually included in a class specification is
    A. a definition of the duties and responsibilities covered
    B. the class title
    C. a description of the recruitment method to be used
    D. a statement of typical tasks performed
    E. the statement of minimum qualifications necessary to perform the work

24.____

25. The one of the following which is usually NOT considered part of a classification survey is
    A. grouping positions on the basis of similarities
    B. preparing job specifications
    C. analyzing and recording specific job duties
    D. adjusting job duties to employee qualifications
    E. allocating individual positions to classes

25.____

26. The one of the following which is MOST generally accepted as a prerequisite to the development of a sound career service is
    A. agreement to accept for all higher positions the senior eligible employee
    B. the recruitment of an adequate proportion of beginning employees who will eventually be capable of performing progressively more difficult duties
    C. strict adherence to the principle of competitive promotion from within for all positions above the entrance level
    D. the development of a program of periodically changing an employee's duties in order to prevent stagnation
    E. the existence of administrators who can stimulate employees and keep their production high

27. The determination of the fitness of a person to fill a position solely on the basis of his experience is
    A. *desirable*; experience is the best test of aptitude for a position when it is rated properly
    B. *undesirable*; the applicant may not be giving correct factual information in regard to his experience
    C. *desirable*; a uniform rating key can be applied to evaluate experience
    D. *undesirable*; it is difficult to evaluate from experience records how much the applicant has gained from his experience
    E. *desirable*; there will be more applicants for a position if no written or oral tests are required

28. The performance rating standards in a city department have been criticized by its employees as unfair.
    The one of the following procedures which would probably be MOST effective in reducing this criticism is to
    A. publish a detailed statement showing how the standards were arrived at
    B. provide for participation by employee representatives in revising the standards
    C. allow individual employees to submit written statements about the standards employed
    D. arrange for periodic meetings of the entire staff at which the standards are discussed
    E. appoint a review board consisting of senior supervisory employees to reconsider the standards

29. The one of the following situations which is MOST likely to result from a too highly specified assignment or definition of responsibility is that
    A. there will be no standard against which to measure the efficiency of the organization
    B. duplication and overlapping of functions will be encouraged
    C. sufficient channels to collect, synthesize, and coordinate all performances may not be provided
    D. essential tasks which have not been explicitly mentioned in the assignment may not get done
    E. there will be a tendency to overlook the need for training

30. Assume that you are interviewing a new entrance level clerical employee for the purpose of determining where he would be best placed.
In making your determination, the characteristic to which you should give greatest weight is the employee's
   A. interest in the jobs you describe to him
   B. mechanical aptitude
   C. poise and self-assurance
   D. fluency of verbal expression
   E. educational background and his hobbies

31. The use of the probationary period in the public service has become an approved practice especially where state tenure laws guarantee long-term continuous employment.
Of the following, the MOST important use of the probationary period is that it
   A. provides supervisory contact which will help the new employee regardless of retention at the end of the probationary period
   B. supplies confirming evidence of academic and cultural fitness not measurable in formal test procedures
   C. introduces the new employee to the office and the work situation which conditions future performance
   D. provides the new employee with a sound basis for self-improvement
   E. reveals aspects of performance and attitude toward the job not adequately measured by formal examination

32. The first prerequisite to the formulation of any compensation plan for a public agency is the collection and analysis of certain basic data.
Data are NOT usually collected for this purpose in regard to
   A. working conditions in the agency
   B. the wage paid in the agency at present
   C. labor turnover in the agency
   D. the cost of living in the area
   E. the age and sex distribution of the employees

33. The one of the following personnel administration techniques which when properly utilized will yield information concerning current training needs of an organization is the
   A. classification plan   B. performance rating
   C. personnel register   D. compensation plan
   E. employee handbook

34. In administering the activities of a personnel office with a staff of fifteen employees, including seven personnel technicians, the personnel officer should
   A. delegate full authority and responsibility to each staff member and discharge those who do not meet his standards
   B. endeavor to keep tab on the work of each individual on his staff
   C. make sure each job is being done properly or do it himself
   D. plan work programs, make assignments, and check on performance
   E. concern himself only with major policies and expect subordinates to carry out actual functions

35. The one of the following factors which is MOST influential in determining the proportion of qualified applicants who refuse public employment when offered is the
    A. interim between application and offer of a position
    B. specific nature of the duties of the position
    C. general nature of economic conditions at the time when the position is offered
    D. salary paid
    E. general undesirable nature of public employment

36. The one of the following which should be the starting point in the development of an accident reduction or prevention program is the
    A. institution of an interorganizational safety contest
    B. improvement of the conditions of work so that accidents are prevented
    C. inauguration of a safety education program to reduce accidents due to carelessness
    D. organization of unit safety committees to bring home the importance of safety to the individual worker
    E. determination of the number, character, and causes of accidents

37. An orientation program for a group of new employees would NOT usually include
    A. a description of the physical layout of the organization
    B. a statement of the rules pertaining to leave, lateness, overtime, and so forth
    C. detailed instruction on the job each employee is to perform
    D. an explanation of the lines of promotions
    E. a talk on the significance of the role the department plays in the governmental structure

38. The device of temporary assignment of an employee to the duties of the higher position is sometimes used to determine promotability.
    The use of this procedure, especially for top positions, is
    A. *desirable*; no test or series of tests can measure fitness to the same extent as actual trial on the job
    B. *undesirable*; the organization will not have a responsible head during the trial period
    C. *desirable*; employees who are on trial tend to operate with greater efficiency
    D. *undesirable*; the organization would tend to deteriorate if no one of the candidates for the position was satisfactory
    E. *desirable*; the procedure outlined is simpler and less expensive than any series of tests

39. Frequently, when accumulating data for a salary standardization study, the salaries for certain basic positions are compared with the salaries paid in other agencies, public and private.
The one of the following which would MOST usually be considered one of these basic positions is
   A. office manager
   B. administrative assistant
   C. chief engineer
   D. junior typist
   E. chemist

39.____

40. The emphasis in public personnel administration during recent years has been less on the
   A. need for the elimination of the spoils system and more on the development of policy and techniques of administration that contribute to employee selection and productivity
   B. development of policy and techniques of administration that contribute to employee selection and productivity and more on the need for the elimination of the spoils system
   C. human relation aspects of personnel administration and more on the technical problems of classification and placement
   D. problems of personnel administration of governmental units in the United States and more on those of international organizations
   E. problems of personnel administration in international organizations and more on those of governmental units in the United States

40.____

41. The recommendation has been made that explicit information be made available to all city employees concerning the procedure to be followed when appealing from a performance rating.
To put this recommendation into effect would be
   A. *desirable*, primarily because employees would tend to have greater confidence in the performance rating system
   B. *undesirable*, primarily because a greater number of employees would submit appeals with no merit
   C. *desirable*, primarily because the additional publicity would spotlight the performance rating system
   D. *undesirable*, primarily because all appeals should be treated as confidential matters and all efforts to make them public should be defeated
   E. *desirable*, primarily because committing the appeal procedure to paper would tend to standardize it

41.____

42. A placement officer in a department follows the procedure of consulting the supervisor of the unit in which a vacancy exists concerning the kind of worker he wants before attempting to fill the vacancy.
This procedure is, in general,
   A. *undesirable*; it makes the selection process dependent on the whim of the supervisor
   B. *desirable*; it will make for a more effectively working organization
   C. *undesirable*; if the kind of worker the supervisor wants is not available, he will be dissatisfied

42.____

D. *desirable*; the more people who are consulted about a matter of this kind, the more chance there is that no mistake will be made
E. *undesirable*; the wishes of the worker, as well as those of the supervisor, should be taken into consideration

43. "In a large organization, proper recruitment is not possible without the existence of an effective position classification system."
The one of the following which BEST explains why this is the case is that otherwise effective means of determining the capabilities and characteristics of prospective employees are of little value
    A. unless these are related to the salary scale and current economic conditions
    B. without a knowledge of the essential character of the work to be performed in each position
    C. where no attempt to classify the different recruitment approaches has been made in advance
    D. if there has been no attempt made to obtain the cooperation of the employees involved
    E. to personnel officers who tend to place new employees in positions without reference to capabilities

44. The recommendation has been made that a department grievance board be set up, which would handle all employee grievances from their inception to conclusion.
Of the following comments for and against the acceptance of his recommendation, the one which is MOST valid is that it is
    A. *desirable*, primarily because it will remove a constant source of friction between supervisor and employee and place the problem in the hands of an objective board
    B. *undesirable*, primarily because handling grievances is an integral part of the supervisory process and the immediate supervisor must be afforded the opportunity to deal with the situation
    C. *desirable*, primarily because no supervisor will have to determine whether he has been unfair to one of his subordinates and no subordinate will have a grievance
    D. *desirable*, primarily because the handling of grievances will tend to be expedited as the board will have only one function
    E. *undesirable*, primarily because the handling of grievances will tend to be delayed as the board will not have all the necessary information available

45. The one of the following which is frequently given as a major argument against a tightly knit promotion-from-within policy is that
    A. it takes too long for an employee in the lower grades to reach the top
    B. all persons both in and out of the government are equally entitled to civil service jobs
    C. persons are placed in executive jobs who are too well acquainted with the existing organization

D. it leads to the presence in executive jobs of clerks who still operate as clerks
E. it is not desirable to guarantee to all employees promotion to new responsibilities from time to time

46. Of the following factors which are influential in determining which employment a young man or woman will choose, government employment is generally considered superior in
    A. incentives to improve efficiency
    B. opportunities to move into other similar organizations
    C. prestige and recognition
    D. leave and retirement benefits
    E. salaries

47. Training programs, to be fully effective, should be concerned not only with the acquisition or improvement of skills but also with
    A. employee attitude and will to work
    B. the personality problems of the individual employees
    C. time and motion studies for the development of new procedures
    D. the recruitment of the best persons available to fill a given position
    E. such theoretical background material as is deemed necessary

48. "Competent civil service personnel cannot come just from initial employment on a competitive basis and 'equal pay for equal work'."
    The one of the following additional factors which is of GREATEST importance in building up a body of competent civil service employees is
    A. analysis of work methods and introduction of streamlined procedures
    B. training for skill improvement and creating a sense of belonging
    C. rotation of employees from organization to organization in order to prevent stagnation
    D. treating personnel problems on a more impersonal basis in order to maintain an objective viewpoint
    E. recruiting for all higher positions from among the body of present employees

49. A comment made by an employee about a training course was: "Half of the group seem to know what the course is about, but the rest of us can't keep up with them."
    The fundamental error in training methods to which this criticism points is
    A. insufficient student participation
    B. failure to develop a feeling of need or active want for the material being presented
    C. that the training sessions may be too long
    D. that no attempt may have been made to connect the new material with what was already known by any member of the group
    E. that insufficient provision has been made by the instructor for individual differences

50. The one of the following which is NOT a major purpose of an employee suggestion plan is to
    A. provide an additional method by means of which an employee's work performance can be evaluated
    B. increase employee interest in the work of the organization
    C. provide an additional channel of communication between the employee and top management
    D. utilize to the greatest extent possible the ideas and proposals of employees
    E. provide a formal method for rewarding the occasional valuable idea

50.____

KEY (CORRECT ANSWERS)

1.	A	11.	B	21.	A	31.	E	41.	A
2.	D	12.	E	22.	C	32.	E	42.	B
3.	E	13.	E	23.	B	33.	B	43.	B
4.	C	14.	A	24.	C	34.	D	44.	B
5.	B	15.	A	25.	D	35.	A	45.	D
6.	A	16.	C	26.	B	36.	E	46.	D
7.	D	17.	B	27.	D	37.	C	47.	A
8.	C	18.	A	28.	B	38.	A	48.	B
9.	C	19.	A	29.	D	39.	D	49.	E
10.	A	20.	C	30.	A	40.	A	50.	A

EXAMINATION SECTION
TEST 1

DIRECTIONS: Each question or incomplete statement is followed by several suggested answers or completions. Select the one that BEST answers the question or completes the statement. *PRINT THE LETTER OF THE CORRECT ANSWER IN THE SPACE AT THE RIGHT.*

1. A management approach widely used today is based on the belief that decisions should be made and actions should be taken by managers closest to the organization's problems.
   This style of management is MOST appropriately called _____ management.
   A. scientific
   B. means-end
   C. decentralized
   D. internal process

   1._____

2. As contrasted with tall organization structures with narrow spans of control, flat organization structures with wide spans of control MOST usually provide
   A. fast communication and information flows
   B. more levels in the organizational hierarchy
   C. fewer workers reporting to supervisors
   D. lower motivation because of tighter control standards

   2._____

3. Use of the systems approach is MOST likely to lead to
   A. consideration of the impact on the whole organization of actions taken in any part of that organization
   B. the placing of restrictions on departmental activity
   C. use of mathematical models to suboptimize production
   D. consideration of the activities of each unit of an organization as a totality without regard to the remainder of the organization

   3._____

4. An administrator, with overall responsibility for all administrative operations in a large operating agency, is considering organizing the agency's personnel office around either of the following two alternative concepts:
   Alternative I: A corps of specialists for each branch of personnel subject matter, whose skills, counsel, or work products are coordinated only by the agency personnel officer
   Alternative II: A crew of so-called *personnel generalists*, who individually work with particular segments of the organization but deal with all subspecialties of the personnel function
   The one of the following which MOST tends to be a DRAWBACK of Alternative I, as compared with Alternative II, is that
   A. training and employee relations work call for education, interests, and talents that differ from those required for classification and compensation work
   B. personnel office staff may develop only superficial familiarity with the specialized areas to which they have been assigned

   4._____

C. supervisors may fail to get continuing overall personnel advice on an integrated basis
D. the personnel specialists are likely to become so interested in and identified with the operating view as to particular cases that they lose their professional objectivity and become merely advocates of what some supervisor wants

5. The matrix summary or decision matrix is a useful tool for making choices. Its effectiveness is MOST dependent upon the user's ability to
   A. write a computer program (Fortran or Cobol)
   B. assign weights representing the relative importance of the objectives
   C. solve a set of two equations with two unknowns
   D. work with matrix algebra

6. An organizational form which is set up only on an *ad hoc* basis to meet specific goals is said PRIMARILY to use
   A. clean break departmentation
   B. matrix or task force organization
   C. scalar specialization
   D. geographic or area-wide decentralization

7. The concept of job enlargement would LEAST properly be implemented by
   A. permitting workers to follow through on tasks or projects from start to finish
   B. delegating the maximum authority possible for decision-making to lower levels in the hierarchy
   C. maximizing the number of professional classes in the classification plan
   D. training employees to grow beyond whatever tasks they have been performing

8. As used in the area of admission, the principle of *unity of command* MOST specifically means that
   A. an individual should report to only one superior for any single activity
   B. individuals make better decisions than do committees
   C. in large organizations, chains of command are normally too long
   D. an individual should not supervise over five subordinates

9. The method of operations research, statistical decision-making, and linear programming have been referred to as the tool kit of the manager. Utilization of these tools is LEAST useful in the performance of which of the following functions?
   A. Elimination of the need for using judgment when making decisions
   B. Facilitation of decision-making without the need for sub-optimization
   C. Quantifying problems for management study
   D. Research and analysis of management operations

10. When acting in their respective managerial capacities, the chief executive officer and the office supervisor both perform the fundamental functions of management.
    Of the following differences between the two, the one which is generally considered to be the LEAST significant is the
    A. breadth of the objectives
    B. complexity of measuring actual efficiency of performance
    C. number of decisions made
    D. organizational relationships affected by actions taken

11. The ability of operations researchers to solve complicated problems rests on their use of models.
    These models can BEST be described as
    A. mathematical statements of the problem
    B. physical constructs that simulate a work layout
    C. toy-like representations of employees in work environments
    D. role-playing simulations

12. Of the following, it is MOST likely to be proper for the agency head to allow the agency personnel officer to make final selection of appointees from certified eligible lists where there are
    A. *small* numbers of employees to be hired in newly-developed professional fields
    B. *large* numbers of persons to be hired for key managerial positions
    C. *large* numbers of persons to be hired in very routine occupations where the individual discretion of operating officials is not vital
    D. *small* numbers of persons to be hired in highly specialized professional occupations which are vital to the agency's operations

13. Of the following, an operating agency personnel office is LEAST likely to be able to exert strong influence or control within the operating agency by
    A. interpreting to the operating agency head what is intended by the directives and rules emanating from the central personnel agency
    B. establishing the key objectives of those line divisions of the operating agency employing large numbers of staff and operating under the management-by-objectives approach
    C. formulating and proposing to the agency head the internal policies and procedures on personnel matters required within the operating agency
    D. exercising certain discretionary authority in the application of the agency head's general personnel policies to actual specific situations

14. PERT is a recently developed system used PRIMARILY to
    A. evaluate the quality of applicants' background
    B. analyze and control the timing aspects of a major project
    C. control the total expenditure of agency funds within a monthly or quarterly time period
    D. analyze and control the differential effect on costs of purchasing different quantities

15. Assume that an operating agency has among its vacant positions two positions, each of which encompasses mixed duties. Both require appointees to have considerable education and experience, but these requirements are essential only for the more difficult duties of these positions. In the place of these positions, an administrator creates two new positions, one in which the higher duties are concentrated and the other with the lesser functions requiring only minimum preparation.
Of the following, it is generally MOST appropriate to characterize the administrator's action as a(n)
    A. *undesirable* example of deliberate downgrading of standards and requirements
    B. *undesirable* manipulation of the classification system for non-merit purposes
    C. *desirable* broadening of the definition of a class of positions
    D. *desirable* example of job redesign

15.____

16. Of the following, the LEAST important stumbling block to the development of personnel mobility among governmental jurisdictions is the
    A. limitations on lateral entry above junior levels in many jurisdictions
    B. continued collection of filing fees for civil service tests by many governmental jurisdictions
    C. absence of reciprocal exchange of retirement benefit eligibility between governments
    D. disparities in salary scales between governments

16.____

17. Of the following, the MAJOR disadvantage of a personnel system that features the *selection out* (forced retirement) of those who have been passed over a number of times for promotion is that such a system
    A. wastes manpower which is perfectly competent at one level but unable to rise above that level
    B. wastes funds by requiring review boards
    C. leads to excessive recruiting of newcomers from outside the system
    D. may not be utilized in *closed* career systems with low maximum age limits for entrance

17.____

18. Of the following, the fields in which operating agency personnel offices generally exercise the MOST stringent controls over first line supervisors in the agency are
    A. methods analysis and work simplification
    B. selection and position classification
    C. vestibule training and Gantt chart
    D. suggestion systems and staff development

18.____

19. Of the following, computers are normally MOST effective in handling
    A. large masses of data requiring simple processing
    B. small amounts of data requiring constantly changing complex processing
    C. data for which reported values are often subject to inaccuracies
    D. large amounts of data requiring continual programming and reprocessing

19.____

20. Contingency planning, which has long been used by the military and is assuming increasing importance in other organizations, may BEST be described as a process which utilizes
    A. alternative plans based on varying assumptions
    B. *crash programs* by organizations departmentalized along process lines
    C. plans which mandate substitution of equipment for manpower at predetermined operational levels
    D. plans that individually and accurately predict future events

21. In the management of inventory, two kinds of costs normally determine when to order and in what amounts.
    The one of the following choices which includes BOTH of these kinds of costs is _____ costs and _____ costs.
    A. carrying; storage
    B. personnel; order
    C. computer; order
    D. personnel; computer

22. At top management levels, the one of the following which is generally the MOST important executive skill is skill in
    A. budgeting procedures
    B. a technical discipline
    C. controlling actions in accordance with previously approved plans
    D. seeing the organization as a whole

23. Of the following, the BEST way to facilitate the successful operation of a committee is to set guidelines establishing its
    A. budget exclusive of personnel costs
    B. location
    C. schedule of meetings or conferences
    D. scope of purpose

24. Executive training programs that single out particular managers and groom them for promotion create the so-called organizational *crown princes*.
    Of the following, the MOST serious problem that arises in connection with this practice is that
    A. the managers chosen for promotion seldom turn out to be the best managers since the future potential of persons cannot be predicted
    B. not enough effort is made to remove organizational obstacles in the way of their development and achievement
    C. the resentment of the managers not selected for the program has an adverse effect on the motivation of those managers not selected
    D. performance appraisal and review are not carried out systematically enough

25. Of the following, the LEAST likely result of the use of the concept of job enlargement is that
    A. coordination will be simplified
    B. the individual's job will become less challenging
    C. worker satisfaction will increase
    D. fewer people will have to give attention to each piece of work

KEY (CORRECT ANSWERS)

1.	C	11.	A
2.	A	12.	C
3.	A	13.	B
4.	C	14.	B
5.	B	15.	D
6.	B	16.	B
7.	C	17.	A
8.	A	18.	B
9.	A	19.	A
10.	C	20.	A

21. A
22. D
23. D
24. C
25. B

TEST 2

DIRECTIONS: Each question or incomplete statement is followed by several suggested answers or completions. Select the one that BEST answers the question or completes the statement. *PRINT THE LETTER OF THE CORRECT ANSWER IN THE SPACE AT THE RIGHT.*

1. The one of the following which is MOST likely to be emphasized in the use of the brainstorming technique is the
   A. early consideration of cost factors of all ideas which may be suggested
   B. avoidance of impractical suggestions
   C. separation of the generation of ideas from their evaluation
   D. appraisal of suggestions concurrently with their initial presentation

   1.____

2. Of the following, the BEST method for assessing managerial performance is generally to
   A. compare the manager's accomplishments against clear, specific, agreed-upon goals
   B. compare the manager's traits with those of his peers on a predetermined objective
   C. measure the manager's behavior against a listing of itemized personal traits
   D. measure the manager's success according to the enumeration of the *satisfaction* principle

   2.____

3. As compared with recruitment from outside, selection from within the service must generally show GREATER concern for the
   A. prestige in which the public service as a whole is held by the public
   B. morale of the candidate group compromising the recruitment field
   C. cost of examining per candidate
   D. benefits of the use of standardized and validated tests

   3.____

4. Performance budgeting focuses PRIMARY attention upon which one of the following? The
   A. things to be acquired, such as supplies and equipment
   B. general character and relative importance of the work to be done or the service to be rendered
   C. list of personnel to be employed, by specific title
   D. separation of employee performance evaluations from employee compensation

   4.____

5. Of the following, the FIRST step in the installation and operation of a performance budgeting system generally should be the
   A. identification of program costs in relationship to the accounting system and operating structure
   B. identification of the specific end results of past programs in other jurisdictions

   5.____

C. identification of work programs that are meaningful for management purposes
D. establishment of organizational structures each containing only one work program

6. Of the following, the MOST important purpose of a system of quarterly allotments of appropriated funds generally is to enable the
   A. head of the judicial branch to determine the legality of agency requests for budget increases
   B. operating agencies of government to upgrade the quality of their services without increasing costs
   C. head of the executive branch to control the rate at which the operating agencies obligate and expend funds
   D. operating agencies of government to avoid payment for services which have not been properly rendered by employees

7. In the preparation of the agency's budget, the agency's central budget office has two responsibilities: program review and management improvement. Which one of the following questions concerning an operating agency's program is MOST closely related to the agency budget officer's program review responsibility?
   A. Can expenditures for supplies, materials, or equipment be reduced?
   B. Will improved work methods contribute to a more effective program?
   C. What is the relative importance of this program as compared to a higher level of program performance?
   D. Will a realignment of responsibilities contribute to a higher level of program performance?

8. Of the following, the method of evaluating relative rates of return normally and generally thought to be MOST useful in evaluating government operations is _____ analysis.
   A. cost-benefit
   B. budget variance
   C. investment capital
   D. budget planning program

9. The one of the following assumptions that is LEAST likely to be made by a democratic or permissive type of leader is that
   A. commitment to goals is seldom a result of monetary rewards alone
   B. people can learn not only to accept, but also to seek, responsibility
   C. the average person prefers security over advancement
   D. creativity may be found in most segments of the population

10. In attempting to motivate subordinates, a manager should PRINCIPALLY be aware of the fact that
    A. the psychological qualities of people, in general, are easily predictable
    B. fear, as a traditional form of motivation, has lost much of its former power to motivate people in our modern industrial society
    C. fear is still the most potent force in motivating the behavior of subordinates in the public service
    D. the worker has very little control over the quality and quantity of his output

3 (#2)

11. Assume that the following figures represent the number of work-unit that were produced during a week by each of sixteen employees in a division:

    12 16 13 18
    21 12 16 13
    16 13 17 21
    13 15 18 20

    If all of the employees of the division who produced thirteen work-units during the week had instead produced fifteen work-units during that same week, then for that week the
    A. mean, median, and mode would all change
    B. mean and mode would change, but the median would remain the same
    C. mode and median would change, but the mean would remain the same
    D. mode, mean, and median would all still remain unchanged in value

11.____

12. An important law in motivation theory is called the *law of effect*. This law says that behavior which satisfies a person's needs tends to be repeated; behavior which does not satisfy a person's needs tends to be eliminated.
    The one of the following which is the BEST interpretation of this law is that
    A. productivity depends on personality traits
    B. diversity of goals leads to instability and motivation
    C. the greater the satisfaction, the more likely it is that the behavior will be reinforced
    D. extrinsic satisfaction is more important than intrinsic reward

12.____

13. Of the following, the MOST acceptable reason an administrator can give for taking advice from other employees in the organization only when he asks for it is that he wants to
    A. encourage creativity and high morale
    B. keep dysfunctional pressures and inconsistent recommendations to a minimum
    C. show his superiors and peers who is in charge
    D. show his subordinates who is in charge

13.____

14. A complete picture of the communication channels in an organization can BEST be revealed by
    A. observing the planned paperwork system
    B. recording the highly intermittent patterns of communication
    C. plotting the entire flow of information over a period of time
    D. monitoring the *grapevine*

14.____

Questions 15-16.

DIRECTIONS: Questions 15 and 16 are to be answered SOLELY on the basis of the following passage.

Management by objectives (MBO) may be defined as the process by which the superior and the subordinate managers of an organization jointly define its common goals, define each individual's major areas of responsibility in terms of the results expected of him and use these measures as guides for operating the unit and assessing the contribution of each of its members.

The MBO approach requires that after organizational goals are established and communicated, targets must be set for each individual position which are congruent with organizational goals. Periodic performance reviews and a final review using the objectives set as criteria are also basic to this approach.

Recent studies have shown that MBO programs are influenced by attitudes and perceptions of the boss, the company, the reward-punishment system, and the program itself. In addition, the manner in which the MBO program is carried out can influence the success of the program. A study done in the late sixties indicates that the best results are obtained when the manager sets goals which deal with significant problem areas in the organizational unit, or with the subordinate's personal deficiencies. These goals must be clear with regard to what is expected of the subordinate. The frequency of feedback is also important in the success of a management-by-objectives program. Generally, the greater the amount of feedback, the more successful the MBO program.

15. According to the above passage, the expected output for individual employees should be determined
    A. after a number of reviews of work performance
    B. after common organizational goals are defined
    C. before common organizational goals are defined
    D. on the basis of an employee's personal qualities

16. According to the above passage, the management-by-objectives approach requires
    A. less feedback than other types of management programs
    B. little review of on-the-job performance after the initial setting of goals
    C. general conformance between individual goals and organizational goals
    D. the setting of goals which deal with minor problem area in the organization

Questions 17-19.

DIRECTIONS: Questions 17 through 19 are to be answered SOLELY on the basis of the following passage.

During the last decade, a great deal of interest has been generated around the phenomenon of organizational development, or the process of developing human resources through conscious organization effort. Organizational development (OD) stresses improving interpersonal relationships and organizational skills, such as communication, to a much greater degree than individual training ever did.

The kind of training that an organization should emphasize depends upon the present and future structure of the organization. If future organizations are to be unstable, shifting coalitions, then individual skills and abilities, particularly those emphasizing innovativeness, creativity, flexibility, and the latest technological knowledge, are crucial, and individual training is most appropriate.

But if there is to be little change in organizational structure, then the main thrust of training should be group-oriented or organizational development. This approach seems better designed for overcoming hierarchical barriers, for developing a degree of interpersonal relationships which make communication along the chain of command possible, and for retaining a modicum of innovation and/or flexibility.

17. According to the above passage, group-oriented training is MOST useful in 17._____
    A. developing a communications system that will facilitate understanding through the chain of command
    B. highly flexible and mobile organizations
    C. preventing the crossing of hierarchical barriers within an organization
    D. saving energy otherwise wasted on developing methods of dealing with rigid hierarchies

18. The one of the following conclusions which can be drawn MOST appropriately from the above passage is that 18._____
    A. behavioral research supports the use of organizational development training method rather than individualized training
    B. it is easier to provide individualized training in specific skills than to set up sensitivity training programs
    C. organizational development eliminates innovative or flexible activity
    D. the nature of an organization greatly influences which training methods will be most effective

19. According to the above passage, the one of the following which is LEAST important for large-scale organizations geared to rapid and abrupt change is 19._____
    A. current technological information
    B. development of a high degree of interpersonal relationships
    C. development of individual skills and abilities
    D. emphasis on creativity

Questions 20-25.

DIRECTIONS: Each of Questions 20 through 25 consist of a statement which contains one word that is incorrectly used because it is not in keeping with the meaning that the quotation is evidently intended to convey. Determine which word is INCORRECTLY used. Select from the choices lettered A, B, C, and D the word which, when substituted for the incorrectly used word, would BEST help to convey the meaning of the statement.

20. One of the considerations likely to affect the currency of classification, particularly in professional and managerial occupations, is the impact of the incumbent's capacities on the job. Some work is highly susceptible to change as the result of the special talents or interests of the classifier. Organization should never be so rigid as not to capitalize on the innovative or unusual proclivities of its key employees. While a machine operator may not be able, even subtly, to change the character or level of his job, the design engineer, the attorney, or the organization and methods analyst might readily do so. Reliance on his judgment and the scope of his assignments may both grow as the result of his skill, insight, and capacity.
    A. unlikely   B. incumbent   C. directly   D. scope

21. The supply of services by the state is not governed by market price. The aim is to supply such services to all who need them and to treat all consumers equally. This objective especially compels the civil servant to maintain a role f strict impartiality, based on the principle of equality of individual citizens vis-à-vis their government. However, there is a clear difference between being neutral and impartial. If the requirement is construed to mean that all civil servants should be political eunuchs, devoid of the drive and motivation essential to dynamic administration, then the concept of impartiality is being seriously utilized. Modern governments should not be stopped from demanding that their hirelings have not only the technical but the emotional qualifications necessary for whole-hearted effort.
    A. determined   B. rule   C. stable   D. misapplied

22. The manager was barely listening. Recently, at the divisional level, several new fronts of troubles had erupted, including a requirement to increase production yet hold down operating costs and somehow raise quality standards. Though the three objectives were basically obsolete, top departmental management was insisting on the simultaneous attainment of them, an insistence not helping the manager's ulcer, an old enemy within. Thus, the manager could not find time for interest in individuals—only in statistics which regiment of individuals, like unconsidered Army privates, added up to.
    A. quantity   B. battalion   C. incompatible   D. quiet

23. When a large volume of data flows directly between operators and first-line supervisors, senior executives tend to be out of the mainstream of work. Summary reports can increase their remoteness. An executive needs to know the volume, quality, and cost of completed work, and exceptional problems. In addition, he may desire information on key operating conditions. Summary reports on these matters are, therefore, essential features of a communications network and make delegation without loss of control possible.
    A. unimportant   B. quantity   C. offset   D. incomplete

24. Of major significance in management is harmony between the overall objectives of the organization and the managerial objectives within that organization. In addition, harmony among goals of managers is impossible; they should not be at cross-purposes. Each manager's goal should supplement and assist the goals of his colleagues. Likewise, the objectives of individuals or non-management members should be harmonized with those of the manager. When this is accomplished, genuine teamwork is the result, and human relations are aided materially. The integration of managers' and individuals' goals aids in achieving greater work satisfaction at all levels.
    A. competition   B. dominate   C. incremental   D. vital

25. Change constantly challenges the manager. Some of this change is evolutionary, some revolutionary, some recognizable, some non-recognizable. Both forces within an enterprise and forces outside the enterprise cause managers to act and react in initiating changes in their immediate working environment. Change invalidates existing operations. Goals are not being accomplished in the best manner, problems develop, and frequently because of the lack of time, only patched-up solutions are followed. The result is that the mode of management is profound in nature and temporary in effectiveness. A complete overhaul of managerial operations should take place. It appears quite likely that we are just beginning to see the real effects of change in our society; the pace probably will accelerate in ways that few really understand or know how to handle.
    A. confirms   B. decline   C. instituting   D. superficial

KEY (CORRECT ANSWERS)

1.	C		11.	B
2.	A		12.	C
3.	B		13.	B
4.	B		14.	C
5.	C		15.	B
6.	C		16.	C
7.	C		17.	A
8.	A		18.	D
9.	C		19.	B
10.	B		20.	B

21. D
22. C
23. C
24. D
25. D

EXAMINATION SECTION
TEST 1

DIRECTIONS: Each question or incomplete statement is followed by several suggested answers or completions. Select the one that BEST answers the question or completes the statement. *PRINT THE LETTER OF THE CORRECT ANSWER IN THE SPACE AT THE RIGHT.*

1. Assume that a manager is preparing a list of reasons to justify making a major change in methods and procedures in his agency.
   Which of the following reasons would be LEAST appropriate on such a list?
   A. Improve the means for satisfying needs and wants of agency personnel
   B. Increase efficiency
   C. Intensify competition and stimulate loyalty to separate work groups
   D. Contribute to the individual and group satisfaction of agency personnel

   1.____

2. Many managers recognize the benefits of decentralization but are concerned about the danger of over-relaxation of control as a result of increased delegation.
   Of the following, the MOST appropriate means of establishing proper control under decentralization is for the manager to
   A. establish detailed standards for all phases of operation
   B. shift his attention from operating details to appraisal of results
   C. keep himself informed by decreasing the time span covered by reports
   D. make unilateral decisions on difficult situations that arise in decentralized locations

   2.____

3. In some agencies, the counsel to the agency head is given the right to bypass the chain of command and issue orders directly to the staff concerning matters that involve certain specific processes and practices.
   This situation MOST NEARLY illustrates the principle of _____ authority.
   A. the acceptance theory of
   B. multiple-linear
   C. splintered
   D. functional

   3.____

4. Assume that a manager is writing a brief report to his superior outlining the advantages of matrix organization.
   Of the following, it would be INCORRECT to state that
   A. in matrix organization, a project is emphasized by designating one individual as the focal point for all matters pertaining to it
   B. utilization of manpower can be flexible in matrix organization because a reservoir of specialists is maintained in the line operations
   C. the usual line staff arrangement is generally reversed in matrix organization
   D. in matrix organization, responsiveness to project needs is generally faster due to establishing needed communication lines and decision points

   4.____

5. It is commonly understood that communication is an important part of the administrative process.
Which of the following is NOT a valid principle of the communication process in administration?
   A. The channels of communication should be spontaneous.
   B. The lines of communication should be as direct and as short as possible.
   C. Communications should be authenticated.
   D. The persons serving in communications centers should be competent.

6. The PRIMARY purpose of the quantitative approach in management is to
   A. identify better alternatives for management decision-making
   B. substitute data for judgment
   C. match opinions to data
   D. match data to opinions

7. If an executive wants to make a strong case for running his agency as a flat type of structure, he should point out that the PRIMARY advantage of doing so is to
   A. provide less experience in decision-making for agency personnel
   B. facilitate frequent contact between each superior and his immediate subordinates
   C. improve communication and unify attitudes
   D. improve communication and diversify attitudes

8. In deciding how detailed his delegation of authority to a subordinate should be, a manager should follow the general principle that
   A. delegation of authority is more detailed at the top of the organizational structure
   B. detailed delegation of authority is associated with detailed work assignments
   C. delegation of authority should be in sufficient detail to prevent overlapping assignments
   D. detailed delegation of authority is associated with broad work assignments

9. In recent years, newer and more fluid types of organizational forms have been developed. One of these is a type of free-form organization.
Another name for this type of organization is the
   A. project organization
   B. semimix organization
   C. naturalistic structure
   D. semipermanent structure

10. Which of the following is the MAJOR objective of operational or management systems audits?
    A. Determining the number of personnel needed
    B. Recommending opportunities for improving operating and management practices
    C. Detecting fraud
    D. Determining organization problems

11. Assume that a manager observes that conflict exists between his agency and another operating agency of government.
    Which of the following statements is the LEAST probable cause of this conflict?
    A. Incompatibility between the agencies' goals but similarity in their resource allocations
    B. Compatibility between agencies' goals and resources
    C. Status differences between agency personnel
    D. Differences in perceptions of each other's policies

11.____

12. Of the following, a MAJOR purpose of brainstorming as a problem-solving technique is to
    A. develop the ability to concentrate
    B. encourage creative thinking
    C. evaluate employees' ideas
    D. develop critical ability

12.____

13. The one of the following requirements which is LEAST likely to accompany regular delegation of work from a manager to a subordinate is a(n)
    A. need to review the organization's workload
    B. indication of what work the subordinate is to do
    C. need to grant authority to the subordinate
    D. obligation for the subordinate who accepts the work to try to complete it

13.____

14. Of the following, the one factor which is generally considered LEAST essential to successful committee operation is
    A. stating a clear definition of the authority and scope of the committee
    B. selecting the committee chairman carefully
    C. limiting the size of the committee to four persons
    D. limiting the subject matter to that which can be handled in group discussion

14.____

15. In using the program evaluation and review technique, the *critical path* is the path that
    A. requires the shortest time
    B. requires the longest time
    C. focuses most attention on social constraints
    D. focuses most attention to repetitious jobs

15.____

16. Which one of the following is LEAST characteristic of the management-by-objectives approach?
    A. The scope within which the employee may exercise decision-making is broadened.
    B. The employee starts with a self-appraisal of his performances, abilities, and potential.
    C. Emphasis is placed on activities performed; activities orientation is maximized.
    D. Each employee participates in determining his own objectives.

16.____

17. The function of management which puts into effect the decisions, plans, and programs that have previously been worked out for achieving the goals of the group is MOST appropriately called
    A. scheduling   B. classifying   C. budgeting   D. directing

18. In the establishment of a plan to improve office productive efficiency, which of the following guidelines is LEAST helpful in setting sound work standards?
    A. Employees must accept the plan's objectives.
    B. Current production averages must be promulgated as work standards for a group.
    C. The work flow must generally be fairly constant.
    D. The operation of the plan must be expressed in terms understandable to the worker.

19. The one of the following activities which, generally speaking, is of *relatively* MAJOR importance at the lower-management level and of *somewhat* LESSER importance at higher-management levels is
    A. actuating   B. forecasting   C. organizing   D. planning

20. Three styles of leadership exist: democratic, authoritarian, and laissez-faire. Of the following work situations, the one in which a democratic approach would normally be the MOST effective is when the work is
    A. routine and moderately complex   B. repetitious and simple
    C. complex and not routine   D. simple and not routine

21. Governmental and business organizations *generally* encounter the GREATEST difficulties in developing tangible measures of which one of the following?
    A. The level of expenditures   B. Contributions to social welfare
    C. Retention rates   D. Causes of labor unrest

22. Of the following, a *management-by-objectives* program is BEST described as
    A. a new comprehensive plan of organization
    B. introduction of budgets and financial controls
    C. introduction of long-range planning
    D. development of future goals with supporting and related progress reviews

23. Research and analysis is probably the most widely used technique for selecting alternatives when major planning decisions are involved.
    Of the following, a VALUABLE characteristic of research and analysis is that this technique
    A. places the problem in a meaningful conceptual framework
    B. involves practical application of the various alternatives
    C. accurately analyzes all important tangibles
    D. is much less expensive than other problem-solving methods

24. If a manager were assigned the task of using a systems approach to designing a new work unit, which of the following should he consider FIRST in carrying out his design?
    A. Networks
    B. Work flows and information processes
    C. Linkages and relationships
    D. Decision points and control loops

25. The MAIN distinction between Theory X and Theory Y approaches to organization, in accordance with Douglas McGregor's view, is that Theory Y
    A. considers that work is natural to people; Theory X assumes that people are lazy and avoid work
    B. leads to a tall, narrow organization structure, while Theory X leads to one that is flat
    C. organizations motivate people with money; Theory X organizations motivate people with good working conditions
    D. represents authoritarian management, while Theory X management is participative

KEY (CORRECT ANSWERS)

1.	C		11.	B
2.	B		12.	B
3.	D		13.	A
4.	C		14.	C
5.	A		15.	B
6.	A		16.	C
7.	C		17.	D
8.	B		18.	B
9.	A		19.	A
10.	B		20.	C

21.	B
22.	D
23.	A
24.	B
25.	A

TEST 2

DIRECTIONS: Each question or incomplete statement is followed by several suggested answers or completions. Select the one that BEST answers the question or completes the statement. *PRINT THE LETTER OF THE CORRECT ANSWER IN THE SPACE AT THE RIGHT.*

1. Of the following, the stage in decision-making which is usually MOST difficult is
    A. stating the alternatives
    B. predicting the possible outcome of each alternative
    C. evaluating the relative merits of each alternative
    D. minimizing the undesirable aspects of the alternative selected

2. In a department where a clerk is reporting both to a senior clerk in charge of the mail room and also to a supervising clerk in charge of the duplicating section, there may be a breakdown of the management principle called
    A. horizontal specialization   B. job enrichment
    C. unity of command   D. Graicunas' Law

3. Of the following, the failure by line managers to accept and appreciate the benefits and limitations of a new program or system VERY frequently can be traced to the
    A. budgetary problems involved
    B. resultant need to reduce staff
    C. lack of controls it engenders
    D. failure of top management to support its implementation

4. Although there is general agreement that *management-by-objectives* has made a major contribution to modern management of large organizations, criticisms of the system during the past few years have resulted in
    A. mounting pressure for relaxation of management goals
    B. renewed concern with human values and the manager's personal needs
    C. over-mechanistic application of the perceptions of the behavioral scientists
    D. disillusionment with *management-by-objectives* on the part of a majority of managers

5. Of the following, which is usually considered to be a MAJOR obstacle to the systematic analysis of potential problems by managers?
    A. Managers have a tendency to think that all the implications of some proposed step cannot be fully understood.
    B. Rewards rarely go to those managers who are most successful at resolving current problems in management.
    C. There is a common conviction of manages that their goals are difficult to achieve.
    D. Managers are far more concerned about correcting today's problems than with preventing tomorrow's.

6. Which of the following should generally have the MOST influence on the selection of supervisors?
   A. Experience within the work unit where the vacancies exist
   B. Amount of money needed to effect the promotion
   C. Personal preferences of the administration
   D. Evaluation of capacity to exercise supervisory responsibilities

6.____

7. In questioning a potential administrator for selection purposes, the one of the following practices which is MOST desirable is to
   A. encourage the job applicant to give primarily *yes* or *no* replies
   B. get the applicant to talk freely and in detail about his background
   C. let the job applicant speak most of the time
   D. probe the applicant's attitudes, motivation, and willingness to accept responsibility

7.____

8. In implementing the managerial function of training subordinates, it is USEFUL to know that a widely agreed-upon definition of human learning is that learning
   A. is a relatively permanent change in behavior that results from reinforced practice or experience
   B. involves an improvement, but not necessarily a change in behavior
   C. involves a change in behavior, but not necessarily an improvement
   D. is a temporary change in behavior which must be subject to practice or experience

8.____

9. If a manager were thinking about using a committee of subordinates to solve an operating problem, which of the following would generally NOT be an advantage of such use of the committee approach?
   A. Improved coordination   B. Low cost
   C. Increased motivation   D. Integrated judgment

9.____

10. Which one of the following management approaches MOST often uses model-building techniques to solve management problems?
    _____ approach.
    A. Behavioral   B. Fiscal   C. Quantitative   D. Process

10.____

11. Of the following, the MOST serious risk in using budgets as a tool for management control is the
    A. probable neglect of other good management practices
    B. likelihood of guesswork because of the need to plan far in advance
    C. possibility of undue emphasis on factors that are easiest to measure
    D. danger of making qualitative rather than quantitative assessments of performance

11.____

12. In government budgeting, the problem of relating financial transactions to the fiscal year in which they are budgeted is BEST met by
    A. determining the cash balance by comparing how much money has been received and how much has been paid out
    B. applying net revenue to the fiscal year in which they are collected as offset by relevant expenses

12.____

C. adopting a system whereby appropriations are entered when they are received and expenditures are entered when they are paid out
D. entering expenditures on the books when the obligation to make the expenditure is made

13. If the agency's bookkeeping system records income when it is received and expenditures when the money is paid out this system is USUALLY known as a _____ system.
    A. cash
    B. flow-payment
    C. deferred
    D. fiscal year income

13._____

14. An audit, as the term applies to budget execution, is MOST NEARLY a
    A. procedure based on the budget estimates
    B. control exercised by the executive on the legislature in the establishment of program priorities
    C. check on the legality of expenditures and is based on the appropriations act
    D. requirement which must be met before funds can be spent

14._____

15. In government budgeting, there is a procedure known as *allotment*.
    Of the following statements which relate to allotment, select the one that is MOST generally considered to be correct.
    Allotment
    A. increases the practice of budget units coming back to the legislature branch for supplemental appropriations
    B. is simply an example of red tape
    C. eliminates the requirement of timing of expenditures
    D. is designed to prevent waste

15._____

16. In government budgeting, the establishment of the schedules of allotments is MOST generally the responsibility of the
    A. budget unit and the legislature
    B. budget unit and the executive
    C. budget unit only
    D. executive and the legislature

16._____

17. Of the following statements relating to preparation of an organization's budget request, which is the MOST generally valid precaution?
    A. Give specific instructions on the format or budget requests and required supporting data
    B. Because of the complexity of preparing a budget request, avoid argumentation to support the requests
    C. Put requests in whatever format is desirable
    D. Consider that final approval will be given to initial estimates

17._____

18. Of the following statements which relate to the budget process in a well-organized government, select the one that is MOST NEARLY correct.
    A. The budget cycle is the step-by-step process which is repeated each and every fiscal year.
    B. Securing approval of the budget does not take place within the budget cycle.

18._____

4 (#2)

C. The development of a new budget and putting it into effect is a two-step process known as the budget cycle.
D. The fiscal period, usually a fiscal year, has no relation to the budget cycle.

19. If a manager were asked what PPBS stands for, he would be RIGHT if he said _____ budgeting system. 19._____
    A. public planning
    B. planning programming
    C. planning projections
    D. programming procedures

Questions 20-21.

DIRECTIONS: Questions 20 and 21 are to be answered on the basis of the following information.

Sample Budget

Refuse Collection	Amount
Personal Services	$30,000
Contractual Services	5,000
Supplies and Materials	5,000
Capital Outlay	10,000
	$50,000

Residential Collections	
Dwellings – 1 pickup per week	1,000
Tons of refuse collected per year	375
Cost of collections per ton	$ 8
Cost per dwelling pickup per year	$ 3
Total annual cost	$3,000

20. The sample budget shown is a simplified example of a _____ budget. 20._____
    A. factorial   B. performance   C. qualitative   D. rational

21. The budget shown in the sample differs CHIEFLY from line-item and program budgets in that it includes 21._____
    A. objects of expenditure but not activities or functions
    B. only activities, functions, and control
    C. activities and functions but not objects of expenditures
    D. levels of service

Question 22.

DIRECTIONS: Question 22 is to be answered on the basis of the following information.

Sample Budget

```
Environmental Safety
    Air Pollution Protection
        Personal Services              $20,000,000
        Contractual Services             4,000,000
        Supplies and Materials           4,000,000
        Capital Outlay                   2,000,000
            Total Air Pollution Protection              $30,000,000

    Water Pollution Protection
        Personal Services              $23,000,000
        Supplies and Materials           4,500,000
        Capital Outlay                  20,500,000
            Total Water Pollution Protection            $48,000,000

    Total Environmental Safety                          $78,000,000
```

22. Based on the above budget, which is the MOST valid statement?
    A. Environmental Safety, Air Pollution Protection, and Water Pollution Protection could all be considered program elements.
    B. The object listings included water pollution protection and capital outlay.
    C. Examples of the program element listings in the above are personal services and supplies and materials
    D. Contractual Services and Environmental Safety were the program element listings.

23. Which of the following is NOT an advantage of a program budget over a line-item budget?
    A program budget
    A. allows us to set up priority lists in deciding what activities we will spend our money on
    B. gives us more control over expenditures than a line-item budget
    C. is more informative in that we know the broad purposes of spending money
    D. enables us to see if one program is getting much less money than the others

24. If a manager were trying to explain the fundamental difference between traditional accounting theory and practice and the newer practice of managerial accounting, he would be MOST accurate if he said that
    A. traditional accounting practice focused on providing information for persons outside organizations, while managerial accounting focuses on providing information for people inside organizations
    B. traditional accounting practice focused on providing information for persons inside organizations while managerial accounting focuses on providing information for persons outside organizations

C. managerial accounting is exclusively concerned with historical facts while traditional accounting stresses future projections exclusively
D. traditional accounting practice is more budget-focused than managerial accounting

25. Which of the following formulas is used to determine the number of days required to process work?
    _____ = Days to Process Work

    A. $\dfrac{\text{Employees} \times \text{Daily Output}}{\text{Volume}}$
    B. $\dfrac{\text{Volume} \times \text{Daily Output}}{\text{Volume}}$
    C. $\dfrac{\text{Volume}}{\text{Employees} \times \text{Daily Output}}$
    D. $\dfrac{\text{Employees} \times \text{Volume}}{\text{Daily Output}}$

25._____

KEY (CORRECT ANSWERS)

1. C
2. C
3. D
4. B
5. D

6. D
7. D
8. A
9. B
10. C

11. C
12. D
13. A
14. C
15. D

16. C
17. A
18. A
19. B
20. B

21. D
22. A
23. B
24. A
25. C

TEST 3

DIRECTIONS: Each question or incomplete statement is followed by several suggested answers or completions. Select the one that BEST answers the question or completes the statement. *PRINT THE LETTER OF THE CORRECT ANSWER IN THE SPACE AT THE RIGHT.*

1. Electronic data processing equipment can produce more information faster than can be generated by any other means.
   In view of this, the MOST important problem faced by management at present is to
   A. keep computers fully occupied
   B. find enough computer personnel
   C. assimilate and properly evaluate the information
   D. obtain funds to establish appropriate information systems

   1.____

2. A well-designed management information system ESSENTIALLY provides each executive and manager the information he needs for
   A. determining computer time requirements
   B. planning and measuring results
   C. drawing a new organization chart
   D. developing a new office layout

   2.____

3. It is generally agreed that management policies should be periodically reappraised and restated in accordance with current conditions.
   Of the following, the approach which would be MOST effective in determining whether a policy should be revised is to
   A. conduct interviews with staff members at all levels in order to ascertain the relationship between the policy and actual practice
   B. make proposed revisions in the policy and apply it to current problems
   C. make up hypothetical situations using both the old policy and a revised version in order to make comparisons
   D. call a meeting of top level staff in order to discuss ways of revising the policy

   3.____

4. Every manager has many occasions to lead a conference or participate in a conference of some sort.
   Of the following statements that pertain to conferences and conference leadership, which is generally considered to be MOST valid?
   A. Since World War II, the trend has been toward fewer shared decisions and more conferences.
   B. The most important part of a conference leader's job is to direct discussion.
   C. In providing opportunities for group interaction, management should avoid consideration of its past management philosophy.
   D. A good administrator cannot lead a good conference if he is a poor public speaker.

   4.____

5. Of the following, it is usually LEAST desirable for a conference leader to
    A. turn the question to the person who asked it
    B. summarize proceedings periodically
    C. make a practice of not repeating questions
    D. ask a question without indicating who is to reply

6. The behavioral school of management thought bases its beliefs on certain assumptions.
   Which of the following is NOT a belief of this school of thought?
    A. People tend to seek and accept responsibility.
    B. Most people can be creative in solving problems.
    C. People prefer security above all else.
    D. Commitment is the most important factor in motivating people.

7. The one of the following objectives which would be LEAST appropriate as a major goal of research in the field of human resources management is to
    A. predict future conditions, events, and manpower needs
    B. evaluate established policies, programs, and practices
    C. evaluate proposed policies, programs, and practices
    D. identify deficient organizational units and apply suitable penalties

8. Of the following general interviewing methods or techniques, the one that is USUALLY considered to be effective in counseling, grievances, and appraisal interviews is the _____ interview.
    A. directed   B. non-directed   C. panel   D. patterned

9. The ESSENTIAL first phase of decision-making is
    A. finding alternative solutions
    B. making a diagnosis of the problem
    C. selecting the plan to follow
    D. analyzing and comparing alternative solutions

10. Assume that, in a certain organization, a situation has developed in which there is little difference in status or authority between individuals.
    Which of the following would be the MOST likely result with regard to communication in this organization?
    A. Both the accuracy and flow of communication will be improved.
    B. Both the accuracy and flow of communication will substantially decrease.
    C. Employees will seek more formal lines of communication.
    D. Neither the flow nor the accuracy of communication will be improved over the former hierarchical structure.

11. The main function of many agency administrative offices is *information management*. Information that is received by an administrative officer may be classified as active or passive, depending upon whether or not it requires the recipient to take some action.

Of the following, the item received which is clearly the MOST active information is
- A. an appointment of a new staff member
- B. a payment voucher for a new desk
- C. a press release concerning a past city event
- D. the minutes of a staff meeting

12. Which one of the following sets BEST describes the general order in which to teach an operation to a new employee?
    - A. Prepare, present, tryout, follow-up
    - B. Prepare, test, tryout, re-test
    - C. Present, test, tryout, follow-up
    - D. Test, present, follow-up, re-test

13. Of the following, public employees may be separated from public service
    - A. for the same reasons which are generally acceptable for discharging employees in private industry
    - B. only under the most trying circumstances
    - C. under procedures that are neither formalized nor subject to review
    - D. solely in extreme cases involving offenses of gravest character

14. Of the following, the one LEAST considered to be a communication barrier is
    - A. group feedback
    - B. charged words
    - C. selective perception
    - D. symbolic meanings

15. Of the following ways for a manager to handle his appointments, the BEST way, according to experts in administration, generally is to
    - A. schedule his own appointments and inform his secretary not to reserve his time without his approval
    - B. encourage everyone to make appointments through his secretary and tell her when he makes his own appointments
    - C. see no one who has not made a previous appointment
    - D. permit anyone to see him without an appointment

16. Assume that a manager decides to examine closely one of five units under his supervision to uncover problems common to all five.
    His research technique is MOST closely related to the method called
    - A. experimentation
    - B. simulation
    - C. linear analysis
    - D. sampling

17. If one views the process of management as a dynamic process, which one of the following functions is NOT a legitimate part of that process?
    - A. Communication
    - B. Decision-making
    - C. Organizational slack
    - D. Motivation

18. Which of the following would be the BEST statement of a budget-oriented purpose for a government administrator? To
    A. provide 200 hours of instruction in basic reading for 3,500 adult illiterates at a cost of $1 million in the next fiscal year
    B. inform the public of adult educational programs
    C. facilitate the transfer to a city agency of certain functions of a federally-funded program which is being phased out
    D. improve the reading skills of the adult citizens in the city

19. Modern management philosophy and practices are changing to accommodate the expectations and motivations of organization personnel.
    Which of the following terms INCORRECTLY describes these newer managerial approaches?
    A. Rational management
    B. Participative management
    C. Decentralization
    D. Democratic supervision

20. Management studies support the hypothesis that, in spite of the tendency of employees to censor the information communicated to their supervisor, subordinates are MORE likely to communicate problem-oriented information upward when they have
    A. a long period of service in the organization
    B. a high degree of trust in the supervisor
    C. a high educational level
    D. low status on the organizational ladder

KEY (CORRECT ANSWERS)

1.	C	11.	A
2.	B	12.	A
3.	A	13.	A
4.	B	14.	A
5.	A	15.	B
6.	C	16.	D
7.	D	17.	C
8.	B	18.	A
9.	B	19.	A
10.	D	20.	B

EXAMINATION SECTION
TEST 1

DIRECTIONS: Each question or incomplete statement is followed by several suggested answers or completions. Select the one that BEST answers the question or completes the statement. *PRINT THE LETTER OF THE CORRECT ANSWER IN THE SPACE AT THE RIGHT.*

1. In many instances, managers deliberately set up procedures and routines that more than one department or more than one employee is required to complete and verify an entire operation or transaction.
   The MAIN reason for establishing such routines is generally to
   A. minimize the chances of gaps and deficiencies in feedback of information to management
   B. expand the individual employee's vision and concern for broader organizational objectives
   C. provide satisfaction of employees' social and egoistic needs through teamwork and horizontal communications
   D. facilitate internal control designed to prevent errors, whether intentional or accidental

2. Committees—sometimes referred to as boards, commissions, or task forces—are widely used in government to investigate certain problems or to manage certain agencies.
   Of the following, the MOST serious limitation of the committee approach to management in government is that
   A. it reflects government's inability to delegate authority effectively to individual executives
   B. committee members do not usually have similar backgrounds, experience, and abilities
   C. it promotes horizontal communication at the expense of vertical communication
   D. the spreading out of responsibility to a committee often results in a willingness to settle for weak, compromise solutions

3. Of the following, the BEST reason for replacing methods of committees on a staggered or partial basis rather than replacing all members simultaneously is that this practice
   A. gives representatives of different interest groups a chance to contribute their ideas
   B. encourages continuity of policy since retained members are familiar with previous actions
   C. prevents the interpersonal frictions from building up and hindering the work of the group
   D. improves the quality of the group's recommendations and decisions by stimulating development of new ideas

4. Assume that in considering a variety of actions to take to solve a given problem, a manager decides to take no action at all.
   According to generally accepted management practice, such a decision would be
   A. *proper*, because under normal circumstances it is better to make no decision
   B. *improper*, because inaction would be rightly construed as shunning one's responsibilities
   C. *proper*, since this would be a decision which might produce more positive results than the other alternatives
   D. *improper*, since such a solution would delay corrective action and exacerbate the problem

5. Some writers in the field of management assume that when a newly promoted manager has been informed by his superior about the subordinates he is to direct and the extent of his authority, that is all that is necessary.
   However, thereafter, this new manager should realize that, for practical purposes, his authority will be effective ONLY when
   A. he accepts full responsibility for the actions of his subordinates
   B. his subordinates are motivated to carry out their assignments
   C. it derives from acceptable personal attributes rather than from his official position
   D. he exercises it in an authoritarian manner

6. A newly appointed manager is assigned to assist the head of a small developing agency handling innovative programs. Although this manager is a diligent worker, he does not delegate authority to middle- and lower-echelon supervisors.
   The MOST important reason why it would be desirable to change this attitude toward delegation is because otherwise
   A. he may have to assume more responsibility for the actions of his subordinates than is implied in the authority delegated to him
   B. his subordinates will tend to produce innovative solutions on their own
   C. the agency will become a decentralized type of organization in which he cannot maintain adequate controls
   D. he may not have time to perform other essential tasks

7. All types of organizations and all functions within them are to varying degrees affected today by the need to understand the application of computer systems to management practices.
   The one of the following purposes for which such systems would be MOST useful is to
   A. lower the costs of problem-solving by utilizing data that is already in the agency's control system correlated with new data
   B. stabilize basic patterns of the organization into long-term structures and relationships
   C. give instant solutions to complex problems
   D. affect savings in labor costs for office tasks involving non-routine complex problems

8. Compared to individual decision-making, group decision-making is burdened with the DISADVANTAGE of
   A. making snap judgments
   B. pressure to examine all relevant elements of the problem
   C. greater motivation needed to implement the decision
   D. the need to clarify problems for the group participants

9. Assume that a manager in an agency, faced with a major administrative problem, has developed a number of alternative solutions to the problem. Which of the following would be MOST effective in helping the manager make the best decision?
   A. *Experience*, because a manager can distill from the past the fundamental reasons for success or failure since the future generally duplicates the past
   B. *Experimentation*, because it is the method used in scientific inquiry and can be tried out economically in limited areas
   C. *Research analysis*, because it is generally less costly than most other methods and involves the interrelationships among the more critical factors that bear upon the goal sought
   D. *Value forecasting*, because it assigns numerical significance to the values of alternative tangible and intangible choices and indicates the degree of risk involved in each choice

10. Management information systems operate more effectively for managers than mere data tabulating systems because information systems
    A. eliminate the need for managers to tell information processors what is required
    B. are used primarily for staff rather than line functions
    C. are less expensive to operate than manual methods of data collection
    D. present and utilize data in a meaningful form

11. Project-type organizations are in widespread use today because they offer a number of advantages.
    The MOST important purpose of the project organization is to
    A. secure a higher degree of coordination than could be obtained in a conventional line structure
    B. provide an orderly way of phrasing projects in and out of organizations
    C. expedite routine administrative processes
    D. allow for rapid assessment of the status of any given project and its effect on agency productivity

12. A manager adjusts his plans for future activity by reviewing information about the performance of his subordinates.
    This is an application of the process of
    A. human factor impact   B. coordinated response
    C. feedback communication   D. reaction control

13. From the viewpoint of the manager in an agency, the one of the following which is the MOST constructive function of a status system or a rank system based on employee performance is that the system
    A. makes possible effective communication, thereby lessening social distances between organizational levels
    B. is helpful to employees of lesser ability because it provides them with an incentive to exceed their capacities
    C. encourages the employees to attain or exceed the goals set for them by the organization
    D. diminishes friction in assignment and work relationships of personnel

14. Some managers ask employees who have been newly hired by their agency and then assigned to their divisions or units such questions as: *What are your personal goals? What do you expect from your job? Why do you want to work for this organization?*
    For a manager to ask these questions is GENERALLY considered
    A. *inadvisable*; these questions should have been asked prior to hiring the employee
    B. *inadvisable*; the answers will arouse subjective prejudices in the manager before he sees what kind of work the employee can do
    C. *advisable*; this approach indicates to the employee that the manager is interested in him as an individual
    D. *advisable*; the manager can judge how much of a disparity exists between the employee's goals and the agency's goals

15. Assume that you have prepared a report to your superior recommending a reorganization of your staff to eliminate two levels of supervision. The total number of employees would remain the same, with the supervisors of the two eliminated levels taking on staff assignments.
    In your report, which one of the following should NOT be listed as an expected result of such a reorganization?
    A. Fewer breakdowns and distortions in communications to staff
    B. Greater need for training
    C. Broader opportunities for development of employee skills
    D. Fewer employee errors due to exercise of closer supervision and control

16. *Administration* has often been criticized as being unproductive in the sense that it seems far removed from the end products of an organization.
    According to modern management thought, this criticism, for the most part, is
    A. *invalid*, because administrators make it possible for subordinates to produce goods or services by directing coordination, and controlling their activities
    B. *valid*, because most subordinates usually do the work required to produce goods and services with only general direction from their immediate superiors
    C. *invalid*, because administrators must see to all of the details associated with the production of services
    D. *valid*, because administrators generally work behind the scenes and are mainly concerned with long-range planning

17. A manager must be able to evaluate the relative importance of his decisions and establish priorities for carrying them out.
    Which one of the following factors bearing on the relative importance of making a decision would indicate to a manager that he can delegate that decision to a subordinate or give it low priority? The
    A. decision concerns a matter on which strict confidentiality must be maintained
    B. community impact of the decision is great
    C. decision can be easily changed
    D. decision commits the agency to heavy expenditure of funds

18. Suppose that you are responsible for reviewing and submitting to your superior the monthly reports from ten field auditors. Despite your repeated warnings to these auditors, most of them hand in their reports close to or after the deadline dates, so that you have no time to return them for revision and find yourself working overtime to make the necessary corrections yourself. The deadline dates for the auditors' reports and your report cannot be changed.
    Of the following, the MOST probable cause for this continuing situation is that
    A. these auditors need retraining in the writing of this type of report
    B. possible disciplinary action as a result of the delay by the auditors has not been impressed upon them
    C. the auditors have had an opportunity to provide you with feedback to explain the reasons for the delays
    D. you, as the manager, have not used disciplinary measures of sufficient severity to change their behavior

19. Assume that an agency desiring to try out a *management-by-objectives* program has set down the guidelines listed below to implement this activity. Which one of these guidelines is MOST likely to present obstacles to the success of this type of program?
    A. Specific work objectives should be determined by top management for employees at all levels.
    B. Objectives should be specific, attainable, and preferably measurable as to units, costs, ratios, time, etc.
    C. Standards of performance should be either qualitative or quantitative, preferably quantitative.
    D. There should be recognition and rewards for successful achievement or objectives.

20. Of the following, the MOST meaningful way to express productivity where employees work a standard number of hours each day is in terms of the relationship between man-
    A. hours expended and number of work-units needed to produce the final product
    B. days expended and goods and services produced
    C. days and energy expended
    D. days expended and number of workers

21. Agencies often develop productivity indices for many of their activities. 21.____
Of the following, the MOST important use for such indices is generally to
    A. measure the agency's output against its own performance
    B. improve quality standards while letting productivity remain unchanged
    C. compare outputs of the agency with outputs in private industry
    D. determine manpower requirements

22. The MOST outstanding characteristic of staff authority, such as that of a public 22.____
relations officer in an agency, as compared with line authority, is generally
accepted to be
    A. reliance upon personal attributes
    B. direct relationship to the primary objectives of the organization
    C. absence of the right to direct or command
    D. responsibility for attention to technical details

23. In the traditional organization structure, there are often more barriers to 23.____
upward communication than to downward communication.
From the viewpoint of a manager whose goal is to overcome obstacles to
communication, this situation should be
    A. *accepted*; the downward system is the more important since it is highly
       directive, giving necessary orders, instructions, and procedures
    B. *changed*; the upward system should receive more emphasis than the
       downward system, which represents stifling bureaucratic authority
    C. *accepted*; it is generally conceded that upward systems supply enough
       feedback for control purposes necessary to the organization's survival
    D. *changed*; research has generally verified the need for an increase in
       upward communications to supply more information about employees'
       ideas, attitudes, and performance

24. A principal difficulty in productivity measurement for local government services 24.____
is in defining and measuring output, a problem familiar to managers. A
measurement that merely looks good, but which may be against the public
interest, is another serious problem. Managers should avoid encouraging
employees to take actions that lead to such measurements.
In accordance with the foregoing statement, it would be MOST desirable for a
manager to develop a productivity measure that
    A. correlates the actual productivity measure with impact on benefit to the
       citizenry
    B. does not allow for a mandated annual increase in productivity
    C. firmly fixes priorities for resource allocations
    D. uses numerical output, by itself, in productivity incentive plans

25. For a manager, the MOST significant finding of the Hawthorne studies and 25.____
experiments is that an employee's productivity is affected MOST favorably
when the
    A. importance of tasks is emphasized and there is a logical arrangement of
       work functions

B. physical surroundings and work conditions are improved
C. organization has a good public relations program
D. employee is given recognition and allowed to participate in decision-making

---

KEY (CORRECT ANSWERS)

1.	D	11.	A
2.	D	12.	C
3.	B	13.	C
4.	C	14.	A
5.	B	15.	D
6.	D	16.	A
7.	A	17.	C
8.	D	18.	D
9.	C	19.	A
10.	D	20.	B

21. A
22. C
23. D
24. A
25. D

TEST 2

DIRECTIONS: Each question or incomplete statement is followed by several suggested answers or completions. Select the one that BEST answers the question or completes the statement. *PRINT THE LETTER OF THE CORRECT ANSWER IN THE SPACE AT THE RIGHT.*

1. Which one of the following is generally accepted by managers as the MOST difficult aspect of a training program in staff supervision?   1.____
    A. Determining training needs of the staff
    B. Evaluating the effectiveness of the courses
    C. Locating capable instructors to teach the courses
    D. Finding adequate space and scheduling acceptable times for all participants

2. Assume that, as a manager, you have decided to start a job enrichment program with the purpose of making jobs more varied and interesting in an effort to increase the motivation of a certain group of workers in your division.   2.____
   Which one of the following should generally NOT be part of this program?
    A. Increasing the accountability of these individuals for their own work
    B. Granting additional authority or job freedom to these employees in their job activities
    C. Mandating increased monthly production goals for this group of employees
    D. Giving each of these employees a complete unit of work

3. Both employer and employee have an important stake in effective preparation for retirement.   3.____
   According to modern management thinking, the one of the following which is probably the MOST important aspect of a sound pre-retirement program is to
    A. make assignments that utilize the employee's abilities fully
    B. reassign the employee to a less demanding position in the organization for the last year or two he is on the job
    C. provide the employee with financial data and other facts that would be pertinent to his retirement planning
    D. encourage the employee to develop interests and hobbies which are connected with the job

4. The civil service system generally emphasizes a policy of *promotion-from-within*. Employees in the direct line of promotion in a given occupational group are eligible for promotion to the next higher title in that occupational group.   4.____
   Which one of the following is LEAST likely to occur as a result of this policy and practice?
    A. Training time will be saved since employees in higher-level positions are already familiar with many agency rules, regulations, and procedures.
    B. The recruitment section will be able to show prospective employees that there are distinct promotional opportunities.

C. Employees will be provided with a clear-cut picture as to their possible career ladder.
D. Employees will be encouraged to seek broad-based training and education to enhance their promotability.

5. From a management point of view, the MAIAN drawback of seniority as opposed to merit as a basis for granting pay increases to workers is that a pay increase system based on seniority
   A. is favored by unions
   B. upsets organizational status relationships
   C. may encourage mediocre performance by employees
   D. is more difficult to administer than a merit plan

5._____

6. One of the actions that is often taken against employees in the non-uniformed forces who are accused of misconduct on the job is suspension without pay. The MOST justifiable reason for taking such action is to
   A. ease an employee out of the agency
   B. enable an investigation to be conducted into the circumstances of the offense
   C. improve the performance of the employee when he returns to the job
   D. punish the employee by imposing a hardship on him

6._____

7. A manager has had difficulty in getting good clerical employees to staff a filing section under his supervision. To add to his problems, one of his most competent senior clerks requests a transfer to the accounting division so that he can utilize his new accounting skill, which he is acquiring by going to college at night. The manager attempts to keep the senior clerk in his filing section by calling the director of personnel and getting him to promise not to authorize any transfer.
   GENERALLY, this manager's action is
   A. *desirable*; he should not help his staff to develop themselves if it means losing good people
   B. *undesirable*; he should recommend that the senior clerk get a raise in the hope of preventing him from transferring to another section
   C. *desirable*; it shows that the manager is concerned about the senior clerk's future performance
   D. *undesirable*; it is good policy to transfer employees to the type of work they are interested in and for which they are acquiring training

7._____

8. One of your subordinates, a unit supervisor, comes to you, the division chief, because he feels that he is working out of title, and he suggests that his competitive class position should be reclassified to a higher title.
   Which one of the following statements that the subordinate has made is generally LEAST likely to be a valid support for his suggestion?
   A. The work he is doing conforms to the general statement of duties and responsibilities as described in the class specification for the next higher title in his occupational group.
   B. Most of the typical tasks he performs are listed in the class specification for a title with a higher salary range and are not listed for his current title.

8._____

C. His education and experience qualifications far exceed the minimum requirements for the position he holds.
D. His duties and responsibilities have changed recently and are now similar to those of his supervisor.

9. Assume that a class specification for a competitive title used exclusively by your agency is outdated, and that no examination for the title has been given since the specification was issued.
Of the following, the MOST appropriate action for your agency to take is to
A. make the necessary changes and submit the revised class specification to the city civil service commission
B. write the personnel director to recommend that the class specification be updated, giving the reasons and suggested revisions
C. prepare a revised class specification and submit it to the office of management and budget for their approval
D. secure approval of the state civil service commission to update the class specification, and then submit the revised specification to the city civil service commission

9._____

10. Assume that an appropriate eligible list has been established and certified to your agency for a title in which a large number of provisionals are serving in your agency.
In order to obtain permission from the personnel director to retain some of them beyond the usual time limit set by rules (two months) following certification of the list, which one of the following conditions MUST apply?
A. The positions are sensitive and require investigation of eligibles prior to appointment.
B. Replacement of all provisionals within two months would impair essential public service.
C. Employees are required to work rotating shifts, including nights and weekends.
D. The duties of the positions require unusual physical effort and endurance.

10._____

11. Under the federally-funded Comprehensive Employment and Training Act (CETA), the hiring by the city of non-civil servants for CETA jobs is PROHIBITED when the
A. applicants are unemployed because of seasonal lay-offs in private industry
B. applicants do not meet U.S. citizenship and city residence requirements
C. jobs have minimum requirements of specialized professional or technical training and experience
D. jobs are comparable to those performed by laid-off civil servants

11._____

12. Assume you are in charge of the duplicating service in your agency. Since employees assigned to this operation lack a sense of accomplishment because the work is highly specialized and repetitive, your superior proposes to enlarge the jobs of these workers and asks you about your reaction to this strategy.

12._____

The MOST appropriate response for you to make is that job enlargement would be
- A. *undesirable*, primarily because it would increase production costs
- B. *undesirable*, primarily because it would diminish the quality of the output
- C. *desirable*, primarily because it might make it possible to add an entire level of management to the organizational structure of your agency
- D. *desirable*, primarily because it might make it possible to decrease the amount of supervision the workers will require

13. According to civil service law, layoff or demotion must be made in inverse order of seniority among employees permanently serving in the same title and layoff unit.
Which one of the following is now the CORRECT formula for computing seniority?
Total continuous service in the
- A. competitive class only
- B. competitive, non-competitive, or labor class
- C. classified or unclassified services
- D. competitive, non-competitive, exempt, and labor classes

13.____

14. Under which of the following conditions would an appointing officer be permitted to consider the sex of a candidate in making an employment decision?
When
- A. the duties of the position require considerable physical effort or strength
- B. the duties of the position are considered inherently dangerous
- C. separate toilet facilities and dressing rooms for the sexes are unavailable and/or cannot be provided in any event
- D. the public has indicated a preference to be served by persons of a specified sex

14.____

15. Assume that an accountant under your supervision signs out to the field to make an agency audit. It is later discovered that, although he had reported himself at work until 5 P.M. that day, he had actually left for home at 3:30 P.M. Although this accountant has worked for the city for ten years and has had an excellent performance record, he is demoted to a lower title in punishment for this breach of duty.
According to generally accepted thinking on personnel management, the disciplinary action taken in this case should be considered
- A. *appropriate*; a lesser penalty might encourage repetition of the offense
- B. *inappropriate*; the correct penalty for such a breach of duty should be dismissal
- C. *appropriate*; the accountant's abilities may be utilized better in the new assignment
- D. *inappropriate*; the impact of a continuing stigma and loss of salary is not commensurate with the offense committed

15.____

5 (#2)

16. Line managers often request more funds for their units than are actually required to attain their current objectives.
Which one of the following is the MOST important reason for such inflated budget requests?
The
    A. expectation that budget examiners will exercise their prerogative of budget cutting
    B. line manager's interest in improving the performance of his unit is thereby indicated to top management
    C. expectation that such requests will make it easier to obtain additional funds in future years
    D. opinion that it makes sense to obtain additional funds and decide later how to use them

16._____

17. Integrating budgeting with program planning and evaluation in a city agency is GENERALLY considered to be
    A. *undesirable*; budgeting must focus on the fiscal year at hand, whereas planning must concern itself with developments over a period of years
    B. *desirable*; budgeting facilitates the choice-making process by evaluating the financial implications of agency programs and forcing cost comparisons among them
    C. *undesirable*; accountants and statisticians with the required budgetary skills have little familiarity with the substantive programs that the agency is conducting
    D. *desirable*; such a partnership increases the budgetary skills of planners, thus promoting more effective use of public resources

17._____

18. An aspect of the managerial function, a budget is described BEST as a
    A. set of qualitative management controls over productivity
    B. tool based on historical accounting reports
    C. type of management plan expressed in quantitative terms
    D. precise estimate of future quantitative and qualitative contingencies

18._____

19. Which one of the following is generally accepted as the MAJOR immediate advantage of installing a system of program budgeting?
It
    A. encourages managers to relate their decisions to the agency's long-range goals
    B. is a replacement for the financial or fiscal budget
    C. decreases the need for managers to make trade-offs in the decision-making process
    D. helps to adjust budget figures to provide for unexpected developments

19._____

20. Of the following, the BEST means for assuring necessary responsiveness of a budgetary program to changing conditions is by
    A. overestimating budgetary expenditures by 15% and assigning the excess to unforeseen problem areas
    B. underestimating budgetary expenditures by at least 20% and setting aside a reserve account in the same amount

20._____

120

C. reviewing and revising the budget at regular intervals so that it retains its character as a current document
D. establishing *budget-by-exception* policies for each division in the agency

21. According to expert thought in the area of budgeting, participation in the preparation of a government agency's budget should GENERALLY involve
    A. only top management
    B. only lower levels of management
    C. all levels of the organization
    D. only a central budget office or bureau

22. Of the following, the MOST useful guide to analysis of budget estimates for the coming fiscal year is a comparison with
    A. appropriations as amended for the current fiscal year
    B. manpower requirements for the previous two years
    C. initial appropriations for the current fiscal year
    D. budget estimates for the preceding five years

23. A manager assigned to analyze the costs and benefits associated with a program which the agency head proposes to undertake may encounter certain factors which cannot be measured in dollar terms.
    In such a case, the manager should GENERALLY
    A. ignore the factors which cannot be quantified
    B. evaluate the factors in accordance with their degree of importance to the overall agency goals
    C. give the factors weight equal to the weight given to measurable costs and benefits
    D. assume that non-measurable costs and benefits will balance out against one another

24. If city employees believe that they are receiving adverse treatment in terms of training and disciplinary actions because of their national origin, they may file charges of discrimination with the Federal government's
    A. Human Rights Commission
    B. Public Employee Relations Board
    C. Equal Employment Opportunity Commission
    D. United States Department of Commerce

25. Under existing employment statutes, the city is obligated, as an employer, to take *affirmative action* in certain instances.
    This requirement has been imposed to ensure that
    A. employees who are members of minority groups, or women, be given special opportunities for training and promotion even though they are not available to other employees
    B. employees or applicants for employment are treated without regard to race, color, religion, sex, or national origin

C. proof exists to show that the city has acted with good intentions in any case where it has disregarded this requirement
D. men and women are treated alike except where State law provides special hour or working conditions for women

KEY (CORRECT ANSWERS)

1.	B	11.	D
2.	C	12.	D
3.	C	13.	D
4.	D	14.	C
5.	C	15.	D
6.	B	16.	A
7.	D	17.	B
8.	C	18.	C
9.	B	19.	A
10.	B	20.	D

21.	C
22.	A
23.	B
24.	C
25.	B

EVALUATING CONCLUSIONS IN LIGHT OF KNOWN FACTS
EXAMINATION SECTION
TEST 1

DIRECTIONS: Each question or incomplete statement is followed by several suggested answers or completions. Select the one that BEST answers the question or completes the statement. *PRINT THE LETTER OF THE CORRECT ANSWER IN THE SPACE AT THE RIGHT.*

Questions 1-9.

DIRECTIONS: In Questions 1 through 9, you will read a set of facts and a conclusion drawn from them. The conclusion may be valid or invalid, based on the facts—it's your task to determine the validity of the conclusion.

For each question, select the letter before the statement that BEST expresses the relationship between the given facts and the conclusion that has been drawn from them. Your choices are:
  A. The facts prove the conclusion;
  B. The facts disprove the conclusion; or
  C. The facts neither prove nor disprove the conclusion.

1. FACTS: If the supervisor retires, James, the assistant supervisor, will not be transferred to another department. James will be promoted to supervisor if he is not transferred. The supervisor retired.

   CONCLUSION: James will be promoted to supervisor.
   A. The facts prove the conclusion.
   B. The facts disprove the conclusion.
   C. The facts neither prove nor disprove the conclusion.

2. FACTS: In the town of Luray, every player on the softball team works at Luray National Bank. In addition, every player on the Luray softball team wear glasses.

   CONCLUSIONS: At least some of the people who work at Luray National Bank wear glasses.
   A. The facts prove the conclusion.
   B. The facts disprove the conclusion.
   C. The facts neither prove nor disprove the conclusion.

3. FACTS: The only time Henry and June go out to dinner is on an evening when they have childbirth classes. Their childbirth classes meet on Tuesdays and Thursdays.

CONCLUSION: Henry and June never go out to dinner on Friday or Saturday.
  A. The facts prove the conclusion.
  B. The facts disprove the conclusion.
  C. The facts neither prove nor disprove the conclusion.

4. FACTS: Every player on the field hockey team has at least one bruise. Everyone on the field hockey team also has scarred knees.

   CONCLUSION: Most people with both bruises and scarred knees are field hockey players.
   A. The facts prove the conclusion.
   B. The facts disprove the conclusion.
   C. The facts neither prove nor disprove the conclusion.

5. FACTS: In the chess tournament, Lance will win his match against Jane if Jane wins her match against Mathias. If Lance wins his match against Jane, Christine will not win her match against Jane.

   CONCLUSION: Christine will not win her match against Jane if Jane wins her match against Mathias.
   A. The facts prove the conclusion.
   B. The facts disprove the conclusion.
   C. The facts neither prove nor disprove the conclusion.

6. FACTS: No green lights on the machine are indicators for the belt drive status. Not all of the lights on the machine's upper panel are green. Some lights on the machine's lower panel are green.

   CONCLUSION: The green lights on the machine's lower panel may be indicators for the belt drive status.
   A. The facts prove the conclusion.
   B. The facts disprove the conclusion.
   C. The facts neither prove nor disprove the conclusion.

7. FACTS: At a small, one-room country school, there are eight students: Amy, Ben, Carla, Dan, Elliot, Francine, Greg, and Hannah. Each student is in either the 6th, 7th, or 8th grade. Either two or three students are in each grade. Amy, Dan, and Francine are all in different grades. Ben and Elliot are both in the 7th grade. Hannah and Carl are in the same grade.

   CONCLUSION: Exactly three students are in the 7th grade.
   A. The facts prove the conclusion.
   B. The facts disprove the conclusion.
   C. The facts neither prove nor disprove the conclusion.

8. **FACTS:** Two married couples are having lunch together. Two of the four people are German and two are Russian, but in each couple the nationality of the spouse is not necessarily the same as the other's. One person in the group is a teacher, the other a lawyer, one an engineer, and the other a writer. The teacher is a Russian man. The writer is Russian, and her husband is an engineer. One of the people, Mr. Stern, is German.

   CONCLUSION: Mr. Stern's wife is a writer.
   A. The facts prove the conclusion.
   B. The facts disprove the conclusion.
   C. The facts neither prove nor disprove the conclusion.

9. **FACTS:** The flume ride at the county fair is open only to children who are at least 36 inches tall. Lisa is 30 inches tall. John is shorter than Henry, but more than 10 inches taller than Lisa.

   CONCLUSION: Lisa is the only one who can't ride the flume ride.
   A. The facts prove the conclusion.
   B. The facts disprove the conclusion.
   C. The facts neither prove nor disprove the conclusion.

Questions 10-17.

DIRECTIONS: Questions 10 through 17 are based on the following reading passage. It is not your knowledge of the particular topic that is being tested, but your ability to reason based on what you have read. The passage is likely to detail several proposed courses of action and factors affecting these proposals. The reading passage is followed by a conclusion or outcome based on the facts in the passage, or a description of a decision taken regarding the situation. The conclusion is followed by a number of statements that have a possible connection to the conclusion. For each statement, you are to determine whether:
   A. The statement proves the conclusion.
   B. The statement supports the conclusion but does not prove it.
   C. The statement disproves the conclusion.
   D. The statement weakens the conclusion but does not disprove it.
   E. The statement has no relevance to the conclusion.

Remember that the conclusion after the passage is to be accepted as the outcome of what actually happened, and that you are being asked to evaluate the impact each statement would have had on the conclusion.

PASSAGE:

The Grand Army of Foreign Wars, a national veteran's organization, is struggling to maintain its National Home, where the widowed spouses and orphans of deceased members are housed together in a small village-like community. The Home is open to spouses and children who are bereaved for any reason, regardless of whether the member's death was related to military service, but a new global conflict has led to a dramatic surge in the number of members' deaths: many veterans who re-enlisted for the conflict have been killed in action.

The Grand Army of Foreign Wars is considering several options for handling the increased number of applications for housing at the National Home, which has been traditionally supported by membership due. At its national convention, it will choose only one of the following:

The first idea is a one-time $50 tax on all members, above and beyond the dues they pay already. Since the organization has more than a million member, this tax should be sufficient for the construction and maintenance of new housing for applicants on the existing grounds of the National Home. The idea is opposed, however, by some older members who live on fixed incomes. These members object in principle to the taxation of Grand Army members. The Grand Army has never imposed a tax on its members.

The second idea is to launch a national fundraising drive the public relations campaign that will attract donations for the National Home. Several national celebrities are members of the organization, and other celebrities could be attracted to the cause. Many Grand Army members are wary of this approach, however: in the past, the net receipts of some fundraising efforts have been relatively insignificant, given the costs of staging them.

A third approach, suggested by many of the younger members, is to have new applicants share some of the costs of construction and maintenance. The spouses and children would pay an up-front "enrollment" fee, based on a sliding scale proportionate to their income and assets, and then a monthly fee adjusted similarly to contribute to maintenance costs. Many older members are strongly opposed to this idea, as it is in direct contradiction to the principles on which the organization was founded more than a century ago.

The fourth option is simply to maintain the status quo, focus the organization's efforts on supporting the families who already live at the National Home, and wait to accept new applicants based on attrition.

CONCLUSION: At its annual national convention, the Grand Army of Foreign Wars votes to impose a one-time tax of $10 on each member for the purpose of expanding and supporting the National Home to welcome a larger number of applicants. The tax is considered to be the solution most likely to produce the funds needed to accommodate the growing number of applicants.

10. Actuarial studies have shown that because the Grand Army's membership consists mostly of older veterans from earlier wars, the organization's membership will suffer a precipitous decline in numbers in about five years. 10._____
    A. The statement proves the conclusion.
    B. The statement supports the conclusion but does not prove it.
    C. The statement disproves the conclusion.
    D. The statement weakens the conclusion but does not disprove it.
    E. The statement has no relevance to the conclusion.

11. After passage of the funding measure, a splinter group of older members appeals for the "sliding scale" provision to be applied to the tax, so that some members may be allowed to contribute less based on their income. 11._____
    A. The statement proves the conclusion.
    B. The statement supports the conclusion but does not prove it.
    C. The statement disproves the conclusion.
    D. The statement weakens the conclusion but does not disprove it.
    E. The statement has no relevance to the conclusion.

5 (#1)

12. The original charter of the Grand Army of Foreign Wars specifically states that the organization will not levy taxes or duties on its members beyond its modest annual dues. It takes a super-majority of attending delegates at the national convention to make alterations to the charter.
    A. The statement proves the conclusion.
    B. The statement supports the conclusion but does not prove it.
    C. The statement disproves the conclusion.
    D. The statement weakens the conclusion but does not disprove it.
    E. The statement has no relevance to the conclusion.

12.____

13. Six months before Grand Army of Foreign Wars' national convention, the Internal Revenue Service rules that because it is an organization that engages in political lobbying, the Grand Army must no longer enjoy its own federal tax-exempt status.
    A. The statement proves the conclusion.
    B. The statement supports the conclusion but does not prove it.
    C. The statement disproves the conclusion.
    D. The statement weakens the conclusion but does not disprove it.
    E. The statement has no relevance to the conclusion.

13.____

14. Two months before the national convention, Dirk Rockwell, arguably the country's most famous film actor, announces in a nationally televised interview that he has been saddened to learn of the plight of the National Home, and that he is going to make it his own personal crusade to see that it is able to house and support a greater number of widowed spouses and orphans in the future.
    A. The statement proves the conclusion.
    B. The statement supports the conclusion but does not prove it.
    C. The statement disproves the conclusion.
    D. The statement weakens the conclusion but does not disprove it.
    E. The statement has no relevance to the conclusion.

14.____

15. The Grand Army's final estimate is that the cost of expanding the National Home to accommodate the increased number of applicants will be about $61 million.
    A. The statement proves the conclusion.
    B. The statement supports the conclusion but does not prove it.
    C. The statement disproves the conclusion.
    D. The statement weakens the conclusion but does not disprove it.
    E. The statement has no relevance to the conclusion.

15.____

16. Just before the national convention, the Federal Department of Veterans Affairs announces steep cuts in the benefits package that is currently offered to the widowed spouses and orphans of veterans.
    A. The statement proves the conclusion.
    B. The statement supports the conclusion but does not prove it.
    C. The statement disproves the conclusion.
    D. The statement weakens the conclusion but does not disprove it.
    E. The statement has no relevance to the conclusion.

16.____

17. After the national convention, the Grand Army of Foreign Wars begins charging a modest "start-up" fee to all families who apply for residence at the national home.
    A. The statement proves the conclusion.
    B. The statement supports the conclusion but does not prove it.
    C. The statement disproves the conclusion.
    D. The statement weakens the conclusion but does not disprove it.
    E. The statement has no relevance to the conclusion.

17.____

Questions 18-25.

DIRECTIONS: Questions 18 through 25 each provide four factual statements and a conclusion based on these statements. After reading the entire question, you will decide whether:
   A. The conclusion is proved by statements I-IV;
   B. The conclusion is disproved by statements I-IV.
   C. The facts are not sufficient to prove or disprove the conclusion.

18. FACTUAL STATEMENTS:
    I. In the Field Day high jump competition, Martha jumped higher than Frank.
    II. Carl jumped higher than Ignacio.
    III. Ignacio jumped higher than Frank.
    IV. Dan jumped higher than Carl.

    CONCLUSION: Frank finished last in the high jump competition.
       A. The conclusion is proved by statements I-IV;
       B. The conclusion is disproved by statements I-IV.
       C. The facts are not sufficient to prove or disprove the conclusion.

18.____

19. FACTUAL STATEMENTS:
    I. The door to the hammer mill chamber is locked if light 6 is red.
    II. The door to the hammer mill chamber is locked only when the mill is operating.
    III. If the mill is not operating, light 6 is blue.
    IV. Light 6 is blue.

    CONCLUSION: The door to the hammer mill chamber is locked.
       A. The conclusion is proved by statements I-IV;
       B. The conclusion is disproved by statements I-IV.
       C. The facts are not sufficient to prove or disprove the conclusion.

19.____

20. FACTUAL STATEMENTS:
    I. Ziegfried, the lion tamer at the circus, has demanded ten additional minutes of performance time during each show.
    II. If Ziegfried is allowed his ten additional minutes per show, he will attempt to teach Kimba the tiger to shoot a basketball.
    III. If Kimba learns how to shoot a basketball, then Ziegfried was not given his ten additional minutes.
    IV. Ziegfried was given his ten additional minutes.

20.____

7 (#1)

CONCLUSION: Despite Ziegfried's efforts, Kimba did not learn how to shoot a basketball.
   A. The conclusion is proved by statements I-IV;
   B. The conclusion is disproved by statements I-IV.
   C. The facts are not sufficient to prove or disprove the conclusion.

21. FACTUAL STATEMENTS:
   I. If Stan goes to counseling, Sara won't divorce him.
   II. If Sara divorces Stan, she'll move back to Texas.
   III. If Sara doesn't divorce Stan, Irene will be disappointed.
   IV. Stan goes to counseling.

   CONCLUSION: Irene will be disappointed.
   A. The conclusion is proved by statements I-IV;
   B. The conclusion is disproved by statements I-IV.
   C. The facts are not sufficient to prove or disprove the conclusion.

22. FACTUAL STATEMENTS:
   I. If Delia is promoted to district manager, Claudia will have to be promoted to team leader.
   II. Delia will be promoted to district manager unless she misses her fourth-quarter sales quota.
   III. If Claudia is promoted to team leader, Thomas will be promoted to assistant team leader.
   IV. Delia meets her fourth-quarter sales quota.

   CONCLUSION: Thomas is promoted to assistant team leader.
   A. The conclusion is proved by statements I-IV;
   B. The conclusion is disproved by statements I-IV.
   C. The facts are not sufficient to prove or disprove the conclusion.

23. FACTUAL STATEMENTS:
   I. Clone D is identical to Clone B.
   II. Clone B is not identical to Clone A.
   III. Clone D is not identical to Clone C.
   IV. Clone E is not identical to the clones that are identical to Clone B.

   CONCLUSION: Clone E is identical to Clone D.
   A. The conclusion is proved by statements I-IV;
   B. The conclusion is disproved by statements I-IV.
   C. The facts are not sufficient to prove or disprove the conclusion.

24. FACTUAL STATEMENTS:
   I. In the Stafford Tower, each floor is occupied by a single business.
   II. Big G Staffing is on a floor between CyberGraphics and MainEvent.
   III. Gasco is on the floor directly below CyberGraphics and three floors above Treehorn Audio.
   IV. MainEvent is five floors below EZ Tax and four floors below Treehorn Audio.

8 (#1)

CONCLUSION: EZ Tax is on a floor between Gasco and MainEvent.
   A. The conclusion is proved by statements I-IV;
   B. The conclusion is disproved by statements I-IV.
   C. The facts are not sufficient to prove or disprove the conclusion.

25. FACTUAL STATEMENTS: 25.____
   I. Only county roads lead to Nicodemus.
   II. All the roads from Hill City to Graham County are federal highways.
   III. Some of the roads from Plainville lead to Nicodemus.
   IV. Some of the roads running from Hill City lead to Strong City.

CONCLUSION: Some of the roads from Plainville are county roads.
   A. The conclusion is proved by statements I-IV;
   B. The conclusion is disproved by statements I-IV.
   C. The facts are not sufficient to prove or disprove the conclusion.

KEY (CORRECT ANSWERS)

1.	A		11.	A
2.	A		12.	D
3.	A		13.	E
4.	C		14.	D
5.	A		15.	B
6.	B		16.	B
7.	A		17.	C
8.	A		18.	A
9.	A		19.	B
10.	E		20.	A

21.	A
22.	A
23.	B
24.	A
25.	A

SOLUTIONS TO PROBLEMS

1. **CORRECT ANSWER: A**
Given Statement 3, we deduce that James will not be transferred to another department. By Statement 2, we can conclude that James will be promoted.

2. **CORRECT ANSWER: A**
Since every player on the softball team wears glasses, these individuals compose some of the people who work at the bank. Although not every person who works at the bank plays softball, those bank employees who do play softball wear glasses.

3. **CORRECT ANSWER: A**
If Henry and June go out to dinner, we conclude that it must be on Tuesday or Thursday, which are the only two days when they have childbirth classes. This implies that if it is not Tuesday or Thursday, then this couple does not go out to dinner.

4. **CORRECT ANSWER: C**
We can only conclude that if a person plays on the field hockey team, then he or she has both bruises and scarred knees. But there are probably a great number of people who have both bruises and scarred knees but do not play on the field hockey team. The given conclusion can neither be proven or disproven.

5. **CORRECT ANSWER: A**
From statement 1, if Jane beats Mathias, then Lance will beat Jane. Using statement 2, we can then conclude that Christine will not win her match against Jane.

6. **CORRECT ANSWER: B**
Statement 1 tells us that no green light can be an indicator of the belt drive status. Thus, the given conclusion must be false.

7. **CORRECT ANSWER: A**
We already know that Ben and Elliot are in the 7th grade. Even though Hannah and Carl are in the same grade, it cannot be the 7th grade because we would then have at least four students in this 7th grade. This would contradict the third statement, which states that either two or three students are in each grade. Since Amy, Dan, and Francine are in different grade, exactly one of them must be in the 7th grade. Thus, Ben, Elliot, and exactly one of Amy, Dan, and Francine are the three students in the 7th grade.

8. **CORRECT ANSWER: A**
One man is a teacher, who is Russian. We know that the writer is female and is Russian. Since her husband is an engineer, he cannot be the Russian teacher. Thus, her husband is of German descent, namely Mr. Stern. This means that Mr. Stern's wife is the writer. Note that one couple consists of a male Russian teacher and a female German lawyer. The other couple consists of a male German engineer and a female Russian writer.

9. **CORRECT ANSWER: A**
Since John is more than 10 inches taller than Lisa, his height is at least 46 inches. Also, John is shorter than Henry, so Henry's height must be greater than 46 inches. Thus, Lisa is the only one whose height is less than 36 inches. Therefore, she is the only one who is not allowed on the flume ride.

18. **CORRECT ANSWER: A**
Dan jumped higher than Carl, who jumped higher than Ignacio, who jumped higher than Frank. Since Martha jumped higher than Frank, every person jumped higher than Frank. Thus, Frank finished last.

19. **CORRECT ANSWER: B**
If the light is red, then the door is locked. If the door is locked, then the mill is operating. Reversing the logical sequence of these statements, if the mill is not operating, then the door is not locked, which means that the light is blue. Thus, the given conclusion is disproved.

20. **CORRECT ANSWER: A**
Using the contrapositive of statement III, Ziegfried was given his ten additional minutes, then Kimba did not learn how to shoot a basketball. Since statement IV is factual, the conclusion is proved.

21. **CORRECT ANSWER: A**
From Statements IV and I, we conclude that Sara doesn't divorce Stan. Then statement III reveals that Irene will be disappointed. Thus, the conclusion is proved.

22. **CORRECT ANSWER: A**
Statement II can be rewritten as "Delia is promoted to district manager or she misses her sales quota." Furthermore, this statement is equivalent to "If Delia makes her sales quota, then she is promoted to district manager." From statement I, we conclude that Claudia is promoted to team leader. Finally, by statement III, Thomas is promoted to assistant team leader.

23. **CORRECT ANSWER: B**
By statement IV, Clone E is not identical to any clones identical to Clone B. Statement I tells us that Clones B and D are identical. Therefore, Clone E cannot be identical to Clone D. The conclusion is disproved.

24. **CORRECT ANSWER: A**
Based on all four statements, CyberGraphics is somewhere below MainEvent. Gasco is one floor below CyberGraphics. EZ Tax is two floors below Gasco. Treehorn Audio is one floor below EZ Tax. MainEvent is four floors below Treehorn Audio. Thus, EZ Tax is two floors below Gasco and five floors above MainEvent. The conclusion is proved.

25. **CORRECT ANSWER: A**
From statement III, we know that some of the roads from Plainville lead to Nicodemus. But statement I tells us that only county roads lead to Nicodemus. Therefore, some of the roads from Plainville must be county roads. The conclusion is proved.

TEST 2

DIRECTIONS: Each question or incomplete statement is followed by several suggested answers or completions. Select the one that BEST answers the question or completes the statement. *PRINT THE LETTER OF THE CORRECT ANSWER IN THE SPACE AT THE RIGHT.*

Questions 1-9.

DIRECTIONS: In Questions 1 through 9, you will read a set of facts and a conclusion drawn from them. The conclusion may be valid or invalid, based on the facts—it's your task to determine the validity of the conclusion.

For each question, select the letter before the statement that BEST expresses the relationship between the given facts and the conclusion that has been drawn from them. Your choices are:
  A. The facts prove the conclusion;
  B. The facts disprove the conclusion; or
  C. The facts neither prove nor disprove the conclusion.

1. FACTS: Some employees in the testing department are statisticians. Most of the statisticians who work in the testing department are projection specialists. Tom Wilks works in the testing department.

   CONCLUSION: Tom Wilks is a statistician.
     A. The facts prove the conclusion.
     B. The facts disprove the conclusion.
     C. The facts neither prove nor disprove the conclusion.

   1.____

2. FACTS: Ten coins are split among Hank, Lawrence, and Gail. If Lawrence gives his coins to Hank, then Hank will have more coins than Gail. If Gail gives her coins to Lawrence, then Lawrence will have more coins than Hank.

   CONCLUSION: Hank has six coins.
     A. The facts prove the conclusion.
     B. The facts disprove the conclusion.
     C. The facts neither prove nor disprove the conclusion.

   2.____

3. FACTS: Nobody loves everybody. Janet loves Ken. Ken loves everybody who loves Janet.

   CONCLUSION: Everybody loves Janet.
     A. The facts prove the conclusion.
     B. The facts disprove the conclusion.
     C. The facts neither prove nor disprove the conclusion.

   3.____

4. **FACTS:** Most of the Torres family lives in East Los Angeles. Many people in East Los Angeles celebrate Cinco de Mayo. Joe is a member of the Torres family.

   CONCLUSION: Joe lives in East Los Angeles.
   A. The facts prove the conclusion.
   B. The facts disprove the conclusion.
   C. The facts neither prove nor disprove the conclusion.

5. **FACTS:** Five professionals each occupy one story of a five-story office building. Dr. Kane's office is above Dr. Assad's. Dr. Johnson's office is between Dr. Kane's and Dr. Conlon's. Dr. Steen's office is between Dr. Conlon's and Dr. Assad's. Dr. Johnson is on the fourth story.

   CONCLUSION: Dr. Kane occupies the top story.
   A. The facts prove the conclusion.
   B. The facts disprove the conclusion.
   C. The facts neither prove nor disprove the conclusion.

6. **FACTS:** To be eligible for membership in the Yukon Society, a person must be able to either tunnel through a snowbank while wearing only a T-shirt and short, or hold his breath for two minutes under water that is 50°F. Ray can only hold his breath for a minute and a half.

   CONCLUSION: Ray can still become a member of the Yukon Society by tunneling through a snowbank while wearing a T-shirt and shorts.
   A. The facts prove the conclusion.
   B. The facts disprove the conclusion.
   C. The facts neither prove nor disprove the conclusion.

7. **FACTS:** A mark is worth five plunks. You can exchange four sharps for a tinplot. It takes eight marks to buy a sharp.

   CONCLUSION: A sharp is the most valuable.
   A. The facts prove the conclusion.
   B. The facts disprove the conclusion.
   C. The facts neither prove nor disprove the conclusion.

8. **FACTS:** There are gibbons, as well as lemurs, who like to play in the trees at the monkey house. All those who like to play in the trees at the monkey house are fed lettuce and bananas.

   CONCLUSION: Lemurs and gibbons are types of monkeys.
   A. The facts prove the conclusion.
   B. The facts disprove the conclusion.
   C. The facts neither prove nor disprove the conclusion.

9. **FACTS:** None of the Blackfoot tribes is a Salishan Indian tribe. Salishan Indians came from the northern Pacific Coast. All Salishan Indians live each of the Continental Divide.

   CONCLUSION: No Blackfoot tribes live east of the Continental Divide.
   A. The facts prove the conclusion.
   B. The facts disprove the conclusion.
   C. The facts neither prove nor disprove the conclusion.

Questions 10-17.

DIRECTIONS: Questions 10 through 17 are based on the following reading passage. It is not your knowledge of the particular topic that is being tested, but your ability to reason based on what you have read. The passage is likely to detail several proposed courses of action and factors affecting these proposals. The reading passage is followed by a conclusion or outcome based on the facts in the passage, or a description of a decision taken regarding the situation. The conclusion is followed by a number of statements that have a possible connection to the conclusion. For each statement, you are to determine whether:
   A. The statement proves the conclusion.
   B. The statement supports the conclusion but does not prove it.
   C. The statement disproves the conclusion.
   D. The statement weakens the conclusion but does not disprove it.
   E. The statement has no relevance to the conclusion.

Remember that the conclusion after the passage is to be accepted as the outcome of what actually happened, and that you are being asked to evaluate the impact each statement would have had on the conclusion.

PASSAGE:

On August 12, Beverly Willey reported that she was in the elevator late on the previous evening after leaving her office on the 16th floor of a large office building. In her report, she states that a man got on the elevator at the 11th floor, pulled her off the elevator, assaulted her, and stole her purse. Ms. Willey reported that she had seen the man in the elevators and hallways of the building before. She believes that the man works in the building. Her description of him is as follows: he is tall, unshaven, with wavy brown hair and a scar on his left cheek. He walks with a pronounced limp, often dragging his left foot behind his right.

CONCLUSION: After Beverly Willey makes her report, the police arrest a 43-year-old man, Barton Black, and charge him with her assault.

4 (#2)

10. Barton Black is a former Marine who served in Vietnam, where he sustained shrapnel wounds to the left side of his face and suffered nerve damage in his left leg.
    A. The statement proves the conclusion.
    B. The statement supports the conclusion but does not prove it.
    C. The statement disproves the conclusion.
    D. The statement weakens the conclusion but does not disprove it.
    E. The statement has no relevance to the conclusion.

10.____

11. When they arrived at his residence to question him, detectives were greeted at the door by Barton Black, who was tall and clean-shaven.
    A. The statement proves the conclusion.
    B. The statement supports the conclusion but does not prove it.
    C. The statement disproves the conclusion.
    D. The statement weakens the conclusion but does not disprove it.
    E. The statement has no relevance to the conclusion.

11.____

12. Barton Black was booked into the county jail several days after Beverly Willey's assault.
    A. The statement proves the conclusion.
    B. The statement supports the conclusion but does not prove it.
    C. The statement disproves the conclusion.
    D. The statement weakens the conclusion but does not disprove it.
    E. The statement has no relevance to the conclusion.

12.____

13. Upon further investigation, detectives discover that Beverly Willey does not work at the office building.
    A. The statement proves the conclusion.
    B. The statement supports the conclusion but does not prove it.
    C. The statement disproves the conclusion.
    D. The statement weakens the conclusion but does not disprove it.
    E. The statement has no relevance to the conclusion.

13.____

14. Upon further investigation, detectives discover that Barton Black does not work at the office building.
    A. The statement proves the conclusion.
    B. The statement supports the conclusion but does not prove it.
    C. The statement disproves the conclusion.
    D. The statement weakens the conclusion but does not disprove it.
    E. The statement has no relevance to the conclusion.

14.____

15. In the spring of the following year, Barton Black is convicted of assaulting Beverly Willey on August 11.
    A. The statement proves the conclusion.
    B. The statement supports the conclusion but does not prove it.
    C. The statement disproves the conclusion.
    D. The statement weakens the conclusion but does not disprove it.
    E. The statement has no relevance to the conclusion.

15.____

16. During their investigation of the assault, detectives determine that Beverly Willey 16.____
    was assaulted on the 12th floor of the office building.
    A. The statement proves the conclusion.
    B. The statement supports the conclusion but does not prove it.
    C. The statement disproves the conclusion.
    D. The statement weakens the conclusion but does not disprove it.
    E. The statement has no relevance to the conclusion.

17. The day after Beverly Willey's assault, Barton Black fled the area and was never 17.____
    seen again.
    A. The statement proves the conclusion.
    B. The statement supports the conclusion but does not prove it.
    C. The statement disproves the conclusion.
    D. The statement weakens the conclusion but does not disprove it.
    E. The statement has no relevance to the conclusion.

Questions 18-25.

DIRECTIONS: Questions 18 through 25 each provide four factual statements and a conclusion based on these statements. After reading the entire question, you will decide whether:
    A. The conclusion is proved by statements I-IV;
    B. The conclusion is disproved by statements I-IV.
    C. The facts are not sufficient to prove or disprove the conclusion.

18. FACTUAL STATEMENTS: 18.____
    I. Among five spice jars on the shelf, the sage is to the right of the parsley.
    II. The pepper is to the left of the basil.
    III. The nutmeg is between the sage and the pepper.
    IV. The pepper is the second spice from the left.

    CONCLUSION: The safe is the farthest to the right.
    A. The conclusion is proved by statements I-IV;
    B. The conclusion is disproved by statements I-IV.
    C. The facts are not sufficient to prove or disprove the conclusion.

19. FACTUAL STATEMENTS: 19.____
    I. Gear X rotates in a clockwise direction if Switch C is in the OFF position.
    II. Gear X will rotate in a counter-clockwise direction is Switch C is ON.
    III. If Gear X is rotating in a clockwise direction, then Gear Y will not be rotating at all.
    IV. Switch C is ON.

    CONCLUSION: Gear X is rotating in a counter-clockwise direction.
    A. The conclusion is proved by statements I-IV;
    B. The conclusion is disproved by statements I-IV.
    C. The facts are not sufficient to prove or disprove the conclusion.

20. FACTUAL STATEMENTS:
   I. Lane will leave for the Toronto meeting today only if Terence, Rourke, and Jackson all file their marketing reports by the end of the work day.
   II. Rourke will file her report on time only if Ganz submits last quarter's data.
   III. If Terence attends the security meeting, he will attend it with Jackson, and they will not file their marketing reports by the end of the work day.

   CONCLUSION: Lane will leave for the Toronto meeting today.
   A. The conclusion is proved by statements I-IV;
   B. The conclusion is disproved by statements I-IV.
   C. The facts are not sufficient to prove or disprove the conclusion.

21. FACTUAL STATEMENTS:
   I. Bob is in second place in the Boston Marathon.
   II. Gregory is winning the Boston Marathon.
   III. There are four miles to go in the race, and Bob is gaining on Gregory at the rate of 100 yards every minute.
   IV. There are 1760 yards in a mile and Gregory's usual pace during the Boston Marathon is one mile every six minutes.

   CONCLUSION: Bob wins the Boston Marathon.
   A. The conclusion is proved by statements I-IV;
   B. The conclusion is disproved by statements I-IV.
   C. The facts are not sufficient to prove or disprove the conclusion.

22. FACTUAL STATEMENTS:
   I. Four brothers are named Earl, John, Gary, and Pete.
   II. Earl and Pete are unmarried.
   III. John is shorter than the youngest of the four.
   IV. The oldest brother is married, and is also the tallest.

   CONCLUSION: Gary is the oldest brother.
   A. The conclusion is proved by statements I-IV;
   B. The conclusion is disproved by statements I-IV.
   C. The facts are not sufficient to prove or disprove the conclusion.

23. FACTUAL STATEMENTS:
   I. Brigade X is ten miles from the demilitarized zone.
   II. If General Woundwort gives the order, Brigade X will advance to the demilitarized zone, but not quickly enough to reach the zone before the conflict begins.
   III. Brigade Y, five miles behind Brigade X, will not advance unless General Woundwort gives the order.
   IV. Brigade Y advances.

7 (#2)

CONCLUSION: Brigade X reaches the demilitarized zone before the conflict begins.
   A. The conclusion is proved by statements I-IV;
   B. The conclusion is disproved by statements I-IV.
   C. The facts are not sufficient to prove or disprove the conclusion.

24. FACTUAL STATEMENTS:
   I. Jerry has decided to take a cab from Fullerton to Elverton.
   II. Chubby Cab charges $5 plus $3 a mile.
   III. Orange Cab charges $7.50 but gives free mileage for the first 5 miles.
   IV. After the first 5 miles, Orange Cab charges $2.50 a mile.

   CONCLUSION: Orange Cab is the cheaper fare from Fullerton to Elverton.
   A. The conclusion is proved by statements I-IV;
   B. The conclusion is disproved by statements I-IV.
   C. The facts are not sufficient to prove or disprove the conclusion.

24.____

25. FACTUAL STATEMENTS:
   I. Dan is never in class when his friend Lucy is absent.
   II. Lucy is never absent unless her mother is sick.
   III. If Lucy is in class, Sergio is in class also.
   IV. Sergio is never in class when Dalton is absent.

   CONCLUSION: If Lucy is absent, Dalton may be in class.
   A. The conclusion is proved by statements I-IV;
   B. The conclusion is disproved by statements I-IV.
   C. The facts are not sufficient to prove or disprove the conclusion.

25.____

KEY (CORRECT ANSWERS)

1. C
2. B
3. B
4. C
5. A

6. A
7. B
8. C
9. C
10. B

11. E
12. B
13. D
14. E
15. A

16. E
17. C
18. B
19. A
20. C

21. C
22. A
23. B
24. A
25. B

9 (#2)

SOLUTIONS TO PROBLEMS

1. CORRECT ANSWER: C
   Statement 1 only tells us that some employees who work in the Testing Department are statisticians. This means that we need to allow the possibility that at least one person in this department is not a statistician. Thus, if a person works in the Testing Department, we cannot conclude whether or not this individual is a statistician.

2. CORRECT ANSWER: B
   If Hank had six coins, then the total of Gail's collection and Lawrence's collection would be four. Thus, if Gail gave all her coins to Lawrence, Lawrence would only have four coins. Thus, it would be impossible for Lawrence to have more coins than Hank.

3. CORRECT ANSWER: B
   Statement 1 tells us that nobody loves everybody. If everybody loved Janet, then Statement 3 would imply that Ken loves everybody. This would contradict statement 1. The conclusion is disproved.

4. CORRECT ANSWER: C
   Although most of the Torres family lives in East Los Angeles, we can assume that some members of this family do not live in East Los Angeles. Thus, we cannot prove or disprove that Joe, who is a member of the Torres family, lives in East Los Angeles.

5. CORRECT ANSWER: A
   Since Dr. Johnson is on the 4th floor, either (a) Dr. Kane is on the 5th floor and Dr. Conlon is on the 3rd floor, or (b) Dr. Kane is on the 3rd floor and Dr. Conlon is on the 5th floor. If option (b) were correct, then since Dr. Assad would be on the 1st floor, it would be impossible for Dr. Steen's office to be between Dr. Conlon and Dr. Assad's office. Therefore, Dr. Kane's office must be on the 5th floor. The order of the doctors' offices, from 5th floor down to the 1st floor is: Dr. Kane, Dr. Johnson, Dr. Conlon, Dr. Steen, Dr. Assad.

6. CORRECT ANSWER: A
   Ray does not satisfy the requirement of holding his breath for two minutes under water, since he can only hold is breath for one minute in that setting. But if he tunnels through a snowbank with just a T-shirt and shorts, he will satisfy the eligibility requirement. Note that the eligibility requirement contains the key word "or." So only one of the two clauses separated by "or" need to be fulfilled.

7. CORRECT ANSWER: B
   Statement 2 says that four sharps is equivalent to one tinplot. This means that a tinplot is worth more than a sharp. The conclusion is disproved. We note that the order of these items, from most valuable to least valuable are: tinplot, sharp, mark, plunk.

8. CORRECT ANSWER: C
   We can only conclude that gibbons and lemurs are fed lettuce and bananas. We can neither prove nor disprove that these animals are types of monkeys.

9. CORRECT ANSWER: C
We know that all Salishan Indians live east of the Continental Divide. But some non-members of this tribe of Indians may also live east of the Continental Divide. Since none of the members of the Blackfoot tribe belong to the Salishan Indian tribe, we cannot draw any conclusion about the location of the Blackfoot tribe with respect to the Continental Divide.

18. CORRECT ANSWER: B
Since the pepper is second from the left and the nutmeg is between the sage and the pepper, the positions 2, 3, and 4 (from the left) are pepper, nutmeg, sage. By statement II, the basil must be in position 5, which implies that the parsley is in position 1. Therefore, the basil, not the sage, is farthest to the right. The conclusion disproved.

19. CORRECT ANSWER: A
Statement II assures us that if switch C is ON, then Gear X is rotating in a counterclockwise direction. The conclusion is proved.

20. CORRECT ANSWER: C
Based on Statement IV, followed by Statement II, we conclude that Ganz and Rourke will file their reports on time. Statement III reveals that if Terence and Jackson attend the security meeting, they will fail to file their reports on time. We have no further information if Terence and Jackson attended the security meeting, so we are not able to either confirm or deny that their reports were filed on time. This implies that we cannot know for certain that Lane will leave for his meeting in Toronto.

21. CORRECT ANSWER: C
Although Bob is in second place behind Gregory, we cannot deduce how far behind Gregory he is running. At Gregory's current pace, he will cover four miles in 24 minutes. If Bob were only 100 yards behind Gregory, he would catch up to Gregory in one minute. But if Bob were very far behind Gregory, for example 5 miles, this is the equivalent of $(5)(1760) = 8800$ yards. Then Bob would need $8800/100 = 88$ minutes to catch up to Gregory. Thus, the given facts are not sufficient to draw a conclusion.

22. CORRECT ANSWER: A
Statement II tells us that neither Earl nor Pete could be the oldest; also, either John or Gary is married. Statement IV reveals that the oldest brother is both married and the tallest. By Statement III, John cannot be the tallest. Since John is not the tallest, he is not the oldest. Thus, the oldest brother must be Gary. The conclusion is proved.

23. CORRECT ANSWER: B
By Statements III and IV, General Woundwort must have given the order to advance. Statement II then tells us that Brigade X will advance to the demilitarized zone, but not soon enough before the conflict begins. Thus, the conclusion is disproved.

24. CORRECT ANSWER: A
If the distance is 5 miles or less, then the cost for the Orange Cab is only $7.50, whereas the cost for the Chubby Cab is $5 + 3x, where x represents the number of miles traveled. For 1 to 5 miles, the cost of the Chubby Cab is between $8 and $20. This means that for a distance of 5 miles, the Orange Cab costs $7.50, whereas the Chubby Cab costs $20. After 5 miles, the cost per mile of the Chubby Cab exceeds the cost per mile of the Orange Cab. Thus, regardless of the actual distance between Fullerton and Elverton, the cost for the Orange Cab will be cheaper than that of the Chubby Cab.

25. CORRECT ANSWER: B
It looks like "Dalton" should be replaced by "Dan" in the conclusion. Then by statement I, if Lucy is absent, Dan is never in class. Thus, the conclusion is disproved.

EVALUATING INFORMATION AND EVIDENCE
EXAMINATION SECTION
TEST 1

DIRECTIONS: Each question or incomplete statement is followed by several suggested answers or completions. Select the one that BEST answers the question or completes the statement. *PRINT THE LETTER OF THE CORRECT ANSWER IN THE SPACE AT THE RIGHT.*

Questions 1-9.

DIRECTIONS: Questions 1 through 9 measure your ability to (1) determine whether statements from witnesses say essentially the same thing and (2) determine the evidence needed to make it reasonably certain that a particular conclusion is true.

1. Which of the following pairs of statements say essentially the same thing in two different ways?
   I. If you get your feet wet, you will catch a cold.
      If you catch a cold, you must have gotten your feet wet.
   II. If I am nominated, I will run for office.
      I will run for office only if I am nominated.
   The CORRECT answer is:
      A. I only   B. I and II   C. II only   D. Neither I nor II

1.____

2. Which of the following pairs of statements say essentially the same thing in two different ways?
   I. The enzyme Rhopsin cannot be present if the bacterium Trilox is absent.
      Rhopsin and Trilox always appear together.
   II. A member of PENSA has an IQ of at least 175.
      A person with an IQ of less than 175 is not a member of PENSA
   The CORRECT answer is;
      A. I only   B. I and II   C. II only   D. Neither I nor II

2.____

3. Which of the following pairs of statements say essentially the same thing in two different ways?
   I. None of Finer High School's sophomores will be going to the prom.
      No student at Finer High School who is going to the prom is a sophomore.
   II. If you have 20/20 vision, you may carry a firearm.
      You may not carry a firearm unless you have 20/20 vision.
   The CORRECT answer is:
      A. I only   B. I and II   C. II only   D. Neither I nor II

3.____

4. Which of the following pairs of statements say essentially the same thing in two different ways?
   I. If the family doesn't pay the ransom, they will never see their son again.
      It is necessary for the family to pay the ransom in order for them to see their son again.
   II. If it is raining, I am carrying an umbrella.
       If I am carrying an umbrella, it is raining.
   The CORRECT answer is:
   A. I only   B. I and II   C. II only   D. Neither I nor II

4._____

5. Summary of Evidence Collected to Date:
   In the county's maternity wards, over the past year, only one baby was born who did not share a birthday with any other baby.
   Prematurely Drawn Conclusion: At least one baby was born on the same day as another baby in the county's maternity wards.
   Which of the following pieces of evidence, if any, would make it reasonably certain that the conclusion drawn is true?
   A. More than 365 babies were born in the county's maternity wards over the past year.
   B. No pairs of twins were born over the past year in the county's maternity wards.
   C. More than one baby was born in the county's maternity wards over the past year.
   D. None of the above

5._____

6. Summary of Evidence Collected to Date:
   Every claims adjustor for MetroLife drives only a Ford sedan when on the job.
   Prematurely Drawn Conclusion: A person who works for MetroLife and drives a Ford sedan is a claims adjustor.
   Which of the following pieces of evidence, if any, would make it reasonably certain that the conclusion drawn is true?
   A. Most people who work for MetroLife are claims adjustors.
   B. Some people who work for MetroLife are not claims adjustors.
   C. Most people who work for MetroLife drive Ford sedans
   D. None of the above

6._____

7. Summary of Evidence Collected to Date:
   Mason will speak to Zisk if Zisk will speak to Ronaldson.
   Prematurely Drawn Conclusion: Jones will not speak to Zisk if Zisk will speak to Ronaldson.
   Which of the following pieces of evidence, if any, would make it reasonably certain that the conclusion drawn is true?
   A. If Zisk will speak to Mason, then Ronaldson will not speak to Jones.
   B. If Mason will speak to Zisk, then Jones will not speak to Zisk.
   C. If Ronaldson will speak to Jones, then Jones will speak to Ronaldson.
   D. None of the above

7._____

8. <u>Summary of Evidence Collected to Date</u>:
No blue lights on the machine are indicators for the belt drive status.
<u>Prematurely Drawn Conclusion</u>: Some of the lights on the lower panel are not indicators for the belt drive status.
Which of the following pieces of evidence, if any, would make it reasonably certain that the conclusion drawn is true?
   A. No lights on the machine's lower panel are blue.
   B. An indicator light for the machine's belt drive status is either green or red.
   C. Some lights on the machine's lower panel are blue.
   D. None of the above

8._____

9. <u>Summary of Evidence Collected to Date</u>:
Of the four Sweeney sisters, two are married, three have brown eyes, and three are doctors.
<u>Prematurely Drawn Conclusion</u>: Two of the Sweeney sisters are brown-eyed, married doctors.
Which of the following pieces of evidence, if any, would make it reasonably certain that the conclusion is true?
   A. The sister who does not have brown eyes is married.
   B. The sister who does not have brown eyes is not a doctor, and one who is not married is not a doctor.
   C. Every Sweeney sister with brown eyes is a doctor.
   D. None of the above

9._____

Questions 10-14.

DIRECTIONS: Questions 10 through 14 refer to Map #5 and measure your ability to orient yourself within a given section of town, neighborhood or particular area. Each of the questions describes a starting point and a destination. Assume that you are driving a car in the area shown on the map accompanying the questions. Use the map as a basis for the shortest way to get from one point to another without breaking the law.

On the map, a street marked by arrows, or by arrows and the words "One Way," indicates one-way travel and should be assumed to be one-way for the entire length, even when there are breaks or jogs in the street. EXCEPTION: A street that does not have the same name over the full length.

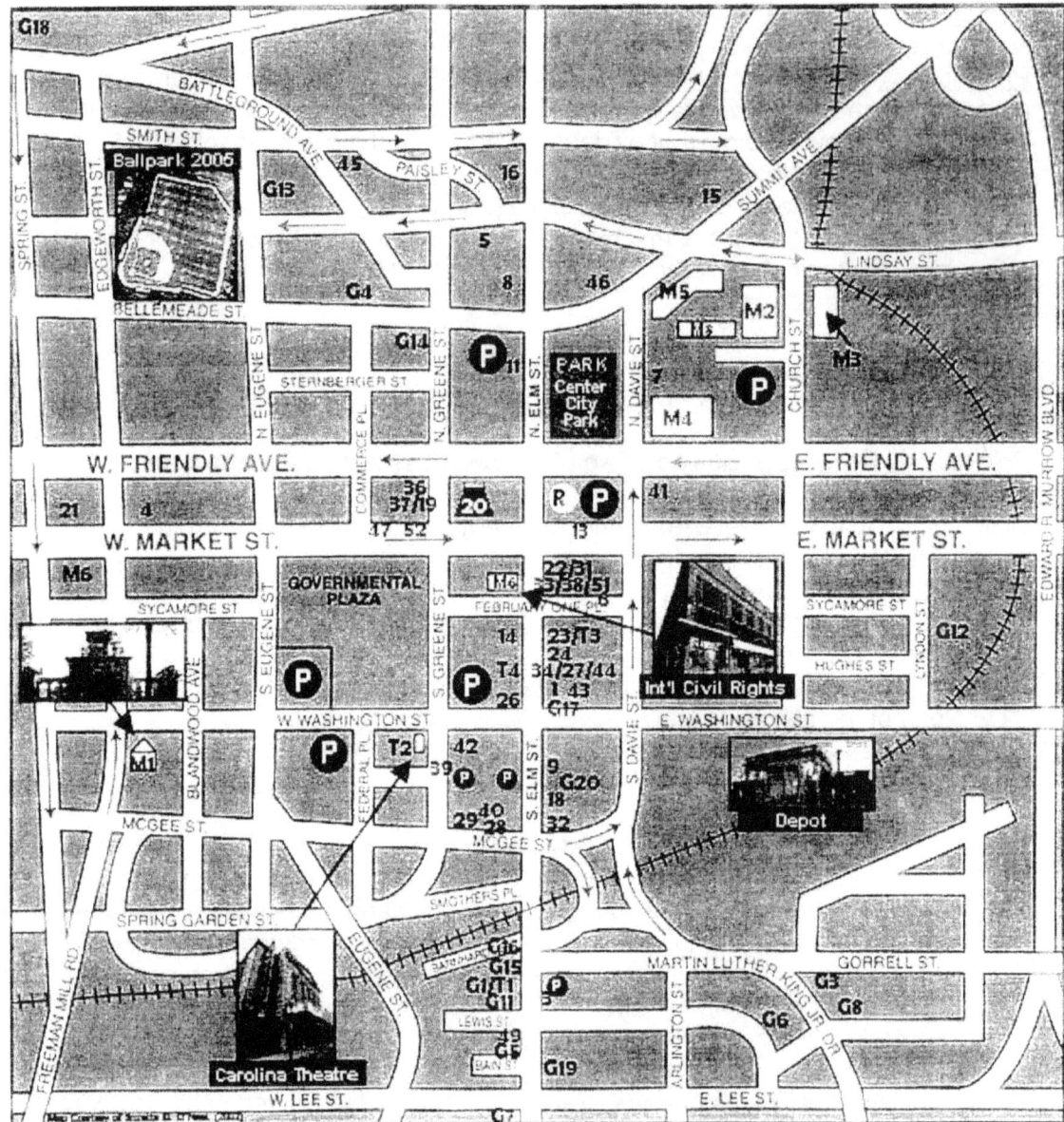

Map #5

10. The SHORTEST legal way from the depot to Center City Park is
    A. north on Church, west on Market, north on Elm
    B. east on Washington, north on Edward R. Murrow Blvd., west on Friendly Ave.
    C. west on Washington, north on Greene, east on Market, north on Davie
    D. north on Church, west on Friendly Ave.

10._____

11. The SHORTEST legal way from the Governmental Plaza to the Ballpark is   11.____
    A. west on Market, north on Edgeworth
    B. west on Market, north on Eugene
    C. north on Greene, west on Lindsay
    D. north on Commerce Place, west on Bellemeade

12. The SHORTEST legal way from the International Civil Rights Building to the   12.____
    building marked "M3" on the map is
    A. east on February One Place, north on Davie, east on Friendly Ave., north on Church
    B. south on Elm, west on Washington, north on Greene, east on Market, north on Church
    C. north on Elm, east on Market, north on Church
    D. north on Elm, east on Lindsay, south on Church

13. The SHORTEST legal way from the Ballpark to the Carolina Theatre is   13.____
    A. east on Lindsay, south on Greene
    B. south on Edgeworth, east on Friendly Ave., south on Greene
    C. east on Bellemeade, south on Elm, west on Washington

14. A car traveling north or south on Church Street may NOT go   14.____
    A. west onto Friendly Ave.   B. west onto Lindsay
    C. east onto Market   D. west onto Smith

Questions 15-19.

DIRECTIONS: Questions 15 through 19 refer to Figure #3, on the following page, and measure your ability to understand written descriptions of events. Each question presents a description of an accident or event and asks you which of the following five drawings in Figure #3 BEST represents it.
In the drawings, the following symbols are used:
Moving vehicle ⌂   Non-moving vehicle ▲
Pedestrian or bicyclist •
The path and direction of travel of a vehicle or pedestrian is indicated by a solid line.
The path and direction of travel of each vehicle or pedestrian directly involved in a collision from the point of impact is indicated by a dotted line.

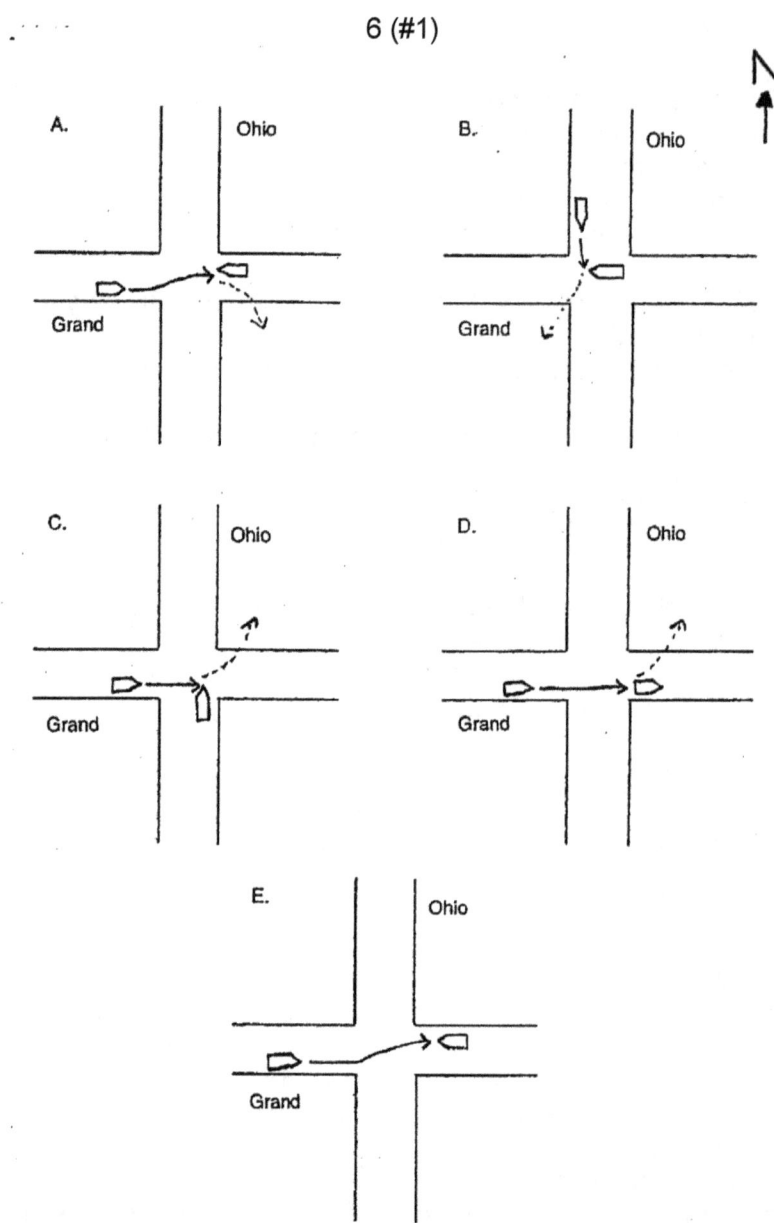

In the space at the right, print the letter of the drawing that BEST fit the descriptions written below.

15. A driver headed south on Ohio runs a red light and strikes the front of a car headed west on Grand. He glances off and leaves the roadway at the southwest corner of Grand and Ohio.

15.____

16. A driver heading east on Grand drifts into the oncoming lane as it travels through the intersection of Grand and Ohio, and strikes an oncoming car head-on

16.____

17. A driver heading east on Grand veers into the oncoming lane, sideswipes a westbound car and overcorrects as he swerves back into his lane. He leaves the roadway near the southeast corner of Grand and Ohio. 17.____

18. A driver heading east on Grand strikes the front of a car that is traveling north on Ohio and has run a red light. After striking the front of the northbound car, the driver veers left and leaves the roadway at the northeast corner of Grand and Ohio. 18.____

19. A driver heading east on Grand is traveling above the speed limit and clips the rear end of another eastbound car. The driver then veers to the left and leaves the roadway at the northeast corner of Grand and Ohio. 19.____

Questions 20-22.

DIRECTIONS: In Questions 20 through 22, choose the word or phrase CLOSEST in meaning to the word or phrase printed in capital letters.

20. PETITION 20.____
    A. appeal   B. law   C. oath   D. opposition

21. MALPRACTICE 21.____
    A. commission   B. mayhem   C. error   D. misconduct

22. EXONERATE 22.____
    A. incriminate   B. accuse   C. lengthen   D. acquit

Questions 23-25.

DIRECTIONS: Questions 23 through 25 measure your ability to do fieldwork-related arithmetic. Each question presents a separate arithmetic problem for you to solve.

23. Officers Lane and Bryant visited another city as part of an investigation. Because each is from a different precinct, they agree to split all expenses. With her credit card, Lane paid $70 for food and $150 for lodging. Bryant wrote checks for gas ($50) and entertainment ($40). 23.____
    How much does Bryant owe Lane?
    A. $65   B. $90   C. $155   D. $210

24. In a remote mountain pass, two search-and-rescue teams, one from Silverton and one from Durango, combine to look for a family that disappeared in a recent snowstorm. The combined team is composed of 20 members. 24.____
    Which of the following statements could NOT be true?
    A. The Durango team has a dozen members.
    B. The Silverton team has only one member.
    C. The Durango team has two more members than the Silverton team.
    D. The Silverton team has one more member than the Durango team.

25. Three people in the department share a vehicle for a period of one year. The average number of miles traveled per month by each person is 150. How many miles will be added to the car's odometer at the end of the year? 25.____
    A. 1,800   B. 2,400   C. 3,600   D. 5,400

KEY (CORRECT ANSWERS)

1.	D	11.	D
2.	C	12.	C
3.	A	13.	D
4.	A	14.	D
5.	A	15.	B
6.	A	16.	E
7.	B	17.	A
8.	C	18.	C
9.	B	19.	D
10.	D	20.	A

21. D
22. D
23. A
24. D
25. D

SOLUTIONS TO QUESTIONS 1-9

P implies Q = original statement

Not Q implies not P = contrapositive of the original statement. A statement and its contrapositive are logically equivalent.

Q implies P = converse of the original statement

Not P implies not Q = inverse of the original statement. The converse and inverse of an original statement are logically equivalent.

P implies Q = Not P or Q.

1. The CORRECT answer is D.
   In items I and II, each statement is the converses of the other. A converse of a statement is not equivalent to its original statement.

2. The CORRECT answer is C.
   In item I, the first statement is equivalent to "If Trilox is absent, then Rhopsin is also absent." But this does NOT imply that if Trilox is present, so too must Rhopsin be present. In item II, each statement is the contrapositive of the other. Thus, they are equivalent.

3. The CORRECT answer is A.
   In item I, the first sentence tells us that if a student is a sophomore, he/she will not go the prom. The second statement is equivalent to "If a student does attend the prom, he/she is not a sophomore." This is the contrapositive of the first statement, (so it is equivalent to it).

4. The CORRECT answer is A.
   In item I, the second statement can be written as "If the family sees their son again, then they must have paid the ransom." This is the contrapositive of the first statement. In item II, these statements are converses of each other; thus, they are not equivalent.

5. The CORRECT answer is A.
   If more than 365 babies were born in the county in one year, then at least two babies must share the same birthday.

6. The CORRECT answer is A.
   Given that most people who work for MetroLife are claims adjustors, plus the fact that all claims adjustors drive only a Ford sedan, it is a reasonable conclusion that any person who drives a Ford sedan and works for MetroLife is a claims adjustor.

7. The CORRECT answer is B.
   Jones will not speak to Zisk if Zisk will speak to Ronaldson, which will happen if Mason will speak to Zisk.

8. The CORRECT answer is C.
We are given that blue lights are never an indicator for the drive belt status. If some of the lights on the lower panel of the machine are blue, then it is reasonable to conclude that some of the lights on the lower panel are not indicators for the drive belt status.

9. The CORRECT answer is B.
There is only one sister that does not have brown eyes and only one sister that is not a doctor, and if the information in answer B is correct, then we learn that the same sister is a non-doctor without brown eyes. We also learn that this same non-doctor is not married. Since this all describes the same sister, we can conclude that two of the other sisters must be married doctors with brown eyes.

TEST 2

DIRECTIONS: Each question or incomplete statement is followed by several suggested answers or completions. Select the one that BEST answers the question or completes the statement. *PRINT THE LETTER OF THE CORRECT ANSWER IN THE SPACE AT THE RIGHT.*

Questions 1-9.

DIRECTIONS: Questions 1 through 9 measure your ability to (1) determine whether statements from witnesses say essentially the same thing and (2) determine the evidence needed to make it reasonably certain that a particular conclusion is true.
To do well on this part of the test, you do NOT have to have a working knowledge of police procedures and techniques. Nor do you have to have any more familiarity with criminals and criminal behavior than that acquired from reading newspapers, listening to radio or watching TV. To do well in this part, you must read and reason carefully.

1. Which of the following pairs of statements say essentially the same thing in two different ways?
   I. If there is life on Mars, we should fund NASA.
      Either there is life on Mars, or we should not fund NASA.
   II. All Eagle Scouts are teenage boys.
       All teenage boy are Eagle Scouts.
   The CORRECT answer is:
   A. I only   B. I and II   C. II only   D. Neither I nor II

2. Which of the following pairs of statements say essentially the same thing in two different ways?
   I. If that notebook is missing its front cover, it definitely belongs to Carter.
      Carter's notebook is the only one missing its front cover.
   II. If it's hot, the pool is open.
       The pool is open if it's hot.
   The CORRECT answer is:
   A. I only   B. I and II   C. II only   D. Neither I nor II

3. Which of the following pairs of statements say essentially the same thing in two different ways?
   I. Nobody who works at the mill is without benefits.
      Everyone who works at the mill has benefits.
   II. We will fund the program only if at least 100 people sign the petition.
       Either we will fund the program or at least 100 people will sign the petition.
   The CORRECT answer is:
   A. I only   B. I and II   C. II only   D. Neither I nor II

4. Which of the following pairs of statements say essentially the same thing in two different ways?
   I. If the new parts arrive, Mr. Luther's request has been answered.
   Mr. Luther requested new parts to arrive.
   II. The machine's test cycle will not run unless the operation cycle is not running.
   The machine's test cycle must be running in order for the operation cycle to run.
   The CORRECT answer is:
   A. I only   B. I and II   C. II only   D. Neither I nor II

5. Summary of Evidence Collected to Date:
   I. To become a member of the East Side Crips, a kid must be either "jumped in" or steal a squad car without getting caught.
   II. Sid, a kid on the East Side, was caught stealing a squad car.
   Prematurely Drawn Conclusion: Sid did not become a member of the East Side Crips.
   Which of the following pieces of evidence, if any, would make it reasonably certain that the conclusion drawn is true?
   A. "Jumping in" is not allowed in prison.
   B. Sid was not "jumped in."
   C. Sid's stealing the squad car had nothing to do with wanting to join the East Side Crips.
   D. None of the above

6. Summary of Evidence Collected to Date:
   I. Jones, a Precinct 8 officer, has more arrests than Smith.
   II. Smith and Watson have exactly the same number of arrests.
   Prematurely Drawn Conclusion: Watson is not a Precinct 8 officer.
   Which of the following pieces of evidence, if any, would make it reasonably certain that the conclusion drawn is true?
   A. All the officers in Precinct 8 have more arrests than Watson.
   B. All the officers in Precinct 8 have fewer arrests than Watson.
   C. Watson has fewer arrests than Jones.
   D. None of the above

7. Summary of Evidence Collected to Date:
   I. Twenty one-dollar bills are divided among Frances, Kerry, and Brian.
   II. If Kerry gives her dollar bills to Frances, then Frances will have more money than Brian.
   Prematurely Drawn Conclusion: Frances has twelve dollars.
   Which of the following pieces of evidence, if any, would make it reasonably certain that the conclusion drawn is true?
   A. If Brian gives his dollars to Kerry, then Kerry will have more money than Frances.
   B. Brian has two dollars.
   C. If Kerry gives her dollars to Brian, Brian will still have less money than Frances.
   D. None of the above

3 (#2)

8. <u>Summary of Evidence Collected to Date</u>:
   I. The street sweepers will be here at noon today.
   II. Residents on the west side of the street should move their cars before noon.
   <u>Prematurely Drawn Conclusion</u>: Today is Wednesday.
   Which of the following pieces of evidence, if any, would make it reasonably certain that the conclusion drawn is true?
   A. The street sweepers never sweep the east side of the street on Wednesday.
   B. The street sweepers arrive at noon every other day.
   C. There is no parking allowed on the west side of the street on Wednesday.
   D. None of the above

8.____

9. <u>Summary of Evidence Collected to Date</u>:
   The only time the warning light comes on is when there is a power surge.
   <u>Prematurely Drawn Conclusion</u>: The warning light does not come on if the air conditioner is not running.
   Which of the following pieces of evidence, if any, would make it reasonably certain that the conclusion drawn is true?
   A. The air conditioner does not turn on if the warning light is on.
   B. Sometimes a power surge is caused by the dishwasher.
   C. There is only a power surge when the air conditioner turns on.
   D. None of the above

9.____

Questions 10-14.

DIRECTIONS: Questions 10 through 14 refer to Map #3 and measure your ability to orient yourself within a given section of town, neighborhood or particular area. Each of the questions describes a starting point and a destination. Assume that you are driving a car in the area shown on the map accompanying the questions. Use the map as a basis for the shortest way to get from one point to another without breaking the law.
On the map, a street marked by arrows, or by arrows and the words "One Way," indicates one-way travel and should be assumed to be one-way for the entire length, even when there are breaks or jogs in the street. EXCEPTION: A street that does not have the same name over the full length.

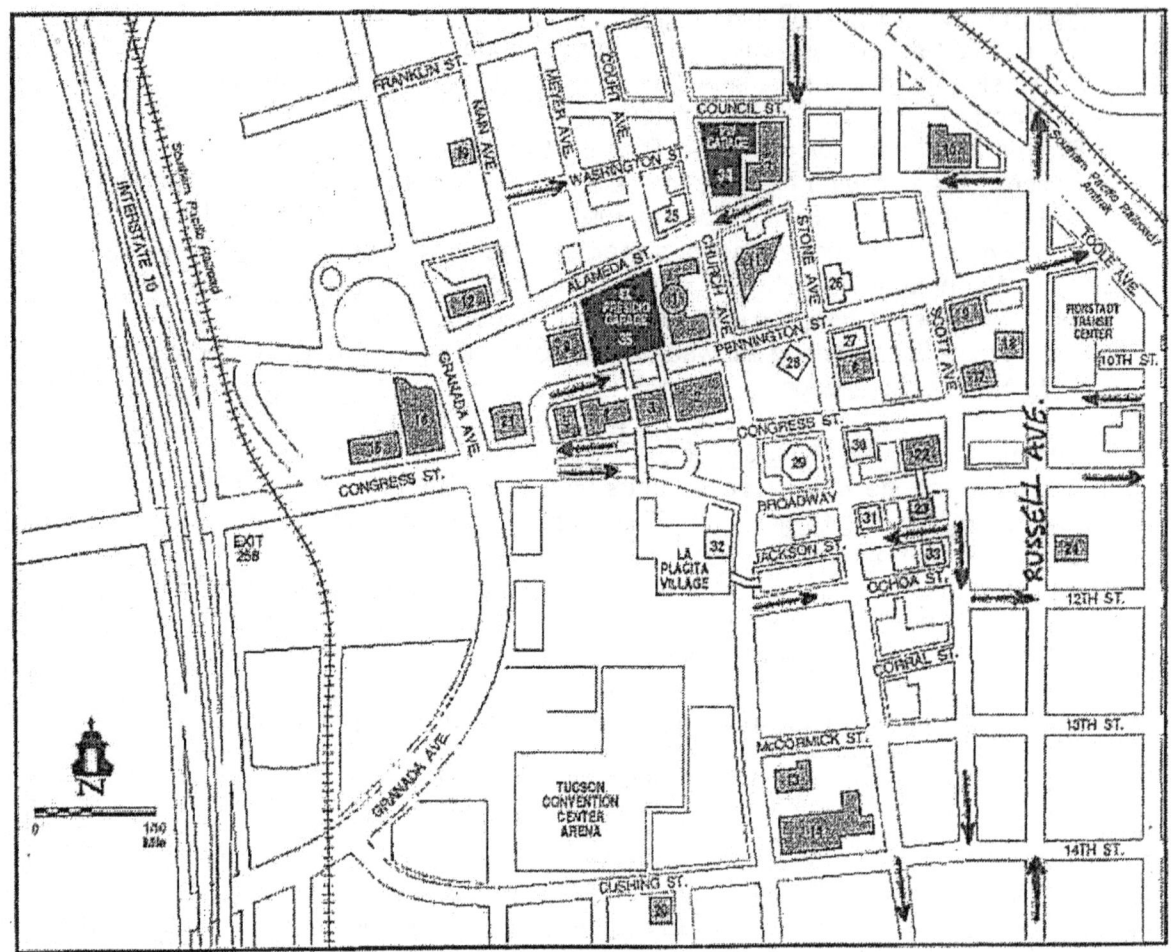

PIMA COUNTY
1. Old Courthouse
2. Superior Court Building
3. Administration Building
4. Health and Welfare Building
5. Mechanical Building
6. Legal Services Building
7. County/City Public Works Center

CITY OF TUCSON
8. City Hall
9. City Hall Annex
10. Alameda Plaza City Court Building
11. Public Library – Main Branch
12. Tucson Water Building
13. Fire Department Headquarters
14. Police Department Building

10. The SHORTEST legal way from the Public Library to the Alameda Plaza City Court Building is
    A. north on Stone Ave., east of Alameda
    B. south on Stone Ave., east on Congress, north on Russell Ave., west on Alameda
    C. south on Stone Ave., east on Pennington, north on Russell Ave., west on Alameda
    D. south on Church Ave., east on Pennington, north on Russell Ave., west on Alameda

11. The SHORTEST legal way from City Hall to the Police Department is 11.____
    A. east on Congress, south on Scott Ave., west on 14th
    B. east on Pennington, south on Stone Ave.
    C. east on Congress, south on Stone Ave.
    D. east on Pennington, south on Church Ave.

12. The SHORTEST legal way from the Tucson Water Building to the Legal Service Building is 12.____
    A. south on Granada Ave., east on Congress, north to east on Pennington, south on Stone Ave.
    B. east on Alameda, south on Church Ave., east on Pennington, south on Stone Ave.
    C. north on Granada Ave., east on Washington, south on Church Ave., east on Pennington, south on Stone Ave.
    D. south on Granada Ave., east on Cushing, north on Stone Ave.

13. The SHORTEST legal way from the Tucson Convention Center Arena to the City Hall Annex is 13.____
    A. west on Cushing, north on Granada Ave., east on Congress east on Broadway
    B. east on Cushing, north on Church Ave., east on Pennington
    C. east on Cushing, north on Russel Ave., west on Pennington
    D. east on Cushing, north on Stone Ave., east on Pennington

14. The SHORTEST legal way from Ronstadt Transit Center to the Fire Department is 14.____
    A. west on Pennington, south on Stone Ave., west on McCormick
    B. west on Congress, south on Russell Ave., west on 13th
    C. west on Congress, south on Church Ave.
    D. west on Pennington, south on Church Ave.

Questions 15-19.

DIRECTIONS: Questions 15 through 19 refer to Figure #3, on the following page, and measure your ability to understand written descriptions of events. Each question presents a description of an accident or event and asks you which of the following five drawings in Figure #3 BEST represents it.
In the drawings, the following symbols are used:
Moving vehicle ⌀   Non-moving vehicle ♦
Pedestrian or bicyclist •
The path and direction of travel of a vehicle or pedestrian is indicated by a solid line.
The path and direction of travel of each vehicle or pedestrian directly involved in a collision from the point of impact is indicated by a dotted line.

In the space at the right, print the letter of the drawing that BEST fit the descriptions written below.

6 (#2)

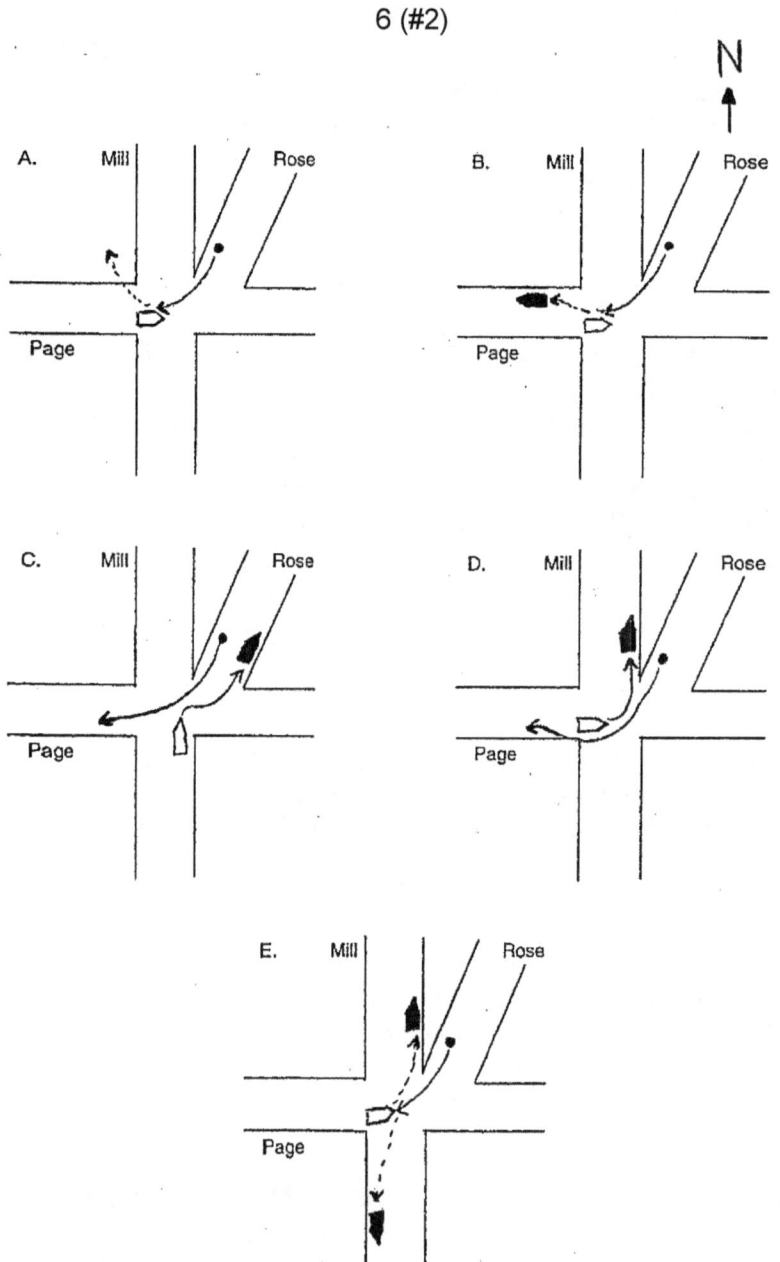

15. A bicyclist heading southwest on Rose travels into the intersection, sideswipes a car that is heading east on Page, and veers right, leaving the roadway at the northwest corner of Page and Mill.

15.____

16. A driver traveling north on Mill swerves right to avoid a bicyclist that is traveling southwest on Rose. The driver strikes the rear end of a car parked on Rose. The bicyclist continues through the intersection and travels west on Page.

16.____

17. A bicyclist heading southwest on Rose travels into the intersection, sideswipes a car that is heading east on Page, and veers right, striking the rear end of a car parked in the westbound lane on Page.

17.____

18. A driver traveling east on Page swerves left to avoid a bicyclist that is traveling southwest on Rose. The driver strikes the rear end of a car parked on Mill. The bicyclist continues through the intersection and travels west on Page.

18.____

19. A bicyclist heading southwest on Rose enters the intersection and sideswipes a car that is swerving left to avoid her. The bicyclist veers left and collides with a car parked in the southbound lane on Mill. The driver of the car veers left and collides with a car parked in the northbound lane on Mill.

19.____

Questions 20-22.

DIRECTIONS: In Questions 20 through 22, choose the word or phrase CLOSEST in meaning to the word or phrase printed in capital letters.

20. WAIVE
    A. cease   B. surrender   C. prevent   D. die

20.____

21. DEPOSITION
    A. settlement   B. deterioration   C. testimony   D. character

21.____

22. IMMUNITY
    A. exposure   B. accusation   C. protection   D. exchange

22.____

Questions 23-25.

DIRECTIONS: Questions 23 through 25 measure your ability to do fieldwork-related arithmetic. Each question presents a separate arithmetic problem for you to solve.

23. Dean, a claims investigator, is reading a 445-page case record in his spare time at work. He has already read 157 pages.
    If Dean reads 24 pages a day, he should finish reading the rest of the record in ____ days.
    A. 7   B. 12   C. 19   D. 24

23.____

24. The Fire Department owns four cars. The Department of Sanitation owns twice as many cars as the Fire Department. The Department of Parks and Recreation owns one fewer car than the Department of Sanitation. The Department of Parks and Recreation is buying new tires for each of its cars. Each tire costs $100.
    How much is the Department of Parks and Recreation going to spend on tires?
    A. $400   B. $2,800   C. $3,200   D. $4,900

24.____

25. A dance hall is about 5,000 square feet. The local ordinance does not allow more than 50 people per every 100 square feet of commercial space. The maximum capacity of the hall is
    A. 500   B. 2,500   C. 5,000   D. 25,000

25.____

KEY (CORRECT ANSWERS)

1.	D	11.	D
2.	B	12.	A
3.	A	13.	B
4.	D	14.	C
5.	B	15.	A
6.	D	16.	C
7.	D	17.	B
8.	A	18.	D
9.	C	19.	E
10.	C	20.	B

21. C
22. C
23. B
24. B
25. B

SOLUTIONS TO QUESTIONS 1-9

P implies Q = original statement

Not Q implies not P = contrapositive of the original statement. A statement and its contrapositive are logically equivalent.

Q implies P = converse of the original statement

Not P implies not Q = inverse of the original statement. The converse and inverse of an original statement are logically equivalent.

P implies Q = Not P or Q.

1. The CORRECT answer is D.
   For item I, the second statement should be "Either there is no life on Mars or we should fund NASA" in order to be logically equivalent to the first statement. For item II, the statements are converses of each other; thus, they are not equivalent.

2. The CORRECT answer is B.
   In item I, this is an example of P implies Q and Q implies P. In this case, P = the notebook is missing its cover and Q = the notebook belongs to Carter. In item II, the ordering of the words is changed, but the If P then Q is exactly the same. P = it is hot and Q = the pool is open.

3. The CORRECT answer is A.
   For item I, if nobody is without benefits, then everybody has benefits. For item II, the second equivalent statement should be "either we will not fund the program or at least 100 people will sign the petition."

4. The CORRECT answer is D.
   For item I, the first statement is an implication, whereas the second statement mentions only one part of the implication (new parts are requested) and says nothing about the other part. For item II, the first statement is equivalent to "if the operating cycle is not running, then the test cycle will run." The second statement is equivalent to "if the operating cycle is running, then the test cycle will run." So, these statements in item II are not equivalent.

5. The CORRECT answer is B.
   Since Sid did not steal a car and avoid getting caught, the only other way he could become a Crips member would be "jumped in." Choice B tells us that Sid was not "jumped in," so we conclude that he did not become a member of the Crips.

6. The CORRECT answer is D.
   Since Smith and Watson have the same number of arrests, Watson must have fewer arrests than Jones. This means that each of choices A and B is impossible. Choice C would also not reveal whether or not Watson is a Precinct 8 officer.

7. The CORRECT answer is D.
Exact dollar amounts still cannot be ascertained by using any of the other choices.

8. The CORRECT answer is A.
The street sweepers never sweep on the east side of the street on Wednesday; however, they will be here at noon today. This implies that they will sweep on the west side of the street. Since the residents should move their cars before noon, we can conclude that today is Wednesday.

9. The CORRECT answer is C.
We start with W implies P, where W = warning light comes on and P = power surge. Choice C would read as P implies A, where A = air conditioning is running. Combining these statements leads to W implies A. The conclusion can be read as: Not A implies Not W, which is equivalent to W implies A.

REPORT WRITING
EXAMINATION SECTION
TEST 1

DIRECTIONS: Each question or incomplete statement is followed by several suggested answers or completions. Select the one that BEST answers the question or completes the statement. *PRINT THE LETTER OF THE CORRECT ANSWER IN THE SPACE AT THE RIGHT.*

Questions 1-4.

DIRECTIONS: Answer Questions 1 through 4 on the basis of the following report which was prepared by a supervisor for inclusion in his agency's annual report.

```
Line #
  1    On Oct. 13, I was assigned to study the salaries paid
  2    to clerical employees in various titles by the city and by
  3    private industry in the area.
  4    In order to get the data I needed, I called Mr. Johnson at
  5    the Bureau of the Budget and the payroll officers at X Corp.—
  6    a brokerage house, Y Co. —an insurance company, and Z Inc. —
  7    a publishing firm. None of them was available and I had to call
  8    all of them again the next day.
  9    When I finally got the information I needed, I drew up a
 10    chart, which is attached. Note that not all of the companies I
 11    contacted employed people at all the different levels used in the
 12    city service.
 13    The conclusions I draw from analyzing this information is
 14    as follows: The city's entry-level salary is about average for
 15    the region; middle-level salaries are generally higher in the
 16    city government plan than in private industry; but salaries at the
 17    highest levels in private industry are better than city em-
 18    ployees' pay.
```

1. Which of the following criticisms about the style in which this report is written is MOST valid?   1.____
   A. It is too informal.   B. It is too concise.
   C. It is too choppy.   D. The syntax is too complex.

2. Judging from the statements made in the report, the method followed by this employee in performing his research was   2.____
   A. *good*; he contacted a representative sample of businesses in the area
   B. *poor*; he should have drawn more definite conclusions
   C. *good*; he was persistent in collecting information
   D. *poor*; he did not make a thorough study

165

3. One sentence in this report contains a grammatical error. This sentence begins on line number
   A. 4   B. 7   C. 10   D. 14

4. The type of information given in this report which should be presented in footnotes or in an appendix is the
   A. purpose of the study
   B. specifics about the businesses contacted
   C. reference to the chart
   D. conclusions drawn by the author

5. The use of a graph to show statistical data in a report is SUPERIOR to a table because it
   A. features approximations
   B. emphasizes facts and relationships more dramatically
   C. presents data more accurately
   D. is easily understood by the average reader

6. Of the following, the degree of formality required of a written report in tone is MOST likely to depend on the
   A. subject matter of the report
   B. frequency of its occurrence
   C. amount of time available for its preparation
   D. audience for whom the report is intended

7. Of the following, a distinguishing characteristic of a written report intended for the head of your agency as compared to a report prepared for a lower-echelon staff member is that the report for the agency head should USUALLY include
   A. considerably more detail, especially statistical data
   B. the essential details in an abbreviated form
   C. all available source material
   D. an annotated bibliography

8. Assume that you are asked to write a lengthy report for use by the administrator of your agency, the subject of which is "The Impact of Proposed New Data Processing Operation on Line Personnel" in your agency. You decide that the *most* appropriate type of report for you to prepare is an analytical report, including recommendations.
   The MAIN reason for your decision is that
   A. the subject of the report is extremely complex
   B. large sums of money are involved
   C. the report is being prepared for the administrator
   D. you intend to include charts and graphs

9. Assume that you are preparing a report based on a survey dealing with the attitudes of employees in Division X regarding proposed new changes in compensating employees for working overtime. Three percent of the respondents to the survey voluntarily offer an unfavorable opinion on the method of assigning overtime work, a question not specifically asked of the employees.
On the basis of this information, the MOST appropriate and significant of the following comments for you to make in the report with regard to employees' attitudes on assigning overtime work is that
    A. an insignificant percentage of employees dislike the method of assigning overtime work
    B. three percent of the employees in Division X dislike the method of assigning overtime work
    C. three percent of the sample selected for the survey voiced an unfavorable opinion on the method of assigning overtime work
    D. some employees voluntarily voiced negative feelings about the method of assigning overtime work, making it impossible to determine the extent of this attitude

10. A supervisor should be able to prepare a report that is well-written and unambiguous.
Of the following sentences that might appear in a report, select the one which communicates MOST clearly the intent of its author.
    A. When your subordinates speak to a group of people, they should be well-informed.
    B. When he asked him to leave, SanMan King told him that he would refuse the request.
    C. Because he is a good worker, Foreman Jefferson assigned Assistant Foreman D'Agostino to replace him.
    D. Each of us is responsible for the actions of our subordinates.

11. In some reports, especially longer ones, a list of the resources (books, papers, magazines, etc.) used to prepare it is included. This list is called the
    A. accreditation   B. bibliography
    C. summary   D. glossary

12. Reports are usually divided into several sections, some of which are more necessary than others.
Of the following, the section which is ABSOLUTELY necessary to include in a report is
    A. a table of contents   B. the body
    C. an index   D. a bibliography

13. Suppose you are writing a report on an interview you have just completed with a particularly hostile applicant.
    Which of the following BEST describes what you should include in this report?
    A. What you think caused the applicant's hostile attitude during the interview
    B. Specific examples of the applicant's hostile remarks and behavior
    C. The relevant information uncovered during the interview
    D. A recommendation that the applicant's request be denied because of his hostility

14. When including recommendations in a report to your supervisor, which of the following is MOST important for you to do?
    A. Provide several alternative courses of action for each recommendation
    B. First present the supporting evidence, then the recommendations
    C. First present the recommendations, then the supporting evidence
    D. Make sure the recommendations arise logically out of the information in the report

15. It is often necessary that the writer of a report present facts and sufficient arguments to gain acceptance of the points, conclusions, or recommendations set forth in the report.
    Of the following, the LEAST advisable step to take in organizing a report, when such argumentation is the important factor, is a(n)
    A. elaborate expression of personal belief
    B. businesslike discussion of the problem as a whole
    C. orderly arrangement of convincing data
    D. reasonable explanation of the primary issues

16. In some types of reports, visual aids add interest, meaning, and support. They also provide an essential means of effectively communicating the message of the report.
    Of the following, the selection of the suitable visual aids to use with a report is LEAST dependent on the
    A. nature and scope of the report
    B. way in which the aid is to be used
    C. aid used in other reports
    D. prospective readers of the report

17. Visual aids used in a report may be placed either in the text material or in the appendix.
    Deciding where to put a chart, table, or any such aid should depend on the
    A. title of the report   B. purpose of the visual aid
    C. title of the visual aid   D. length of the report

18. A report is often revised several times before final preparation and distribution in an effort to make certain the report meets the needs of the situation for which it is designed.
    Which of the following is the BEST way for the author to be sure that a report covers the areas he intended?

A. Obtain a coworker's opinion
B. Compare it with a content checklist
C. Test it on a subordinate
D. Check his bibliography

19. In which of the following situations is an oral report preferable to a written report? When a(n)
    A. recommendation is being made for a future plan of action
    B. department head requests immediate information
    C. long-standing policy change is made
    D. analysis of complicated statistical data is involved

20. When an applicant is approved, the supervisor must fill in standard forms with certain information.
    The GREATEST advantage of using standard forms in this situation rather than having the supervisor write the report as he sees fit is that
    A. the report can be acted on quickly
    B. the report can be written without directions from a supervisor
    C. needed information is less likely to be left out of the report
    D. information that is written up this way is more likely to be verified

21. Assume that it is part of your job to prepare a monthly report for your unit head that eventually goes to the director. The report contains information on the number of applicants you have interviewed that have been approved and the number of applicants you have interviewed that have been turned down.
    Errors on such reports are serious because
    A. you are expected to be able to prove how many applicants you have interviewed each month
    B. accurate statistics are needed for effective management of the department
    C. they may not be discovered before the report is transmitted to the director
    D. they may result in loss to the applicants left out of the report

22. The frequency with which job reports are submitted should depend MAINLY on
    A. how comprehensive the report has to be
    B. the amount of information in the report
    C. the availability of an experienced man to write the report
    D. the importance of changes in the information included in the report

23. The CHIEF purpose in preparing an outline for a report is usually to insure that
    A. the report will be grammatically correct
    B. every point will be given equal emphasis
    C. principal and secondary points will be properly integrated
    D. the language of the report will be of the same level and include the same technical terms

24. The MAIN reason for requiring written job reports is to 24._____
    A. avoid the necessity of oral orders
    B. develop better methods of doing the work
    C. provide a permanent record of what was done
    D. increase the amount of work that can be done

25. Assume you are recommending in a report to your supervisor that a radical 25._____
    change in a standard maintenance procedure should be adopted.
    Of the following, the MOST important information to be included in this report is
    A. a list of the reasons for making this change
    B. the names of others who favor the change
    C. a complete description of the present procedure
    D. amount of training time needed for the new procedure

KEY (CORRECT ANSWERS)

1.	A		11.	B
2.	D		12.	B
3.	D		13.	C
4.	B		14.	D
5.	B		15.	A
6.	D		16.	C
7.	B		17.	B
8.	A		18.	B
9.	D		19.	B
10.	D		20.	C

21. B
22. D
23. C
24. C
25. A

TEST 2

DIRECTIONS: Each question or incomplete statement is followed by several suggested answers or completions. Select the one that BEST answers the question or completes the statement. *PRINT THE LETTER OF THE CORRECT ANSWER IN THE SPACE AT THE RIGHT.*

1. It is often necessary that the writer of a report present facts and sufficient arguments to gain acceptance of the points, conclusions, or recommendations set forth in the report.
   Of the following, the LEAST advisable step to take in organizing a report, when such argumentation is the important factor, is a(n)
   A. elaborate expression of personal belief
   B. businesslike discussion of the problem as a whole
   C. orderly arrangement of convincing data
   D. reasonable explanation of the primary issues

   1.____

2. Of the following, the factor which is generally considered to be LEAST characteristic of a good control report is that it
   A. stresses performance that adheres to standard rather than emphasizing the exception
   B. supplies information intended to serve as the basis for corrective action
   C. provides feedback for the planning process
   D. includes data that reflect trends as well as current status

   2.____

3. An administrative assistant has been asked by his superior to write a concise, factual report with objective conclusions and recommendations based on facts assembled by other researchers.
   Of the following factors, the administrative assistant should give LEAST consideration to
   A. the educational level of the person or persons for whom the report is being prepared
   B. the use to be made of the report
   C. the complexity of the problem
   D. his own feelings about the importance of the problem

   3.____

4. When making a written report, it is often recommended that the findings or conclusions be presented near the beginning of the report.
   Of the following, the MOST important reason for doing this is that it
   A. facilitates organizing the material clearly
   B. assures that all the topics will be covered
   C. avoids unnecessary repetition of ideas
   D. prepares the reader for the facts that will follow

   4.____

171

5. You have been asked to write a report on methods of hiring and training new employees. Your report is going to be about ten pages long.
   For the convenience of your readers, a brief summary of your findings should
   A. appear at the beginning of your report
   B. be appended to the report as a postscript
   C. be circulated in a separate memo
   D. be inserted in tabular form in the middle of your report

6. In preparing a report, the MAIN reason for writing an outline is usually to
   A. help organize thoughts in a logical sequence
   B. provide a guide for the typing of the report
   C. allow the ultimate user to review the report in advance
   D. ensure that the report is being prepared on schedule

7. The one of the following which is MOST appropriate as a reason for including footnotes in a report is to
   A. correct capitalization
   B. delete passages
   C. improve punctuation
   D. cite references

8. A completed formal report may contain all of the following EXCEPT
   A. a synopsis
   B. a preface
   C. marginal notes
   D. bibliographical references

9. Of the following, the MAIN use of proofreaders' marks is to
   A. explain corrections to be made
   B. indicate that a manuscript has been read and approved
   C. let the reader know who proofread the report
   D. indicate the format of the report

10. Informative, readable, and concise reports have been found to observe the following rules:
    Rule I.   Keep the report short and easy to understand
    Rule II. Vary the length of sentences.
    Rule III. Vary the style of sentences so that, for example, they are not all just subject-verb, subject-verb.
    Consider this hospital laboratory report: The experiment was started in January. The apparatus was put together in six weeks. At that time, the synthesizing process was begun. The synthetic chemicals were separated. Then they were used in tests on patients.
    Which one of the following choices MOST accurately classifies the above rules into those which are violated by this report ad those which are not?
    A. II is violated, but I and III are not.
    B. III is violated, but I and II are not.
    C. II and III are violated, but I is not.
    D. I, II, and III are violated,

Questions 11-13.

DIRECTIONS: Questions 11 through 13 are based on the following example of a report. The report consists of eight numbered sentences, some of which are not consistent with the principles of good report writing.

(1) I interviewed Mrs. Loretta Crawford in Room 424 of County Hospital. (2) She had collapsed on the street and been brought into emergency. (3) She is an attractive woman with many friends judging by the cards she had received. (4) She did not know what her husband's last job had been, or what their present income was. (5) The first thing that Mrs. Crawford said was that she had never worked and that her husband was presently unemployed. (6) She did not know if they had any medical coverage or if they could pay the bill. (7) She said that her husband could not be reached by telephone but that he would be in to see her that afternoon. (8) I left word at the nursing station to be called when he arrived.

11. A good report should be arranged in logical order.
Which of the following sentences from the report does NOT appear in its proper sequence in the report?
    A. 1   B. 4   C. 7   D. 8

12. Only material that is relevant to the main thought of a report should be included. Which of the following sentences from the report contains material which is LEAST relevant to this report? Sentence
    A. 3   B. 4   C. 6   D. 8

13. Reports should include all essential information.
Of the following, the MOST important fact that is missing from this report is:
    A. Who was involved in the interview
    B. What was discovered at the interview
    C. When the interview took place
    D. Where the interview took place

Questions 14-15.

DIRECTIONS: Each of Questions 14 and 15 consists of four numbered sentences which constitute a paragraph in a report. They are not in the right order. Choose the numbered arrangement appearing after letter A, B, C, or D which is MOST logical and which BEST expresses the thought of the paragraph.

14.
 I. Congress made the commitment explicit in the Housing Act of 1949, establishing as a national goal the realization of a decent home and suitable environment for every American family.
 II. The result has been that the goal of decent home and suitable environment is still as far distant as ever for the disadvantaged urban family
 III. In spite of this action by Congress, federal housing programs have continued to be fragmented and grossly under-funded.
 IV. The passage of the National Housing Act signaled a new federal commitment to provide housing for the nation's citizens.

The CORRECT answer is:
A. I, IV, III, II   B. IV, I, III, II   C. IV, I, III, II   D. II, IV, I, III

15. I. The greater expense does not necessarily involve "exploitation," but it is often perceived as exploitative and unfair by those who are aware of the price differences involved, but unaware of operating costs.
    II. Ghetto residents believe they are "exploited" by local merchants, and evidence substantiates some of these beliefs.
    III. However, stores in low-income areas were more likely to be small independents, which could not achieve the economies available to supermarket chains and were, therefore, more likely to charge higher prices, and the customers were more likely to buy smaller-sized packages which are more expensive per unit of measure.
    IV. A study conducted in one city showed that distinctly higher prices were charged for goods sold in ghetto stores than in other areas.

    The CORRECT answer is:
    A. IV, II, I, III   B. IV, I, III, II   C. II, IV, III, I   D. II, III, IV, I

16. In organizing data to be presented in a formal report, the FIRST of the following steps should be
    A. determining the conclusions to be drawn
    B. establishing the time sequence of the data
    C. sorting and arranging like data into groups
    D. evaluating how consistently the data support the recommendations

17. All reports should be prepared with at least one copy so that
    A. there is one copy for your file
    B. there is a copy for your supervisor
    C. the report can be sent to more than one person
    D. the person getting the report can forward a copy to someone else

18. Before turning in a report of an investigation he has made, a supervisor discovers some additional information he did not include in this report. Whether he rewrites this report to include this additional information should PRIMARILY depend on the
    A. importance of the report itself
    B. number of people who will eventually review this report
    C. established policy covering the subject matter of the report
    D. bearing this new information has on the conclusions of the report

KEY (CORRECT ANSWERS)

1.	A	11.	B
2.	A	12.	A
3.	D	13.	C
4.	D	14.	B
5.	A	15.	C
6.	A	16.	C
7.	D	17.	A
8.	C	18.	D
9.	A		
10.	C		

PREPARING WRITTEN MATERIAL
EXAMINATION SECTION
TEST 1

DIRECTIONS: Each question consists of a sentence which may or may not be an example of good English usage. Examine each sentence, considering grammar, punctuation, spelling, capitalization, and awkwardness. Then choose the correct statement about it from the four choices below it. If the English usage in the sentence given is better than any of the changes suggested in choices B, C, or D, pick choice A. (Do not pick a choice that will change the meaning of the sentence.) *PRINT THE LETTER OF THE CORRECT ANSWER IN THE SPACE AT THE RIGHT.*

1. We attended a staff conference on Wednesday the new safety and fire rules were discussed.   1.____
   A. This is an example of acceptable writing.
   B. The words "safety," "fire," and "rules" should begin with capital letters.
   C. There should be a comma after the word "Wednesday."
   D. There should be a period after the word "Wednesday" and the word "the" should begin with a capital letter.

2. Neither the dictionary or the telephone directory could be found in the office library.   2.____
   A. This is an example of acceptable writing.
   B. The word "or" should be changed to "nor."
   C. The word "library" should be spelled "libery."
   D. The word "neither" should be changed to "either."

3. The report would have been typed correctly if the typist could read the draft.   3.____
   A. This is an example of acceptable writing.
   B. The word "would" should be removed.
   C. The word "have" should be inserted after the word "could."
   D. The word "correctly" should be changed to "correct."

4. The supervisor brought the reports and forms to an employees desk.   4.____
   A. This is an example of acceptable writing.
   B. The word "brought" should be changed to "took."
   C. There should be a comma after the word "reports" and a comma after the word "forms."
   D. The word "employees" should be spelled "employee's."

5. It's important for all the office personnel to submit their vacation schedules on time.   5.____
   A. This is an example of acceptable writing.
   B. The word "It's" should be spelled "Its."
   C. The word "their" should be spelled "they're."
   D. The word "personnel" should be spelled "personal."

6. The report, along with the accompanying documents, were submitted for review.
   A. This is an example of acceptable writing.
   B. The words "were submitted" should be changed to "was submitted."
   C. The word "accompanying" should be spelled "accompaning."
   D. The comma after the word "report" should be taken out.

7. If others must use your files, be certain that they understand how the system works, but insist that you do all the filing and refiling.
   A. This is an example of acceptable writing.
   B. There should be a period after the word "works," and the word "but" should start a new sentence.
   C. The words "filing" and "refiling" should be spelled "fileing" and "refileing."
   D. There should be a comma after the word "but."

8. The appeal was not considered because of its late arrival.
   A. This is an example of acceptable writing.
   B. The word "its" should be changed to "it's."
   C. The word "its" should be changed to "the."
   D. The words "late arrival" should be changed to "arrival late."

9. The letter must be read carefuly to determine under which subject it should be filed.
   A. This is an example of acceptable writing.
   B. The word "under" should be changed to "at."
   C. The word "determine" should be spelled "determin."
   D. The word "carefuly" should be spelled "carefully."

10. He showed potential as an office manager, but he lacked skill in delegating work.
    A. This is an example of acceptable writing.
    B. The word "delegating" should be spelled "delagating."
    C. The word "potential" should be spelled "potencial."
    D. The words "he lacked" should be changed to "was lacking."

KEY (CORRECT ANSWERS)

1.	D	6.	B
2.	B	7.	A
3.	C	8.	A
4.	D	9.	D
5.	A	10.	A

TEST 2

DIRECTIONS: Each question consists of a sentence which may or may not be an example of good English usage. Examine each sentence, considering grammar, punctuation, spelling, capitalization, and awkwardness. Then choose the correct statement about it from the four choices below it. If the English usage in the sentence given is better than any of the changes suggested in choices B, C, or D, pick choice A. (Do not pick a choice that will change the meaning of the sentence.) *PRINT THE LETTER OF THE CORRECT ANSWER IN THE SPACE AT THE RIGHT.*

1. The supervisor wants that all staff members report to the office at 9:00 A.M. 1.____
   A. This is an example of acceptable writing.
   B. The word "that" should be removed and the word "to" should be inserted after the word "members."
   C. There should be a comma after the word "wants" and a comma after the word "office."
   D. The word "wants" should be changed to "want" and the word "shall" should be inserted after the word "members."

2. Every morning the clerk opens the office mail and distributes it. 2.____
   A. This is an example of acceptable writing.
   B. The word "opens" should be changed to "open."
   C. The word "mail" should be changed to "letters."
   D. The word "it" should be changed to "them."

3. The secretary typed more fast on a desktop computer than on a laptop computer. 3.____
   A. This is an example of acceptable writing.
   B. The words "more fast" should be changed to "faster."
   C. There should be a comma after the words "desktop computer."
   D. The word "than" should be changed to "then."

4. The new stenographer needed a desk a computer, a chair and a blotter. 4.____
   A. This is an example of acceptable writing.
   B. The word "blotter" should be spelled "blodder."
   C. The word "stenographer" should begin with a capital letter.
   D. There should be a comma after the word "desk."

5. The recruiting officer said, "There are many different goverment jobs available." 5.____
   A. This is an example of acceptable writing.
   B. The word "There" should not be capitalized.
   C. The word "government" should be spelled "government."
   D. The comma after the word "said" should be removed.

6. He can recommend a mechanic whose work is reliable. 6.____
   A. This is an example of acceptable writing.
   B. The word "reliable" should be spelled "relyable."
   C. The word "whose" should be spelled "who's."
   D. The word "mechanic should be spelled "mecanic."

7. She typed quickly; like someone who had not a moment to lose.
    A. This is an example of acceptable writing.
    B. The word "not" should be removed.
    C. The semicolon should be changed to a comma.
    D. The word "quickly" should be placed before instead of after the word "typed."

8. She insisted that she had to much work to do.
    A. This is an example of acceptable writing.
    B. The word "insisted" should be spelled "incisted."
    C. The word "to" used in front of "much" should be spelled "too."
    D. The word "do" should be changed to "be done."

9. He excepted praise from his supervisor for a job well done.
    A. This is an example of acceptable writing.
    B. The word "excepted" should be spelled "accepted."
    C. The order of the words "well done" should be changed to "done well."
    D. There should be a comma after the word "supervisor."

10. What appears to be intentional errors in grammar occur several times in the passage.
    A. This is an example of acceptable writing.
    B. The word "occur" should be spelled "occurr."
    C. The word "appears" should be changed to "appear."
    D. The phrase "several times" should be changed to "from time to time."

KEY (CORRECT ANSWERS)

1.	B	6.	A
2.	A	7.	C
3.	B	8.	C
4.	D	9.	B
5.	C	10.	C

TEST 3

DIRECTIONS: Each question consists of a sentence which may or may not be an example of good English usage. Examine each sentence, considering grammar, punctuation, spelling, capitalization, and awkwardness. Then choose the correct statement about it from the four choices below it. If the English usage in the sentence given is better than any of the changes suggested in choices B, C, or D, pick choice A. (Do not pick a choice that will change the meaning of the sentence.) *PRINT THE LETTER OF THE CORRECT ANSWER IN THE SPACE AT THE RIGHT.*

1. The clerk could have completed the assignment on time if he knows where these materials were located.
    A. This is an example of acceptable writing.
    B. The word "knows" should be replaced by "had known."
    C. The word "were" should be replaced by "had been."
    D. The words "where these materials were located" should be replaced by "the location of these materials."

1.____

2. All employees should be given safety training. Not just those who accidents.
    A. This is an example of acceptable writing.
    B. The period after the word "training" should be changed to a colon.
    C. The period after the word "training" should be changed to a semicolon, and the first letter of the word "Not" should be changed to a small "n."
    D. The period after the word "training" should be changed to a comma, and the first letter of the word "Not" should be changed to a small "n."

2.____

3. This proposal is designed to promote employee awareness of the suggestion program, to encourage employee participation in the program, and to increase the number of suggestions submitted.
    A. This is an example of acceptable writing.
    B. The word "proposal" should be spelled "proposal."
    C. The words "to increase the number of suggestions submitted" should be changed to "an increase in the number of suggestions is expected."
    D. The word "promote" should be changed to "enhance" and the word "increase" should be changed to "add to."

3.____

4. The introduction of inovative managerial techniques should be preceded by careful analysis of the specific circumstances and conditions in each department.
    A. This is an example of acceptable writing.
    B. The word "technique" should be spelled "techneques."
    C. The word "inovative" should be spelled "innovative."
    D. A comma should be placed after the word "circumstances" and after the word "conditions."

4.____

5. This occurrence indicates that such criticism embarrasses him.
   A. This is an example of acceptable writing.
   B. The word "occurrence" should be spelled "occurence."
   C. The word "criticism" should be spelled "critisism."
   D. The word "embarrasses" should be spelled "embarasses."

KEY (CORRECT ANSWERS)

1. B
2. D
3. A
4. C
5. A

WRITTEN ENGLISH EXPRESSION
EXAMINATION SECTION
TEST 1

DIRECTIONS: In each of the sentences below, four portions are underlined and lettered. Read each sentence and decide whether any of the underlined parts contains an error in spelling, punctuation, or capitalization, or employs grammatical usage which would be inappropriate for carefully written English. If so, note the letter printed under the unacceptable form and print it in the space at the right. If all four of the underlined portions are acceptable as they stand, print the letter E. No sentences contains more than one unacceptable form.

1. A low ceiling <u>is</u> <u>when</u> the atmospheric conditions <u>make</u> <u>flying</u> inadvisable.   1.____
              A   B   C   D

2. <u>They</u> couldn't <u>tell</u> <u>who</u> the card was <u>from</u>.   2.____
    A   B C   D

3. No one <u>but</u> you and <u>I</u> <u>are</u> <u>to help</u> them.   3.____
           A   B C D

4. To <u>him</u> <u>fall</u> the <u>duties</u> of <u>foster parent</u>.   4.____
     A. B.   C   D

5. If the word <u>should</u> somehow find peace <u>within itself</u>, so that all <u>her</u> people   5.____
               A   B   C
<u>would</u> stop fighting everlastingly…that would be the day!
 D

6. <u>Everyone</u> of the <u>teachers</u> prepared <u>his</u> lesson in a <u>consummate</u> manner.   6.____
    A   B   C   D

7. <u>Didn't</u> <u>they</u> <u>used</u> to <u>pay</u> promptly?   7.____
    A   B   C   D

8. The services <u>rendered</u> by these people and <u>their</u> share <u>in making</u> the work a   8.____
                 A   B   C
success <u>is</u> to be commended.
     D

9. <u>They</u> <u>couldn't</u> tell <u>whom</u> the cable was <u>recieved</u> from…   9.____
   A   B   C   D

10. We like <u>these</u> <u>better</u> than <u>those</u> <u>kind</u>.   10.____
      A   B   C D

11. It is a test of you more than I.
    A   B   C   D

12. The person in charge being him there can be no change in policy.
         A   B   C   D

13. A large amount of information and news are to be found there.
      A   B   C   D

14. I should have liked to have seen it again.
        A   B   C D

15. The desire to travel made him restless.
                A   B   C   D

16. Should that effect their decision?
    A   B   C   D

17. Do as we do for the celebration of the childrens' event.
    A B   C   D

18. Do either of you care to join us?
    A B   C   D

19. A child's food requirements differ from the adult.
       A   B   C   D

20. A large family, including two uncles and four grandparents live at the hotel.
            A   B   C   D

21. If they would have done that, they might have succeeded.
              A   B   C   D

22. Neither the hot days or the humid nights annoy our Southern visitor.
        A   B   C   D

23. Some people do not gain favor because they are kind of tactless.
      A   B   C   D

24. No sooner had the turning point come than a new embarassing issue arose.
        A   B   C   D

25. An usher seldom rises above a theatre manager.
              A   B   C   D

184

KEY (CORRECT ANSWERS)

1.	B	11.	D
2.	C	12.	C
3.	B	13.	C
4.	E	14.	B
5.	C	15.	E
6.	D	16.	B
7.	C	17.	D
8.	D	18.	A
9.	D	19.	D
10.	C	20.	C

21.	A
22.	B
23.	D
24.	D
25.	C

TEST 2

DIRECTIONS: In each of the sentences below, four portions are underlined and lettered. Read each sentence and decide whether any of the underlined parts contains an error in spelling, punctuation, or capitalization, or employs grammatical usage which would be inappropriate for carefully written English. If so, note the letter printed under the unacceptable form and print it in the space at the right. If all four of the underlined portions are acceptable as they stand, print the letter E. No sentences contains more than one unacceptable form.

1. The <u>epic,</u> "Gone With the <u>Wind,"</u> deals with events that <u>ocurred</u> during the Civil War <u>era</u>.
    A   B   C   D
    1.____

2. <u>Shall</u> you <u>be</u> <u>at home,</u> <u>let us say</u>, on Sunday at two o'clock?
    A   B   C   D
    2.____

3. We <u>see</u> Mr. <u>Lewis'</u> <u>take</u> his car <u>out of the garage</u> daily.
        A   B   C   D
    3.____

4. We <u>have</u> <u>no</u> place <u>to keep</u> our rubbers, <u>only</u> in the hall closet.
        A   B   C   D
    4.____

5. <u>Isn't it</u> true <u>what</u> <u>you</u> <u>told</u> me about the best way to prepare for an examination?
    A   B   C   D
    5.____

6. "<u>Who</u> <u>shall</u> I say called," the butler <u>asked</u> <u>?</u>
       A   B   C   D
    6.____

7. The museum <u>is</u> often visited by students who <u>are</u> fond of <u>Primitive</u> paintings, and by <u>patent</u> attorneys.
                   A   B   C   D
    7.____

8. I <u>rose</u> <u>to nominate</u> the <u>superintendant,</u> the man <u>who</u> most of us felt was the best.
       A   B   C   D
    8.____

9. The child <u>was</u> sent to the store to <u>purchase</u> a bottle of milk and <u>brought</u> home fresh rolls, <u>too</u>.
                A   B   C   D
    9.____

10. The garden tool <u>was sent</u> <u>to be sharpened</u> and a new handle <u>to be</u> <u>put on</u>.
                       A   B   C   D
    10.____

2 (#2)

11. At the end of her vacation, Joan came home with little money, nevertheless , 11._____
                                                            A   B   C
    it was a joyous occasion.
                    D

12. We people have opportunities to show the rest of the world how real 12._____
       A   B
    democracy functions and leads to the perfectability of man.
                            C   D

13. The guide paddled along and then fell into a reverie where he related the 13._____
                                     A   B   C   D
    history of the region.

14. We should have investigated the cause of the noise in the Hotel by bringing 14._____
         A   B   C   D
    the car to a halt.

15. The first few strokes of the brush were enough to convince me that Tom 15._____
                                      A   B
    could paint much better than me.
                  C   D

16. We inquired whether we could see the owner of the store, after we waited 16._____
                A   B   C
    for one hour.
    D

17. The irratation of the high-strung parent was aggravated by the slightest 17._____
           A   B   C
    noise that the baby made.
                         D

18. There is a large demand for men interested in the field of Information Retrieval. 18._____
             A   B   C   D

19. Snow after the rains delay the coming crops. 19._____
    A   B   C   D

20. They intend to partially do away with ceremonies. 20._____
    A   B C   D

21. If that be done and turns out badly we shall see horror. 21._____
    A   B   C   D

22. The new plant is to be electrically lighted; increasing brightness by 50%. 22._____
                   A   B   C D

187

23. The <u>reason</u> the speaker was offended <u>was</u> <u>that</u> the audience <u>was</u> inattentive.   23.____
        A   B C   D

24. There <u>appear</u> <u>to be</u> conditions <u>that</u> govern the behavioral <u>Sciences.</u>   24.____
            A   B   C   D

25. <u>Either</u> of the men <u>are</u> influential <u>enough</u> <u>to control</u> the situation.   25.____
        A   B   C   D

KEY (CORRECT ANSWERS)

1.	C		11.	A
2.	E		12.	D
3.	B		13.	C
4.	D		14.	C
5.	B		15.	D
6.	D		16.	C
7.	C		17.	A
8.	C		18.	D
9.	C		19.	C
10.	C		20.	E

21. C
22. C
23. E
24. D
25. B

TEST 3

DIRECTIONS: In each of the sentences below, four portions are underlined and lettered. Read each sentence and decide whether any of the underlined parts contains an error in spelling, punctuation, or capitalization, or employs grammatical usage which would be inappropriate for carefully written English. If so, note the letter printed under the unacceptable form and print it in the space at the right. If all four of the underlined portions are acceptable as they stand, print the letter E. No sentences contains more than one unacceptable form.

1. Who did you predict would win the election this year?
   A B   C   D   1._____

2. It takes a lot more effort to sell houses this year than last year.
   A   B   C   D   2._____

3. Having pranced into the arena with little grace and unsteady hoof
   A   B
   for the jumps ahead, the driver reined his horse.
   C   D   3._____

4. Once the dog wagged it's tail, you knew it was a friendly animal.
                        A   B   C D   4._____

5. The record of the winning team was among the most noteworthy
                                   A   B   C
   of the season.
   D   5._____

6. When asked to choose corn, cabbage, or potatoes, the diner selected the
   A   B   C
   latter.
   D   6._____

7. The maid wasn't so small that she couldn't reach the top window for cleaning.
            A   B   C   D   7._____

8. Many people feel that powdered coffee produces a really abhorent flavor.
                A   B   C   D   8._____

9. Would you mind me trying that coat on for size?
   A   B   C   D   9._____

10. This chair looks much different than the chair we selected in the store.
               A   B   C   D   10._____

11. After trying unsuccessfully to land a job in the city, Will settled in the
          A   B   C   D
    country on a farm.   11._____

189

12. On the last attempt, the pole-vaulter came nearly to getting hurt.   12._____
        　　　　　　　　　　　　　　　　　　 A   B   C   D

13. The observance of armistice day throughout the world offers an opportunity   13._____
        　　　A　　　　　B　　　　　　C
    to reflect on the horrors of war.
    　D

14. Outside of the mistakes in spelling, the child's letter was a very good one.   14._____
    　　A　　　　　　　　　　　　　　　　　　　　　　 B　　C　　　　D

15. Scissors are always dangerous for a child to handle.   15._____
    　　A　　B　　　　　　　　　　C　　　　　　D

16. I assure you that I will not yield to pressure to sell my interest.   16._____
    　　　　　A　　B　　　C　　　　　　　　D

17. Ask him if he recalls the incident which took place at our first meeting.   17._____
    　　　A　B　　　C　　　　　　　　　　　D

18. The manager felt like as not to order his usher-captain to surrender his   18._____
    　　　　　　　　A　　　　　B　　　　　　　C　　　　　　D
    uniform.

19. The mother of the bride climaxed the occasion by exclaiming, "I want my   19._____
    　　　　　　　　　　　　A　　　　　B　　　　　C
    children should be happy forever."
    　　　　D

20. We read in the papers where the prospects for peace are improving.   20._____
    　　　A　　B　　　　C　　　　　　　　　　　　　D

21. "Can I share the cab with you?" was frequently heard during the period of   21._____
    　　A　　B　　　　C　　　　　D
    gas rationing.

22. Had the police suspected the ruse, they would have taken relevant   22._____
    　A　　　　　　　B　　　　　　　　　　C　　　　　D
    precautions.

23. The teacher admonished the other students neither to speak to John, nor   23._____
    　　　　　　　　　　　　　　A　　　　　　　B　　　　　　　　　　　　　C
    should they annoy him.
    　　D

24. Fortunately, we had been told that there was but one availible service   24._____
    　　　　　　　　A　　　　　B　　　　　　　C　　　　D
    station in that area.

25. We haven't hardly enough time to make it.   25. ____
     A   B   C   D

KEY (CORRECT ANSWERS)

1.	E	11.	B
2.	B	12.	B
3.	D	13.	B
4.	A	14.	A
5.	E	15.	A
6.	D	16.	E
7.	B	17.	B
8.	D	18.	B
9.	B	19.	D
10.	A	20.	C

21. A
22. D
23. D
24. D
25. A

TEST 4

DIRECTIONS: In each of the sentences below, four portions are underlined and lettered. Read each sentence and decide whether any of the underlined parts contains an error in spelling, punctuation, or capitalization, or employs grammatical usage which would be inappropriate for carefully written English. If so, note the letter printed under the unacceptable form and print it in the space at the right. If all four of the underlined portions are acceptable as they stand, print the letter E. No sentences contains more than one unacceptable form.

1. He either will fail in his attempt or will seek other Government employment. 1.____
        A   B   C   D

2. After each side gave their version, the case was closed. 2.____
    A   B C   D

3. Every one of the cars were tagged by the police. 3.____
     A   B   C   D

4. They can't seem to see it when I explain the theory. 4.____
       A   B   C D

5. It is difficult to find the genuine signature between all those submitted. 5.____
    A   B   C   D

6. She can't understand why they don't remember who to give the letter to. 6.____
                            A   B   C   D

7. Every man and woman in America is interested in his tax bill. 7.____
    A   B   C   D

8. A guard was called to prevent them carrying away souvenirs. 8.____
         A   B   C   D

9. Neither you nor I am to blame for the sudden slump in business. 9.____
    A   B C D

10. To you and him belong the credit. 10.____
       A   B   C   D

11. The auctioneer had less items to sell this year than last year. 11.____
                   A   B   C   D

12. Theirs instead of his instructions will be followed. 12.____
      A   B   C   D

13. It is the same at his local broker's Frank Smith. 13.____
     A   B   C   D

2 (#4)

14. The teacher <u>politely</u> <u>requested</u> <u>each</u> pupil to <u>step in</u> the room.   14._____
              A   B   C   D

15. <u>Too</u> many parents <u>leave</u> <u>their</u> children do as <u>they</u> please.   15._____
     A   B   C   D

16. <u>He</u> arrived <u>safe,</u> his papers <u>untouched,</u> his composure <u>unrufled</u>.   16._____
     A   B   C   D

17. I <u>do not</u> have <u>any</u> faith in <u>John</u> <u>running</u> for office.   17._____
        A   B   C   D

18. The musicians began to play <u>tunefully</u> <u>;</u> <u>keeping</u> the proper tempo <u>indicated</u>   18._____
                                 A   B   C   D
    for the selection.

19. <u>Mary's</u> maid of honor bought the <u>kind of</u> <u>an</u> <u>outfit</u> suitable for an afternoon   19._____
     A   B   C   D
    wedding.

20. After the debate, <u>every one</u> of the <u>Speakers</u> realized that, <u>given</u> another   20._____
                      A   B   C
    chance, he <u>could have done</u> better.
                D

21. The reason <u>given</u> by the physician for the patient's trouble <u>was</u> <u>because</u> of   21._____
               A   B   C
    his poor eating <u>habits</u>.
                    D

22. The fog was so <u>thick</u> that the driver <u>couldn't</u> <u>hardly</u> see more than ten feet   22._____
                   A   B   C
    <u>ahead.</u>
    D

23. I suggest that you <u>present</u> the medal to <u>who</u> you <u>deem</u> <u>best</u>.   23._____
                       A   B   C   D

24. A decision made by a man <u>without much deliberation</u> is sometimes <u>no</u>   24._____
                              A   B
    different <u>than</u> a <u>slow one</u>.
              C   D

25. <u>By the time</u> Jones <u>graduates</u> from <u>Dental School,</u> he <u>will be</u> twenty-six years   25._____
     A   B   C   D
    of age.

KEY (CORRECT ANSWERS)

1. D
2. C
3. C
4. C
5. C

6. C
7. E
8. C
9. E
10. C

11. A
12. A
13. D
14. D
15. B

16. D
17. C
18. B
19. C
20. B

21. C
22. B
23. B
24. D
25. C

TEST 5

Questions 1-18.

DIRECTIONS: Each of the sentences numbered 1 through 18 may be classified most appropriately under one of the following three categories:
  A. faulty because of incorrect grammar
  B. faulty because of incorrect punctuation
  C. correct

Examine each sentence carefully. Then, in the space at the right, print the letter preceding the option which is BEST of those suggested above. All incorrect sentences contain but one type of error. Consider a sentence correct if it contains none of the types of errors mentioned, even though there may be other correct ways of expressing the same thought.

1. He sent the notice to the clerk who you hired yesterday. 1._____

2. It must be admitted, however that you were not informed of this change. 2._____

3. Only the employees who have served in this grade for at least two years are eligible for promotion. 3._____

4. The work was divided equally between she and Mary. 4._____

5. He thought that you were not available at that time. 5._____

6. When the messenger returns; please give him this package. 6._____

7. The new secretary prepared, typed, addressed, and delivered, the notices. 7._____

8. Walking into the room, his desk can be seen at the rear. 8._____

9. Although John has worked here longer than she, he produces a smaller amount of work. 9._____

10. She said she could of typed this report yesterday. 10._____

11. Neither one of these procedures are adequate for the efficient performance of this task. 11._____

12. The typewriter is the tool of the typist; the cash register, the tool of the cashier. 12._____

13. "The assignment must be completed as soon as possible" said the supervisor. 13._____

14. As you know, office handbooks are issued to all new employees. 14._____

15. Writing a speech is sometimes easier than to deliver it before an audience. 15._____

16. Mr. Brown our accountant, will audit the accounts next week. 16._____

17. Give the assignment to whomever is able to do it most efficiently. 17._____

18. The supervisor expected either your or I to file these reports. 18._____

Questions 19-28.

DIRECTIONS: Each of the following sentences may be classified most appropriately under one of the following four categories:
- A. faulty because of incorrect grammar
- B. faulty because of incorrect punctuation
- C. faulty because of incorrect spelling
- D. correct

Examine each sentence carefully. Then, in the space at the right, print the letter preceding the option which is BEST of those suggested above. All incorrect sentences contain but one type of error. Consider a sentence correct if it contains none of the types of errors mentioned, even though there may be other correct ways of expressing the same thought.

19. The fire apparently started in the storeroom, which is usually locked. 19._____

20. On approaching the victim two bruises were noticed by the officer. 20._____

21. The officer, who was there examined the report with great care. 21._____

22. Each employee in the office had a separate desk. 22._____

23. All employees including members of the clerical staff, were invited to the lecture. 23._____

24. The suggested procedure is similar to the one now in use. 24._____

25. No one was more pleased with the new procedure than the chauffeur. 25._____

26. He tried to pursuade her to change the procedure. 26._____

27. The total of the expenses charged to petty cash were high. 27._____

28. An understanding between him and I was finally reached. 28._____

KEY (CORRECT ANSWERS)

1.	A	11.	A	21.	B
2.	B	12.	C	22.	C
3.	C	13.	B	23.	B
4.	A	14.	C	24.	D
5.	C	15.	A	25.	D
6.	B	16.	B	26.	C
7.	B	17.	A	27.	A
8.	A	18.	A	28.	A
9.	C	19.	D		
10.	A	20.	A		

WRITTEN ENGLISH EXPRESSION
EXAMINATION SECTION
TEST 1

Questions 1-5.

DIRECTIONS: Each of the following sentences may be classified under one of the following four categories:
- A. faulty because of incorrect grammar
- B. faulty because of incorrect punctuation
- C. faulty because of incorrect capitalization or incorrect spelling
- D. correct

Examine each sentence carefully. Then, in the space at the right, print the letter preceding the option which is BEST of those suggested above. All incorrect sentences contain but one type of error. Consider a sentence correct if it contains none of the types of errors mentioned, even though there may be other correct ways of expressing the same thought.

1. They told both he and I that the prisoner had escaped. 1._____

2. Any superior officer, who, disregards the just complaints of his subordinates, is remiss in the performance of his duty. 2._____

3. Only those members of the national organization who resided in the Middle West attended the conference in Chicago. 3._____

4. We told him to give the investigation assignment to whoever was available. 4._____

5. Please do not disappoint and embarrass us by not appearing in court. 5._____

Questions 6-10.

DIRECTIONS: Each of the following sentences may be classified under one of the following four categories:
- A. faulty because of incorrect spelling only
- B. faulty because of incorrect grammar or word usage only
- C. faulty because of one error in spelling and one error in grammar or word usage
- D. correct

Examine each sentence carefully. Then, in the space at the right, print the letter preceding the option which is BEST of those suggested above. All incorrect sentences contain but one type of error. Consider a sentence correct if it contains none of the types of errors mentioned, even though there may be other correct ways of expressing the same thought.

6. Although the officer's speech proved to be entertaining, the topic was not relevant to the main theme of the conference.   6.____

7. In February all new officers attended a training course in which they were learned their principal duties and the fundamental operating procedures of the department.   7.____

8. I personally seen inmate Jones threaten inmates Smith and Green with bodily harm if they refused to participate in the plot.   8.____

9. To the layman, who on a chance visit to the prison observes everything functioning smoothly, the maintenance of prison discipline may seem to be a relatively easily realizable objective.   9.____

10. The prisoners in cell block fourty were forbidden to lay on the cell cots during the recreation hour.   10.____

Questions 11-22.

DIRECTIONS: Each of the following sentences may be classified under one of the following four categories:
- A. faulty because of incorrect grammar
- B. faulty because of incorrect punctuation
- C. faulty because of incorrect capitalization or incorrect spelling
- D. correct

Examine each sentence carefully. Then, in the space at the right, print the letter preceding the option which is BEST of those suggested above. All incorrect sentences contain but one type of error. Consider a sentence correct if it contains none of the types of errors mentioned, even though there may be other correct ways of expressing the same thought.

11. I cannot encourage you any.   11.____

12. You always look well in those sort of clothes.   12.____

13. Shall we go to the park?   13.____

14. The man whome he introduced was Mr. Carey.   14.____

15. She saw the letter laying here this morning.   15.____

16. It should rain before the Afternoon is over.   16.____

17. They have already went home.   17.____

18. That Jackson will be elected is evident.   18.____

19. He does not hardly approve of us.   19.____

20. It was he, who won the prize. 20.____
21. Shall we go to the park. 21.____
22. They are, alike, in this particular. 22.____

KEY (CORRECT ANSWERS)

1.	A	11.	A
2.	B	12.	A
3.	C	13.	D
4.	D	14.	C
5.	C	15.	A
6.	A	16.	C
7.	C	17.	A
8.	B	18.	D
9.	D	19.	A
10.	C	20.	B

21. B
22. B

TEST 2

DIRECTIONS: Among the sentences in this test are some which cannot be accepted inn formal, written English for one or another of the following reasons:

POOR DICTION: The use of a word which is improper either because its meaning does not fit the sentence or because it is not acceptable in formal writing.
Example: The audience was strongly effected by the senator's speech.

VERBOSITY: Repetitious elements adding nothing to the meaning of the sentence and not justified by any need for special emphasis.
Example: At that time there was then no right of petition.

FAULTY GRAMMAR: Word forms and expressions which do not conform to the grammatical and structural usages required by formal written English (errors in case, number, parallelisms, and the like).
Example: Everyone in the delegation had their reasons for opposing the measure.

No sentence has more than one kind of error. Some sentences have no errors. Read each sentence carefully; then, in the space at the right, print the letter:
    D, if the sentence contains an error in diction
    V, if the sentence is verbose
    G, if the sentence contains faulty grammar
    O, if the sentence contains none of these errors

1. I will not go unless I receive a special invitation.   1.____

2. The pilot shouted decisive orders to his assistant as the plane burst into flames.   2.____

3. She acts like her feelings were hurt.   3.____

4. Please come here and try and help me finish this piece of work.   4.____

5. As long as you are ready, you may as well start promptly and on time.   5.____

6. My younger brother insists that he is as tall as me.   6.____

7. A spiritual person is usually deeply concerned with mundane affairs.   7.____

8. Speaking from practical experience, I advise you to give up those unquestionably quixotic schemes.   8.____

9. We walked as long as there was any light to guide us.   9.____

10. Realizing I had forgotten my gloves, I returned to the theatre, using a flashlight and turned down every seat.   10.____

11. The winters were hard and dreary, nothing could live without shelter.   11.____

2 (#2)

12. Not one in a thousand readers take the matter seriously. 12.____
13. This tire has so many defections that it is worthless. 13.____
14. The jury were divided in their views. 14.____
15. He was so credulous that his friends found it hard to deceive him. 15.____
16. The emperor's latest ukase is sure to stir up such resentment that the people will revolt. 16.____
17. When you go to the library tomorrow, please bring this book to the librarian in the reference room. 17.____
18. His speech is so precise as to seem infected. 18.____
19. I had sooner serve overseas before I remain inactive at home. 19.____
20. We read each others' letters together. 20.____

KEY (CORRECT ANSWERS)

1. O
2. V Eliminate decisive
3. G Use *as though* instead of like
4. V Eliminate and try
5. V Eliminate and on time
6. G *I* instead of me
7. D Mundane means worldly; what is needed here is *religious* or *ethereal*
8. O
9. O
10. G To achieve parallelism and balance, rewrite as follows: "…*and, using a flashlight, turned down every seat.*"
11. G Semicolon (;) after dreary instead of comma (,)
12. G *Takes*, not take
13. D *Defects*, not defections
14. O
15. D *Easy*, not hard
16. O
17. D *Take*, not bring
18. D *Affected*, not infected
19. G Replace before I by *than*
20. V Eliminate *together*

203

TEST 3

DIRECTIONS: Among the sentences in this test are some which cannot be accepted inn formal, written English for one or another of the following reasons:

POOR DICTION: The use of a word which is improper either because its meaning does not fit the sentence or because it is not acceptable in formal writing.
Example: The audience was strongly <u>effected</u> by the senator's speech.

VERBOSITY: Repetitious elements adding nothing to the meaning of the sentence and not justified by any need for special emphasis.
Example: At that time there was <u>then</u> no right of petition.

FAULTY GRAMMAR: Word forms and expressions which do not conform to the grammatical and structural usages required by formal written English (errors in case, number, parallelisms, and the like).
Example: Everyone in the delegation had <u>their</u> reasons for opposing the measure.

No sentence has more than one kind of error. Some sentences have no errors. Read each sentence carefully; then, in the space at the right, print the letter:
- D, if the sentence contains an error in <u>diction</u>
- V, if the sentence is <u>verbose</u>
- G, if the sentence contains <u>faulty grammar</u>
- O, if the sentence contains <u>none</u> of these errors

1. Choose an author as you choose a friend.   1.____

2. Home is home, be it ever so humble and so plain.   2.____

3. Invidious smokers usually find it difficult to break the habit.   3.____

4. You always look devastating in that sort of clothes.   4.____

5. We had no sooner entered the room when the bell rang.   5.____

6. A box of choice figs was sent him for Christmas.   6.____

7. Neither Charles or his brother finished his assignment.   7.____

8. There goes the last piece of cake and the last spoonful of ice cream.   8.____

9. Diamonds are more desired than any precious stones.   9.____

10. The administrator's unconscionable demands elated the workers.   10.____

11. Never before, to the best of my recollection, has there been such promising students.   11.____

2 (#3)

12. It is only because your manners are so objectionable that you are not invited to the party. 12.____

13. An altruistic proverb is: "God helps those who help themselves." 13.____

14. I fully expected that the children would be at their desks and to find them ready to begin work. 14.____

15. A complete system of railroads covers and crisscrosses the entire country. 15.____

16. Our vacation being over, I am sorry to say. 16.____

17. It is so dark that I can't hardly see. 17.____

18. Either you or I am right; we cannot both be right. 18.____

19. After it had laid in the rain all night, it was not fit for use again. 19.____

20. Although the meaning was implicit, the statement required further explanation. 20.____

KEY (CORRECT ANSWERS)

1. O
2. V   Eliminate <u>and so plain</u>
3. D   *Inveterate*, not <u>invidious</u>
4. D   *Well*, not <u>devastating</u>
5. G   *Than*, for <u>well</u>
6. O
7. G   *Nor*, for <u>or</u>
8. G   *Go*, for <u>goes</u>
9. G   Insert *other* after <u>any</u>
10. D   *Embittered*, not <u>elated</u>
11. G   *Have*, not <u>has</u>
12. O
13. D   Not <u>altruistic</u>, *selfish*
14. G   To assure parallelism and balance, place comma (,) after desks, and eliminate <u>and to find them</u>
15. V   Eliminate <u>and crisscrosses</u>
16. G   Replace <u>being</u> by *is*
17. G   *Can hardly see*, not <u>can't hardly see</u>
18. O
19. D,G   *Lain*, not <u>laid</u>
20. O

TEST 4

DIRECTIONS: Among the sentences in this test are some which cannot be accepted inn formal, written English for one or another of the following reasons:

POOR DICTION: The use of a word which is improper either because its meaning does not fit the sentence or because it is not acceptable in formal writing.
Example: The audience was strongly effected by the senator's speech.

VERBOSITY: Repetitious elements adding nothing to the meaning of the sentence and not justified by any need for special emphasis.
Example: At that time there was then no right of petition.

FAULTY GRAMMAR: Word forms and expressions which do not conform to the grammatical and structural usages required by formal written English (errors in case, number, parallelisms, and the like).
Example: Everyone in the delegation had their reasons for opposing the measure.

No sentence has more than one kind of error. Some sentences have no errors. Read each sentence carefully; then, in the space at the right, print the letter:
  D, if the sentence contains an error in diction
  V, if the sentence is verbose
  G, if the sentence contains faulty grammar
  O, if the sentence contains none of these errors

1. Neither Tom nor John were present for the rehearsal. 1.____

2. She admired the cavalier manner with which her husband treated her. 2.____

3. The happiness or misery of men's lives depend on their early training. 3.____

4. Honor as well as profit are to be gained by those studies. 4.____

5. The egg business is only incidental to the regular business of the general store. 5.____

6. It was superior in every way to the book previously read. 6.____

7. We found his captious suggestions to be friendly and constructive. 7.____

8. His testimony today is completely and radically different from that of yesterday. 8.____

9. If you would have studied the problem carefully you would have found the solution more quickly. 9.____

10. The large tips he received made the job a highly lucid one despite its long hours. 10.____

11. The flowers smelled so sweet that the whole house was perfumed. 11.____

12. When either or both habits becomes fixed, the student improves. 12.____
13. Neither his words nor his action were justifiable. 13.____
14. A calm almost always comes before a storm. 14.____
15. The gallery with all its pictures were destroyed. 15.____
16. Those trees which are not deciduous remain green and attractive all winter. 16.____
17. Whom did they say won? 17.____
18. The man whom I thought was my friend deceived me. 18.____
19. Send whoever will do the work. 19.____
20. The question of who should be the leader arose and the power he should have. 20.____

KEY (CORRECT ANSWERS)

1. G *Was*, not <u>were</u>
2. D *Resented* for <u>admired</u>
3. G *Depends* for <u>depend</u>
4. G *Is* for <u>are</u>
5. O
6. O
7. D *Careful*, not <u>captious</u>
8. V Eliminate <u>completely and radically</u>
9. G *Had you studied…* is to be submitted for <u>If you would have studied</u>
10. D *Lucrative*, not <u>lucid</u>
11. O
12. G *Become*, not <u>becomes</u>
13. G Use *was* instead of <u>were</u>
14. O
15. G *Was destroyed*, not <u>were destroyed</u>
16. O
17. G *Who*, not <u>whom</u>
18. G *Who*, not <u>whom</u>
19. O
20. G Attain parallelism by placing <u>arose</u> at the end of this sentence

TEST 5

DIRECTIONS: Among the sentences in this test are some which cannot be accepted inn formal, written English for one or another of the following reasons:

POOR DICTION: The use of a word which is improper either because its meaning does not fit the sentence or because it is not acceptable in formal writing.
Example: The audience was strongly <u>effected</u> by the senator's speech.

VERBOSITY: Repetitious elements adding nothing to the meaning of the sentence and not justified by any need for special emphasis.
Example: At that time there was <u>then</u> no right of petition.

FAULTY GRAMMAR: Word forms and expressions which do not conform to the grammatical and structural usages required by formal written English (errors in case, number, parallelisms, and the like).
Example: Everyone in the delegation had <u>their</u> reasons for opposing the measure.

No sentence has more than one kind of error. Some sentences have no errors. Read each sentence carefully; then, in the space at the right, print the letter:
  D, if the sentence contains an error in <u>diction</u>
  V, if the sentence is <u>verbose</u>
  G, if the sentence contains <u>faulty grammar</u>
  O, if the sentence contains <u>none</u> of these errors

1. The town consists of three distinct sections, of which the western one is by far the larger.   1.____

2. Of London and Paris, the former is the wealthiest.   2.____

3. The omniscient clap of thunder was not followed by a storm.   3.____

4. Chicago is larger than any city in Illinois.   4.____

5. America is the greatest nation, and of all other nations England is the greater.   5.____

6. Amalgamating their forces helped the two generals to defeat the enemy.   6.____

7. There are very good and sufficient grounds for such a decision.   7.____

8. Due to bad weather, the game was postponed.   8.____

9. The door opens, and in walks John and Mary.   9.____

10. Where but America is there greater prosperity?   10.____

11. The coffee grounds left a sedentary deposit in the cup.   11.____

2 (#5)

12. I can but do my best. 12.____
13. I cannot help but comparing him with his predecessor. 13.____
14. Many of Aesop's Fables are parodies from which we can profit. 14.____
15. I wish that I was in Florida now. 15.____
16. I like this kind of grapes better than any other. 16.____
17. The remainder of the time was spent in prayer. 17.____
18. Immigration is when people come into a foreign country to live. 18.____
19. He coughed continuously last winter. 19.____
20. The method is different than the one that was formerly used. 20.____

KEY (CORRECT ANSWERS)

1. G *Largest* for <u>larger</u>
2. G *Wealthier* for <u>wealthiest</u>
3. D *Ominous*, not <u>omniscient</u>
4. G Insert *other* before <u>city</u>
5. G *Greatest* should replace <u>greater</u> at the end of this sentence
6. O
7. V Eliminate <u>and sufficient</u>
8. G *Because of*, not <u>due to</u>
9. G *Walk*, not <u>walks</u>
10. G Insert *in* before <u>America</u>
11. D *Sedimentary*, not <u>sedentary</u>
12. O
13. G Eliminate <u>but</u>
14. D *Parables* not <u>parodies</u>
15. G *Were*, not <u>was</u>
16. O
17. O
18. G Rewrite: *Immigration denotes people coming into…*
19. D *Continually*, not <u>continuously</u>
20. G *From*, not <u>than</u>

WRITTEN ENGLISH EXPRESSION
EXAMINATION SECTION
TEST 1

DIRECTIONS: In each of the following groups of sentences, one of the four sentences is faulty in grammar, punctuation, or capitalization. Select the INCORRECT sentence in each case. *PRINT THE LETTER OF THE CORRECT ANSWER IN THE SPACE AT THE RIGHT.*

1. A. If you had stood at home and done your homework, you would not have failed in arithmetic.
    B. Her affected manner annoyed every member of the audience.
    C. How will the new law affect our income taxes?
    D. The plants were not affected by the long, cold winter, but they succumbed to the drought of summer.

    1.____

2. A. He is one of the most able men who have been in the Senate.
    B. It is he who is to blame for the lamentable mistake.
    C. Haven't you a helpful suggestion to make at this time?
    D. The money was robbed from the blind man's cup.

    2.____

3. A. The amount of children in this school is steadily increasing.
    B. After taking an apple from the table, she went out to play.
    C. He borrowed a dollar from me.
    D. I had hoped my brother would arrive before me.

    3.____

4. A. Whom do you think I hear from every week?
    B. Who do you think is the right man for the job?
    C. Who do you think I found in the room?
    D. He is the man whom we considered a good candidate for the presidency.

    4.____

5. A. Quietly the puppy laid down before the fireplace.
    B. You have made your bed; now lie in it.
    C. I was badly sunburned because I had lain too long in the sun.
    D. I laid the doll on the bed and left the room.

    5.____

6. A. Sailing down the bay was a thrilling experience for me.
    B. He was not consulted about your joining the club.
    C. This story is different than the one I told you yesterday.
    D. There is no doubt about his being the best player.

    6.____

7. A. He maintains there is but one road to world peace.
   B. It is common knowledge that a child sees much he is not supposed to see.
   C. Much of the bitterness might have been avoided if arbitration had been restored to earlier in the meeting.
   D. The man decided it would be advisable to marry a girl somewhat younger than him.

   7.____

8. A. In this book, the incident I liked least is where the hero tries to put out the forest fire.
   B. Learning a foreign language will undoubtedly give a person a better understanding of his mother tongue.
   C. His actions made us wonder what he planned to do next.
   D. Because of the war, we were unable to travel during the summer vacation.

   8.____

9. A. The class had no sooner become interested in the lesson than the dismissal bell rang.
   B. There is little agreement about the kind of world to be planned at the peace conference.
   C. "Today," said the teacher, "we shall read 'The Wind in the Willows.' I am sure you'll like it."
   D. The terms of the legal settlement of the family quarrel handicapped both sides for many years.

   9.____

10. A. I was so surprised that I was not able to say a word.
    B. She is taller than any other member of the class.
    C. It would be much more preferable if you were never seen in his company.
    D. We had no choice but to excuse her for being late.

    10.____

KEY (CORRECT ANSWERS)

1.	A	6.	C
2.	D	7.	D
3.	A	8.	A
4.	C	9.	C
5.	A	10.	C

TEST 2

DIRECTIONS: In each of the following groups of sentences, one of the four sentences is faulty in grammar, punctuation, or capitalization. Select the INCORRECT sentence in each case. *PRINT THE LETTER OF THE CORRECT ANSWER IN THE SPACE AT THE RIGHT.*

1. A. Please send me these data at the earliest opportunity. 1.____
   B. The loss of their material proved to be a severe handicap.
   C. My principal objection to this plan is that it is impracticable.
   D. The doll had laid in the rain for an hour and was ruined.

2. A. The garden scissors, left out all night in the rain, were in a badly rusted condition. 2.____
   B. The girls felt bad about the misunderstanding which had arisen.
   C. Sitting near the campfire, the old man told John and I about many exciting adventures he had had.
   D. Neither of us is in a position to undertake a task of that magnitude.

3. A. The general concluded that one of the three roads would lead to the besieged city. 3.____
   B. The children didn't, as a rule, do hardly anything beyond what they were told to do.
   C. The reason the girl gave for her negligence was that she had acted on the spur of the moment.
   D. The daffodils and tulips look beautiful in that blue vase.

4. A. If I was ten years older, I should be interested in this work. 4.____
   B. Give the prize to whoever has drawn the best picture.
   C. When you have finished reading the book, take it back to the library.
   D. My drawing is as good as or better than yours.

5. A. He asked me whether the substance was animal or vegetable. 5.____
   B. An apple which is unripe should not be eaten by a child.
   C. That was an insult to me who am your friend.
   D. Some spy must of reported the matter to the enemy.

6. A. Limited time makes quoting the entire message impossible. 6.____
   B. Who did she say was going?
   C. The girls in your class have dressed more dolls this year than we.
   D. There was such a large amount of books on the floor that I couldn't find a place for my rocking chair.

7. A. What with his sleeplessness and his ill health, he was unable to assume any responsibility for the success of the meeting. 7.____
   B. If I had been born in February, I should be celebrating my birthday soon.
   C. In order to prevent breakage, she placed a sheet of paper between each of the plates when she packed them.
   D. After the spring shower, the violets smelled very sweet.

8. A. He had laid the book down very reluctantly before the end of the lesson.
    B. The dog, I am sorry to say, had lain on the bed all night.
    C. The cloth was first lain on a flat surface; then it was pressed with a hot iron.
    D. While we were in Florida, we lay in the sun until we were noticeably tanned.

9. A. If John was in New York during the recent holiday season, I have no doubt he spent most of time with his parents.
    B. How could he enjoy the television program; the dog was barking and the baby was crying.
    C. When the problem was explained to the class, he must have been asleep.
    D. She wished that her new dress were finished so that she could go to the party.

10. A. The engine not only furnishes power but light and heat as well.
    B. You're aware that we've forgotten whose guilt was established, aren't you?
    C. Everybody knows that the woman made many sacrifices for her children.
    D. A man with his dog and gun is a familiar sight in this neighborhood.

KEY (CORRECT ANSWERS)

1. D 6. D
2. C 7. B
3. B 8. C
4. A 9. B
5. D 10. A

TEST 3

DIRECTIONS: Each of sentences 1 through 18 may be classified most appropriately under one of the following three categories:
- A. faulty because of incorrect grammar
- B. faulty because of incorrect punctuation
- C. correct

Examine each sentence carefully. Then, in the space at the right, print the capital letter preceding the option which is BEST of the three suggested above. All incorrect sentences contain but one type of error. Consider a sentence correct if it contains none of the types of errors mentioned, even though there may be other correct ways of expressing the same thought.

1. He sent the notice to the clerk who you hired yesterday. 1.____

2. It must be admitted, however that you were not informed of this change. 2.____

3. Only the employees who have served in this grade for at least two years are eligible for promotion. 3.____

4. The work was divided equally between she and Mary. 4.____

5. He thought that you were not available at that time. 5.____

6. When the messenger returns; please give him this package. 6.____

7. The new secretary prepared, typed, addressed, and delivered, the notices. 7.____

8. Walking into the room, his desk can be seen at the rear. 8.____

9. Although John has worked here longer than she, he produces a smaller amount of work. 9.____

10. She said she could of typed this report yesterday. 10.____

11. Neither one of these procedures are adequate for the efficient performance of this task. 11.____

12. The typewriter is the tool of the typist; the cash register, the tool of the cashier. 12.____

13. "The assignment must be completed as soon as possible" said the supervisor. 13.____

14. As you know, office handbooks are issued to all new employees. 14.____

15. Writing a speech is sometimes easier than to deliver it before an audience. 15.____

16. Mr. Brown, our accountant, will audit the accounts next week.   16.____

17. Give the assignment to whomever is able to do it most efficiently.   17.____

18. The supervisor expected either your or I to file these reports.   18.____

KEY (CORRECT ANSWERS)

1. A   11. A
2. B   12. C
3. C   13. B
4. A   14. C
5. C   15. A

6. B   16. B
7. B   17. A
8. A   18. A
9. C
10. A

TEST 4

DIRECTIONS: Each sentence may be classified most appropriately under one of the following four categories:
- A. faulty because of incorrect grammar
- B. faulty because of incorrect punctuation
- C. faulty because of incorrect spelling
- D. correct

Examine each sentence carefully. Then, in the space at the right, print the capital letter preceding the BEST of the four suggested above. All incorrect sentences contain but one type of error. Consider a sentence correct if it contains none of the types of errors mentioned, even though there may be other correct ways of expressing the same thought.

1. The fire apparently started in the storeroom, which is usually locked.   1.____
2. On approaching the victim two bruises were noticed by this officer.   2.____
3. The officer, who was there examined the report with great care.   3.____
4. Each employee in the office had a seperate desk.   4.____
5. All employees including members of the clerical staff, were invited to the lecture. 5.____
6. The suggested procedure is similar to the one now in use.   6.____
7. No one was more pleased with the new procedure than the chauffeur.   7.____
8. He tried to pursuade her to change the procedure.   8.____
9. The total of the expenses charged to petty cash were high.   9.____
10. An understanding between him and I was finally reached.   10.____

KEY (CORRECT ANSWERS)

1. D   6. D
2. A   7. D
3. B   8. C
4. C   9. A
5. B   10. A

TEST 5

Questions 1-5.

DIRECTIONS: Each of sentences 1 to 5 may be classified under one of the following four categories:
    A. faulty because of incorrect grammar
    B. faulty because of incorrect punctuation
    C. faulty because of incorrect capitalization or incorrect spelling
    D. correct

Examine each sentence carefully to determine under which of the above four options it is best classified. Then, in the space at the right, print the capital letter preceding the option which is the BEST of the four suggested above. Each faulty sentence contains but one type of error. Consider a sentence to be correct if it contains none of the types of errors mentioned, even though there may be other correct ways of expressing the same thought.

1. They told both he and I that the prisoner had escaped.   1.____

2. Any superior officer, who, disregards the just complaints of his subordinates, is remiss in the performance of his duty.   2.____

3. Only those members of the National organization who resided in the Middle West attended the conference in Chicago.   3.____

4. We told him to give the investigation assignment to whoever was available.   4.____

5. Please do not disappoint and embarass us by not appearing in court.   5.____

Questions 6-10.

DIRECTIONS: Each of questions 6 through 10 consists of a sentence. Read each sentence carefully and then write your answer to each question according to the following scheme:
    A. Sentence contains an error in spelling only
    B. Sentence contains an error in grammar or word usage only
    C. Sentence contains one error in spelling and one error in grammar or word usage
    D. Sentence is correct; contains no errors

6. Although the officer's speech proved to be entertaining, the topic was not relevant to the main theme of the conference.   6.____

7. In February all new officers attended a training course in which they were learned their principal duties and the fundamental operating procedures of the department.   7.____

8. I personally seen inmate Jones threaten inmates Smith and Green with bodily harm if they refused to participate in the plot. 8.____

9. To the layman, who on a chance visit to the prison observes everything functioning smoothly, the maintenance of prison discipline may seem to be a relatively easily realizable objective. 9.____

10. The prisoners in cell block fourty were forbidden to lay on the cell cots during the recreation hour. 10.____

KEY (CORRECT ANSWERS)

1.	A	6.	D
2.	B	7.	C
3.	C	8.	B
4.	D	9.	D
5.	C	10.	C

TEST 6

DIRECTIONS: Each of the following sentences may be classified under one of the following four categories:
- A. faulty because of incorrect grammar
- B. faulty because of incorrect punctuation
- C. faulty because of incorrect capitalization or incorrect spelling
- D. correct

Examine each sentence carefully to determine under which of the above four options it is best classified. Then, in the space at the right, print the capital letter preceding the option which is the BEST of the four suggested above. Each faulty sentence contains but one type of error. Consider a sentence to be correct if it contains none of the types of errors mentioned, even though there may be other correct ways of expressing the same thought.

1. I cannot encourage you any. 1.____
2. You always look well in those sort of clothes. 2.____
3. Shall we go to the park? 3.____
4. The man whome he introduced was Mr. Carey. 4.____
5. She saw the letter laying here this morning. 5.____
6. It should rain before the Afternoon is over. 6.____
7. They have already went home. 7.____
8. That Jackson will be elected is evident. 8.____
9. He does not hardly approve of us. 9.____
10. It was he, who won the prize. 10.____

KEY (CORRECT ANSWERS)

1.	A	6.	C
2.	A	7.	A
3.	D	8.	D
4.	C	9.	A
5.	A	10.	B

TEST 7

DIRECTIONS: Each of the following sentences may be classified under one of the following four categories:
- A. faulty because of incorrect grammar
- B. faulty because of incorrect punctuation
- C. faulty because of incorrect capitalization or incorrect spelling
- D. correct

Examine each sentence carefully to determine under which of the above four options it is best classified. Then, in the space at the right, print the capital letter preceding the option which is the BEST of the four suggested above. Each faulty sentence contains but one type of error. Consider a sentence to be correct if it contains none of the types of errors mentioned, even though there may be other correct ways of expressing the same thought.

1. Shall we go to the park. 1.____
2. They are, alike, in this particular. 2.____
3. They gave the poor man sume food when he knocked on the door. 3.____
4. I regret the loss caused by the error. 4.____
5. The students' will have a new teacher. 5.____
6. They sweared to bring out all the facts. 6.____
7. He decided to open a branch store on 33rd street. 7.____
8. His speed is equal and more than that of a racehorse. 8.____
9. He felt very warm on that Summer day. 9.____
10. He was assisted by his friend, who lives in the next house. 10.____

KEY (CORRECT ANSWERS)

1. B   6. A
2. B   7. C
3. C   8. A
4. D   9. C
5. B   10. D

TEST 8

DIRECTIONS: Each of the following sentences may be classified under one of the following four categories:
- A. faulty because of incorrect grammar
- B. faulty because of incorrect punctuation
- C. faulty because of incorrect capitalization or incorrect spelling
- D. correct

Examine each sentence carefully to determine under which of the above four options it is best classified. Then, in the space at the right, print the capital letter preceding the option which is the BEST of the four suggested above. Each faulty sentence contains but one type of error. Consider a sentence to be correct if it contains none of the types of errors mentioned, even though there may be other correct ways of expressing the same thought.

1. The climate of New York is colder than California. 1.____
2. I shall wait for you on the corner. 2.____
3. Did we see the boy who, we think, is the leader. 3.____
4. Being a modest person, John seldom talks about his invention. 4.____
5. The gang is called the smith street boys. 5.____
6. He seen the man break into the store. 6.____
7. We expected to lay still there for quite a while. 7.____
8. He is considered to be the Leader of his organization. 8.____
9. Although I recieved an invitation, I won't go. 9.____
10. The letter must be here some place. 10.____

KEY (CORRECT ANSWERS)

1.	A	6.	A
2.	D	7.	A
3.	B	8.	C
4.	D	9.	C
5.	C	10.	A

TEST 9

DIRECTIONS: Each of the following sentences may be classified under one of the following four categories:
- A. faulty because of incorrect grammar
- B. faulty because of incorrect punctuation
- C. faulty because of incorrect capitalization or incorrect spelling
- D. correct

Examine each sentence carefully to determine under which of the above four options it is best classified. Then, in the space at the right, print the capital letter preceding the option which is the BEST of the four suggested above. Each faulty sentence contains but one type of error. Consider a sentence to be correct if it contains none of the types of errors mentioned, even though there may be other correct ways of expressing the same thought.

1. I thought it to be he. 1.____
2. We expect to remain here for a long time. 2.____
3. The committee was agreed. 3.____
4. Two-thirds of the building are finished. 4.____
5. The water was froze. 5.____
6. Everyone of the salesmen must supply their own car. 6.____
7. Who is the author of Gone With The Wind? 7.____
8. He marched on and declaring that he would never surrender. 8.____
9. Who shall I say called? 9.____
10. Everyone has left but they. 10.____

KEY (CORRECT ANSWERS)

1.	A	6.	A
2.	D	7.	B
3.	A	8.	A
4.	A	9.	D
5.	A	10.	D

TEST 10

DIRECTIONS: Each of the following sentences may be classified under one of the following four categories:
- A. faulty because of incorrect grammar
- B. faulty because of incorrect punctuation
- C. faulty because of incorrect capitalization or incorrect spelling
- D. correct

Examine each sentence carefully to determine under which of the above four options it is best classified. Then, in the space at the right, print the capital letter preceding the option which is the BEST of the four suggested above. Each faulty sentence contains but one type of error. Consider a sentence to be correct if it contains none of the types of errors mentioned, even though there may be other correct ways of expressing the same thought.

1. Who did we give the order to?   1.____
2. Send your order in immediately.   2.____
3. I believe I paid the Bill.   3.____
4. I have not met but one person.   4.____
5. Why aren't Tom, and Fred, going to the dance?   5.____
6. What reason is there for him not going?   6.____
7. The seige of Malta was a tremendous event.   7.____
8. I was there yesterday I assure you.   8.____
9. Your ukulele is better than mine.   9.____
10. No one was there only Mary.   10.____

KEY (CORRECT ANSWERS)

1.	A	6.	A
2.	D	7.	C
3.	C	8.	B
4.	A	9.	C
5.	B	10.	A

INTERPRETING STATISTICAL DATA GRAPHS, CHARTS, AND TABLES

EXAMINATION SECTION

TEST 1

DIRECTIONS: Each question or incomplete statement is followed by several suggested answers or completions. Select the one that BEST answers the question or completes the statement. *PRINT THE LETTER OF THE CORRECT ANSWER IN THE SPACE AT THE RIGHT.*

Questions 1-5.

DIRECTIONS: Questions 1 through 5 are to be answered SOLELY on the basis of the following chart.

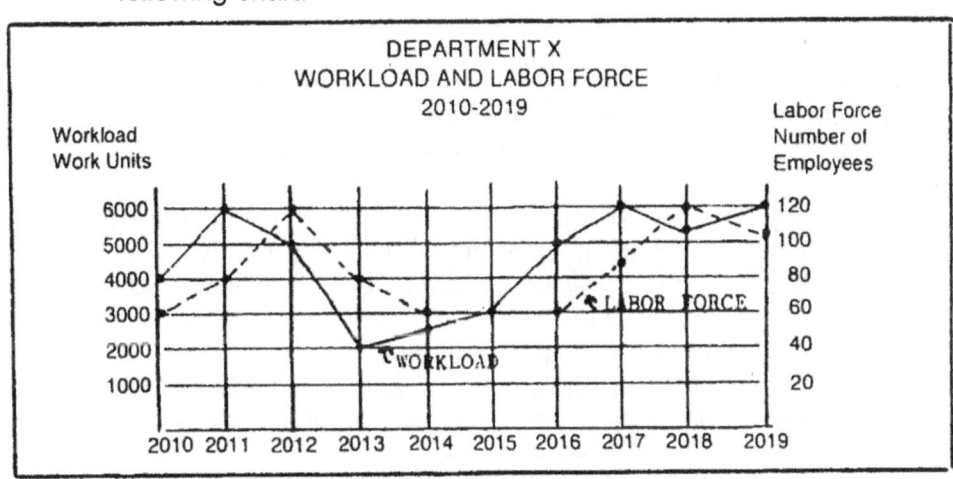

1. The one of the following years for which average employee production was LOWEST was
   A. 2011 B. 2013 C. 2015 D. 2017

1.____

2. The average annual employee production for the ten-year period was, in terms of work units, MOST NEARLY
   A. 30 B. 50 C. 70 D. 80

2.____

3. On the basis of the chart, it can be deduced that personnel needs for the coming year are budgeted on the basis of
   A. workload for the current year
   B. expected workload for the coming year
   C. no set plan]
   D. average workload over the five years immediately preceding the period

3.____

225

4. The chart indicates that the operation is carefully programmed and that the labor force has been used properly.
This opinion is
   A. *supported* by the chart; the organization has been able to meet emergency situations requiring more additional work without commensurate increases in staff
   B. *not supported* by the chart; the irregular workload shows a complete absence of planning
   C. *supported* by the chart; the similar shapes of the WORKLOAD and LABOR FORCE curves show that these important factors are closely related
   D. *not supported* by the chart; poor planning with respect to labor requirements is obvious from the chart

5. The chart indicates that the department may be organized in such a way as to require a permanent minimum staff which is too large for the type of operation indicated.
This opinion is
   A. *supported* by the chart; there is no indication that the operation calls for an irreducible minimum number of employees and application of the most favorable work production records show this to be too high for normal operation
   B. *not supported* by the chart; the absence of any sort of regularity makes it impossible to express any opinion with any degree of certainty
   C. *supported* by the chart; the expected close relationship between workload and labor force is displaced somewhat, a phenomenon which usually occurs as a result of a fixed minimum requirement
   D. *not supported* by the chart; the violent movement of the LABOR FORCE curve makes it evident that no minimum requirements are in effect

4.____

5.____

KEY (CORRECT ANSWERS)

1. B
2. B
3. A
4. D
5. A

TEST 2

Questions 1-4.

DIRECTIONS: Questions 1 through 4 are to be answered SOLELY on the basis of the chart below, which shows the annual average number of administrative actions completed for the four divisions of a bureau. Assume that the figures remain stable from year to year.

Administrative Actions	DIVISIONS				TOTALS
	W	X	Y	Z	
Telephone Inquiries Answered	8,000	6,800	7,500	4,800	27,100
Interviews Conducted	500	630	550	500	2,180
Applications Processed	15,000	18,000	14,500	9,500	57,000
Letters Typed	2,500	4,400	4,350	3,250	14,500
Reports Completed	200	250	100	50	600
Totals	26,200	30,080	27,000	18,100	101,380

1. In which division is the number of Applications Processed the GREATEST percentage of the total Administrative Actions for that division?
   A. W B. C. Y D. Z

2. The bureau chief is considering a plan that would consolidate the typing of letters in a separate unit. This unit would be responsible for the typing of letters for all divisions in which the number of letters typed exceeds 15% of the total number of administrative actions.
   Under this plan, which of the following divisions would CONTINUE to type its own letters?
   A. W and X   B. W, X, and Y   C. X and Y   D. X and Z

3. The setting up of a central information service that would be capable of answering 25% of the whole bureau's telephone inquiries is under consideration. Under such a plan, the divisions would gain for other activities that time previously spent on telephone inquiries.
   Approximately how much total time would such a service gain for all four divisions if it requires 5 minutes to answer the average telephone inquiry?
   _____ hours,
   A. 500   B. 515   C. 565   D. 585

4. Assume that the rate of production shown in the table can be projected as accurate for the coming year and that monthly output is constant for each type of administrative action within a division. Division Y is scheduled to work exclusively on a four-month long special project during that year. During the period of the project, Division Y's regular workload will be divided evenly among the remaining divisions.
   Using the figures in the table, what would be MOST NEARLY the percentage increase in the total Administrative Actions completed by Division Z for the year?
   A. 8%   B. 16%   C. 25%   D. 50%

KEY (CORRECT ANSWERS)

1. B
2. A
3. C
4. B

TEST 3

Questions 1-3.

DIRECTIONS: The management study of employee absence due to sickness is an effective tool in planning. Questions 1 through 3 are to be answered SOLELY on the basis of the data below.

Number of Days Absent Per Worker (Sickness)	1	2	3	4	5	6	7	8 OR OVER
Number of Workers	76	23	6	3	1	0	1	0
Total Number of Workers: 400									
Period Covered: Jan. 1 – Dec. 31									

1. The TOTAL number of man days lost due to illness was
    A. 110   B. 137   C. 144   D. 164

2. What percent of the workers had 4 or more days absence due to sickness?
    A. .25%   B. 2.5%   C. 1.25%   D. 12.5%

3. Of the 400 workers studied, the number who lost no days due to sickness was
    A. 190   B. 236   C. 290   D. 346

KEY (CORRECT ANSWERS)

1. D
2. C
3. C

TEST 4

Questions 1-3.

DIRECTIONS: In the graph below, the lines labeled A and B represent the cumulative progress in the work of two file clerks, each of whom was given 500 consecutively numbered applications to file in the proper cabinets over a five-day work week. Questions 1 through 3 are to be answered SOLELY on the basis of the data provided in the graph.

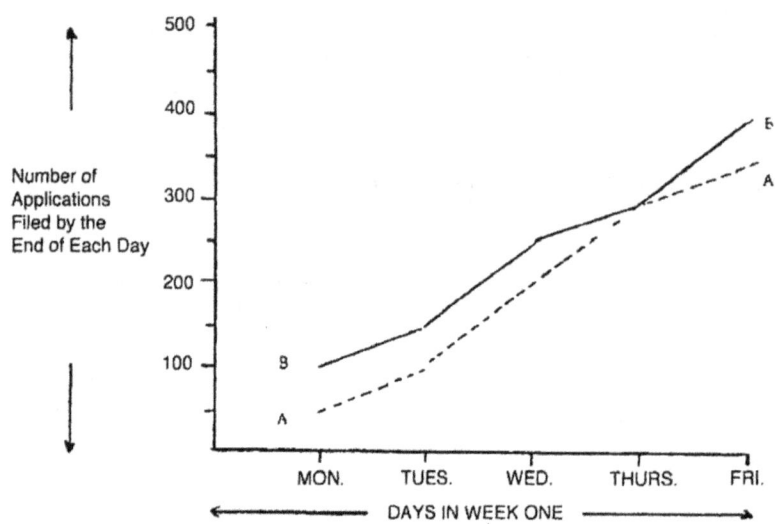

1. The day during which the LARGEST number of applications was filed by both clerks was
   A. Monday   B. Tuesday   C. Wednesday   D. Friday

2. At the end of the second day, the percentage of applications still to be filed was
   A. 25%   B. 50%   C. 66%   D. 75%

3. Assuming that the production pattern is the same the following week as the week shown in the chart, the day on which the file clerks will finish this assignment will be
   A. Monday   B. Tuesday   C. Wednesday   D. Friday

KEY (CORRECT ANSWERS)

1. C
2. D
3. B

TEST 5

Questions 1-3.

DIRECTIONS: Questions 1 through 3 are to be answered SOLELY on the basis of the following information given in the following chart.

Number of Employees Producing Work-Units Within Range in 2009	Number of Work-Units Produced	Number of Employees Producing Work-Units Within Range in 2019
7	500-1000	4
14	1001-1500	11
26	1501-2000	28
22	2001-2500	36
17	2501-3000	39
10	3001-3500	23
4	3501-4000	9

1. Assuming that within each range of work-units produced, the average production was at the mid-point at that range (e.g., category 500-1000 = 750), then the AVERAGE number of work-units produced per employee in 2019 fell into the range
    A. 1001-1500   B. 1501-2000   C. 2001-2500   D. 2501-3000

2. The ratio of the number of employees producing more than 2000 work-units in 2009 to the number of employees producing more than 2000 work units in 2019 is MOST NEARLY
    A. 1:2   B. 2:3   C. 3:4   D. 4:5

3. In Department D, which of the following were GREATER in 2019 than in 2009?
    I. Total number of employees
    II. Total number of work-units produced
    III. Number of employees producing 2000 or fewer work-units
    The CORRECT answer is:
    A. I, II, and III
    B. I and II, but not III
    C. I and III, but not II
    D. II and III, but not I

KEY (CORRECT ANSWERS)
1. C
2. A
3. B

TEST 6

Questions 1-9.

DIRECTIONS: Questions 1 through 9 are to be answered SOLELY on the basis of the information contained in the following four charts which relate to a municipal department. These charts show for the fiscal year the total departmental expenditures for salaries for all its employees; the distribution of expenditures for salaries for permanent employees by title; the distribution of all employees, both permanent and temporary by title; and the distribution of temporary employees by title.

For Departmental Expenditures
For Salaries For Fiscal Year.
Total: $129,000,000

Distribution of Expenditures
For Salaries For Permanent
Employees, By Title.

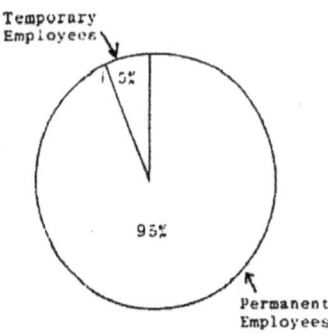
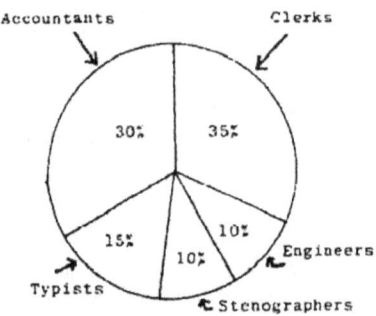

Distribution of All Employees, Both Permanent and Temporary, By Title.
Total Number of Employees: 3,200

Distribution of Temporary Employees, By Title.
Total Number of Temporary Employees: 150

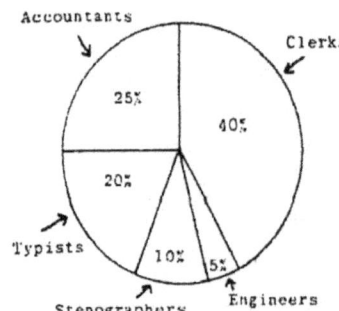
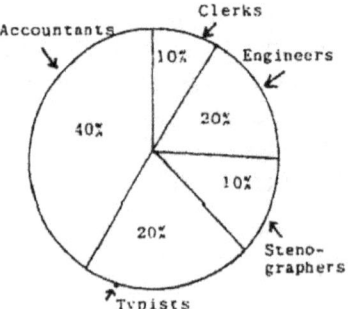

SAMPLE COMPUTATION
The total amount of money expended for the salaries of all the permanent typists can be computed as follows:

By taking 95% of $129,000,000, the total amount of money expended for the salaries of all permanent employees can be obtained. The total amount of money expended for the salaries of all the permanent typists can then be obtained by taking 15% of the money expended for the salaries of all permanent employees.

2 (#6)

The answer is $18,382,500.
Candidates may find it useful to arrange their computations on their scratch paper in an orderly manner since the correct computations for one question may also be helpful in answering another question.

1. The TOTAL number of permanent typists is
   A. 640 B. 670 C. 608 D. 610

   1.____

2. Of the total departmental expenditures for salaries for both permanent and temporary employees, the percentage allotted to permanent clerks is MOST NEARLY
   A. 25% B. 31% C. 33% D. 35%

   2.____

3. The number of permanent employees who are NOT engineers is
   A. 2,890 B. 3,070 C. 3,040 D. 2,920

   3.____

4. Assume that the average annual salary of the temporary accountants is $40000. Then, the average annual salary of the permanent accountants exceeds the average annual salary of the temporary accountants by MOST NEARLY
   A. 25% B. 20% C. 75% D. 40%

   4.____

5. The average annual salary of the permanent clerks is MOST NEARLY
   A. $33,300 B. $33,900 C. $35,250 D. $35,700

   5.____

6. If the temporary stenographers receive 8% of the total salaries allotted to temporary employees, then the average annual salary of the temporary stenographers is MOST NEARLY
   A. $34,500 B. $38,500 C. $36,000 D. $40,000

   6.____

7. Assume that the temporary typists receive an average annual salary that is 3% less than the average annual salary that is paid to the permanent typists. Then, the average annual salary of the temporary typists is MOST NEARLY
   A. $27,850 B. $29,250 C. $30,000 D. $32,150

   7.____

8. Assume that the average annual salary of the permanent engineers exceeds the average annual salary of the temporary engineers by $30,000. Then, the percentage of the total departmental expenditures for salaries for temporary employees that is allotted to temporary engineers is MOST NEARLY
   A. 15% B. 20% C. 25% D. 30%

   8.____

9. If one-half of the permanent accountants earn an average of $45,000 per annum, then the average annual salary of the other permanent accounts is MOST NEARLY
   A. $51,150 B. $51,750 C. $54,350 D. $57,100

   9.____

KEY (CORRECT ANSWERS)

1. D 6. A
2. C 7. B
3. D 8. D
4. A 9. C
5. B

TEST 7

Questions 1-6.

DIRECTIONS: Questions 1 through 6 are to be answered SOLELY on the basis of the information contained in the five charts below.

NUMBER OF UNITS OF WORK PRODUCED IN THE BUREAU PER YEAR

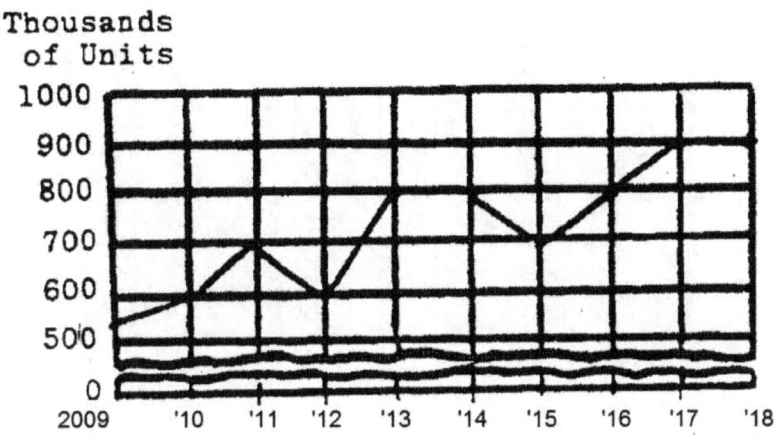

INCREASE IN THE NUMBER OF UNITS OF WORK PRODUCED IN 2018 OVER THE NUMBER PRODUCED IN 2009, BY BOROUGH

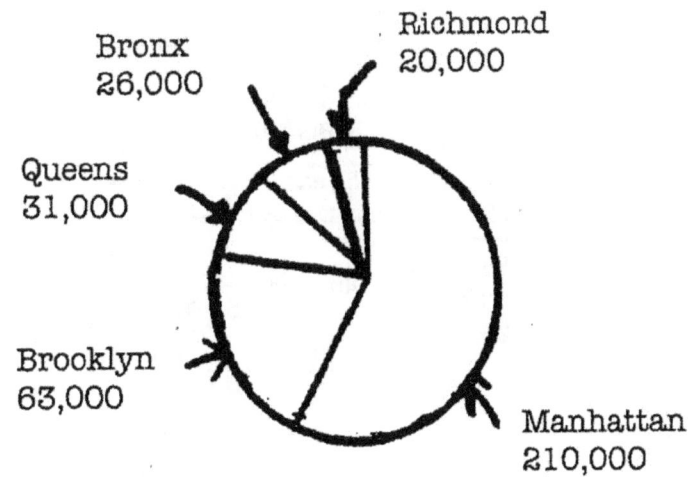

Bronx 26,000
Richmond 20,000
Queens 31,000
Brooklyn 63,000
Manhattan 210,000

NUMBER OF MALE AND FEMALE EMPLOYEES PRODUCING THE UNITS OF WORK IN THE BUREAU PER YEAR

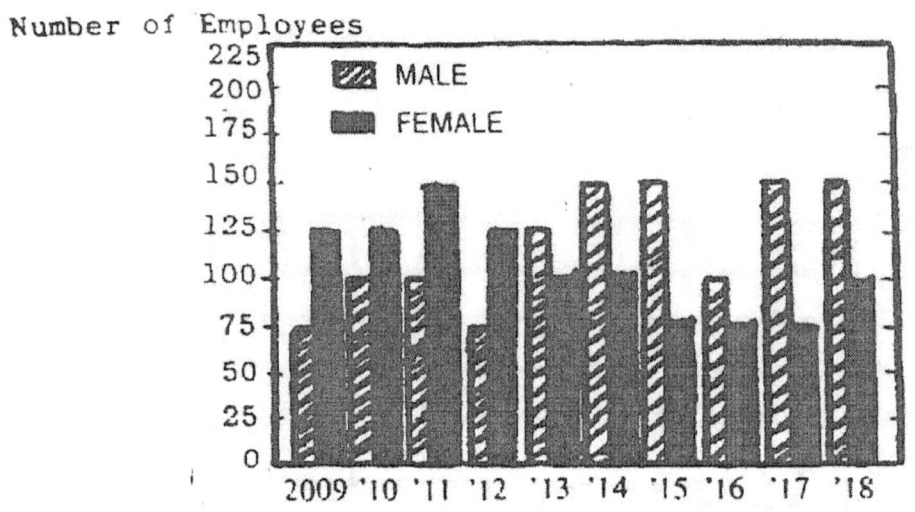

DISTRIBUTION OF THE AGES BY PERCENT OF EMPLOYEES ASSIGNED TO PRODUCE THE UNITS OF WORK IN THE YEARS 2009 AND 2018

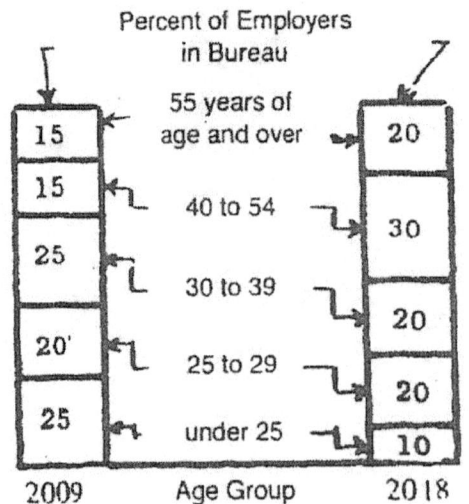

3 (#7)

TOTAL SALARIES PAID PER YEAR TO EMPLOYEES ASSIGNED TO PRODUCE THE UNITS OF WORK IN THE BUREAU

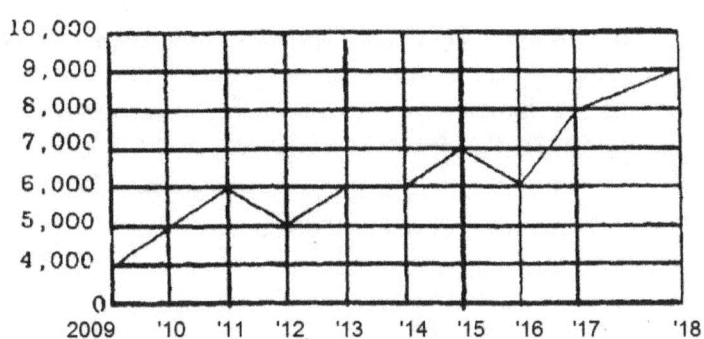

1. The information contained in the charts is sufficient to determine the
   A. amount of money paid in salaries to employees working in Richmond in 2018
   B. difference between the average annual salary of employees in the Bureau in 2018 and their average annual salary in 2017
   C. number of female employees in the Bureau between 30 and 39 years of age who were employed in 2009
   D. cost, in salary for the average male employee in the Bureau to produce 100 units of work in 2014

   1.____

2. The one of the following which was GREATER, in the Bureau, in 2014 than it was in 2012 was the
   A. cost, in salaries, of producing a unit of work
   B. units of work produced annually per employee
   C. proportion of female employees to total number of employees
   D. average annual salary per employee

   2.____

3. If, in 2018, one-half of the employees in the Bureau 55 years of age and over each earned an annual salary of $42,000, then the average annual salary of all the remaining employees in the Bureau was MOST NEARLY
   A. $31,750   B. $34,500   C. $35,300   D. $35,800

   3.____

4. Assume that, in 2009, the offices in Richmond and the Bronx each produced the same number of units of work. Also assume that, in 2009, the offices in Brooklyn, Manhattan, and Queens each produced twice as many units of work as were produced in either of the other two boroughs.
   Then, the number of units of work produced in Brooklyn in 2008 was MOST NEARLY
   A. 69,000   B. 138,000   C. 201,000   D. 225,000

   4.____

4 (#7)

5. If, in 2016, the average annual salary of the female employees in the Bureau was four-fifths as large as the average annual salary of the male employees, then the average annual salary of the female employees in that year was
   A. $37,500   B. $31,000   C. $30,500   D. $30,000

5._____

6. Of the total number of employees in the Bureau who were 30 years of age and over in 2009, _____ must have been _____.
   A. at least 35; females
   B. less than 75; males
   C. no more than 100; females
   D. more than 15; males

6._____

KEY (CORRECT ANSWERS)

1. B
2. B
3. C
4. C
5. D
6. A

INTERPRETING STATISTICAL DATA
GRAPHS, CHARTS AND TABLES

EXAMINATION SECTION

TEST 1

DIRECTIONS: Each question or incomplete statement is followed by several suggested answers or completions. Select the one that BEST answers the question or completes the statement. *PRINT THE LETTER OF THE CORRECT ANSWER IN THE SPACE AT THE RIGHT.*

Questions 1-5.

DIRECTIONS: Questions 1 through 5 are to be answered on the basis of the following chart.

DEPT	MIN BAL	AUTO ALLOC	JAN	FEB	MARCH	APRIL	MAY	JUNE	BEG BAL	JAN	FEB	MARCH	APRIL	MAY	JUNE
A	300	600	300	350	200	150	400	250	800	500	750	550	400	600	350
B	500	900	400	350	600	500	450	300	1100						V
C	200	300	150	100	200	200	100	200	400						W
D	800	1200	600	700	500	450	350	700	1600						X
E	600	900	600	700	650	400	550	700	1400						Y
F	400	700	400	350	200	450	300	250	500						Z

     The above table gives hypothetical information regarding monthly allocations, by department, for a certain agency. Each department has begun the year with money left over from 2018. The second column gives the minimum balance allowable for each department. As soon as expenses for a given month would bring the account below this minimum, the amount entered in the third column would automatically be put into that department's account. Columns 4-9 give each department's expenses for the first half of 2019. Column 10 gives the beginning balance for the year (the amount left over from 2018); the remaining columns show how much money is left in each department's account at the end of each month

     By doing the operations necessary to fill in this table, you will be able to answer Questions 1 through 5.

1. Find the value of V.
      A. $1,200   B. $1,000   C. $1,100   D. $1,300

   1._____

2. Find the value of W.
      A. $450   B. $300   C. $350   D. $250

   2._____

3. Find the value of X.
      A. $800   B. $950   C. $1,600   D. $1,500

   3._____

4. Find the value of Y.
      A. $1,300   B. $1,400   C. $750   D. $1,150

   4._____

5. Find the value of Z.
      A. $550   B. $1,000   C. $700   D. $650

   5._____

Questions 6-15.

DIRECTIONS: Questions 6 through 15 are to be answered on the basis of the following information and charts. The paragraphs below give hypothetical information regarding the number, by age groups, of individuals using five state-run lake facilities for the months of July and August 2019. Assume that no one participated in more than one activity. Also, if an activity is not mentioned, assume that it is not offered at that particular lake.

JULY

Seventy-five hundred people under the age of 13 swam in Lake Catharine while 50 people in that age group rowed. Of those 13-19, 5,400 swam in Lake Catharine, 170 canoed there, and 120 rowed. Sailing was more popular with people 20 and over, with 150 people over 60 and 350 people in the 20 to 60 age group using the lake for sailing. In the grouping of people over 60, 2,300 people swam, 50 people rowed, and 200 people canoed. Of those 20 to 60, 40 people rowed, 350 canoed, and 13,500 swam.

Lake Herman is a much smaller and more remote lake and the figures bear this out. No one under 13 was reported using the lake, and the activities are more limited. Of those over 60, most (400) fished from the pier. The remainder used small crafts: 350 canoed and 200 sailed. In the 20-60 age group, there were also more people (1,100) fishing from the pier than were occupied in other activities. Of the remaining people in this age group, 650 canoed and 400 sailed. Those in the 13 to 19 age group did not use the lake in great number, but those that did were more likely to canoe (75) than to sail (60) or to fish from the pier (10).

Lake Manichee is the largest and most developed lake of the five. The least represented group were those over 60. Thirty-five hundred swam in the lake, while 600 canoed, 600 more fished from the pier, 350 sailed, and 300 rowed. The numbers were also not as great for the 13-19 age group. Seventy-eight hundred young people swam on the lake but few people used small crafts. Only 200 canoed and 400 rowed. A very small number (30) fished from the pier. A great number of people in the other two age categories used the lake. Nine thousand children under 13 swam in the lake, 1,100 fished from the pier, and 40 rowed. Of those people 20 to 60, 15,400 swam, 1,000 canoed, 600 fished from the pier, 500 rowed, and 400 sailed.

Swimming, canoeing, and rowing are possible at Dragon Lake. Forty-five hundred children under 13 swam in the lake, while 100 rowed. Of those 13-19, 3,700 swam, 400 rowed, and 350 canoed. In the 20-60 age group, 7,300 swam, 900 canoed, and 750 rowed. Of those over 60, 2,300 swam, 450 canoed, and 250 rowed.

One thousand children under 13 swam in Dream Lake. Six hundred people aged 13 to 19 swam in the lake, while 25 people fished from the pier. Nine hundred people over 60 swam in the lake, 400 canoed there, and 300 fished from the pier. In the 20-60 age group, 2,500 swam, 950 canoed, and 640 fished from the pier.

AUGUST

In August, significantly more people used the facilities at the five lakes. The only exception to this was Lake Herman. Fishing in the lake was prohibited as of August first and that may have had something to do with the minimal increase in use of that facility. Of those who canoed, 80 were 13-19, 400 were over 60, and 750 were in the 20-60 age group. Of those using sailboats, 250 were over 60 years of age, 60 were 13-19, and 450 were 20-60.

Lake Manichee continued to be more popular than any other lake in the group. Record numbers of adults between the ages of 20 and 60 used the lake. Nearly nineteen thousand (18,850) swam in the lake, while 1,200 canoed, 600 rowed, 750 fished, and 450 sailed. The next highest group were the children under 13. More than 10,000 (10,500) swam in the lake, 50 rowed there, and 1,300 fished from the pier. Ninety-four hundred young people between the ages of 13 and 19 swam in the lake, 480 rowed, and 250 canoed, but only 45 fished from the pier. Forty-two hundred people over 60 swam in the lake. Those over 60 seemed to be the most well-rounded in terms of the other activities available. Seven hundred and twenty canoed, 650 fished, 400 rowed, and 370 sailed.

As in July, Lake Catharine was second in popularity to Lake Manichee. As usual, the largest numbers were found in the 20-60 age group. Sixteen thousand people in that age group swam in the lake, 870 canoed, 500 sailed, and 50 rowed. The lake was also very popular with children. Sixty children under 13 rowed on the lake, while 9,150 swam in it. Next, came the 13-19 age group. Two hundred young adults canoed on the lake, 140 rowed on it, and 6,450 swam in it. No one in this age group sailed on the lake. Finally, of those over 60, 2,700 swam, 220 canoed, 180 sailed, and 50 rowed.

Dream Lake also attracted significantly more people (about 19% more) in August than it had in July. Again, only those over 19 canoed on the lake (20-60: 1,000; over 60: 450). Twelve hundred children under 13 swam in the lake, while 750 of those between the ages of 13 and 19 swam. In addition, 40 people in the 13-19 age group rowed on the lake. Of those 20 to 60, 2,900 swam in the lake, and 750 fished from the pier. Eleven hundred people over 60 swam in the lake and 350 fished from the pier.

Finally, 5,200 children under 13 swam in Dragon Lake and 150 rowed there. Of those in the 13-19 age group, 4,100 swam, 500 rowed, and 400 canoed. Of those adults 20 to 60, 7,800 swam, 1,100 canoed, and 850 rowed. In the over 60 age group, 2,500 swam, 550 canoed, and 300 rowed.

By filling in the tables that follow, you will be able to answer Questions 6 through 15.

4 (#1)

	0-12	13-19	20-60	Over 60	TOTAL
Swim					A
Row					B
Canoe					C
Sail					D
Fish					E
TOTAL	F	G	H	I	J

6. Find the value of A.
    A. 190,000   B. 143,000   C. 173,000   D. 145,000

6._____

7. Find the value of C.
    A. 14,855   B. 13,945   C. 15,855   D. 14,845

7._____

8. Find the value of D.
    A. 4,220   B. 5,620   C. 5,200   D. 4,170

8._____

9. Find the value of G.
    A. 50,850   B. 42,255   C. 38,385   43,280

9._____

10. Find the value of I.
    A. 28,990   B. 38,230   C. 27,370   D. 35,290

10._____

Listed below are per person fees for swimming and fishing privileges at the five lakes. Use this information and the information from the preceding chart to fill in the table below. Again, assume that no one participated in more than one activity, and that those activities which are not mentioned are not offered.

5 (#1)

LAKE CATHERINE	0-12	13-19	20-60	Over 60
Swimming	.25	.50	1.00	.50

LAKE HERMAN	0-12	13-19	20-60	Over 60
Fishing	Free	.50	1.50	.50

LAKE MANICHEE	0-12	13-19	20-60	Over 60
Swimming	.50	1.00	1.00	Free
Fishing	Free	1.00	1.00	Free

DREAM LAKE	0-12	13-19	20-60	Over 60
Swimming	Free	.50	1.00	Free
Fishing	Free	Free	1.00	Free

DRAGON LAKE	0-12	13-19	20-60	Over 60
Swimming	.50	1.00	2.00	1.00

TOTAL REVENUES IN THE FIVE-LAKE REGION: SUMMER 2019					
	0-12	13-19	20-60	Over 60	TOTAL
Swimming					A
Fishing					B
Boat Rental					
Sailboat	N/A	$200	$12,750	$8,800	C
Canoe	N/A	$2,095	$20,000	$7,800	D
Rowboat	$350	$2,050	$3,750	$900	E
TOTAL	F	G	H	I	J

11. Find the value of A.
    A. $163,662.50
    B. $186,625.50
    C. $160,862.50
    D. $140,060.50

11._____

12. Find the value of B.
    A. $4,670   B. $46,700   C. $5,220   D. $4,570

12._____

13. Find the value of G.
    A. $27,925   B. $36,025   C. $33,845   D. $16,035

13._____

14. Find the value of H.
    A. $132,940   B. $140,240   C. $133,870   D. $143,990

14._____

15. Find the value of J.
    A. $195,397.50
    B. $199,297.50
    C. $190,227.50
    D. $224,227.50

15._____

Questions 16-20.

DIRECTIONS: Questions 16 through 20 are to be answered on the basis of the following information. The hypothetical information below concerns the 2019 operating budgets for three units in a particular department. Consolidate this information in the table on the next page and use your findings to answer Questions 16 through 20.

UNIT A

1st Quarter 　　Postal Fees: 250; Utilities, Elec.: 150; Utilities, Phone: 300; Expense Accounts: 1,500; Maintenance: 400; Non-Paper Supplies: 450; Paper Supplies: 500
2nd Quarter 　　Postal Fees: 200; Utilities, Elec.: 150; Utilities, Phone: 200; Expense Accounts: 1,700; Maintenance: 450; Paper Supplies: 200; Non-Paper Supplies: 150
3rd Quarter 　　Postal Fees: 150; Utilities, Elec.: 225; Utilities, Phone: 150; Expense Accounts: 1,000; Maintenance: 400; Paper Supplies: 150; Non-Paper Supplies: 100
4th Quarter 　　Postal Fees: 300; Utilities, Elec.: 200; Utilities, Phone: 350; Expense Accounts: 2,100; Maintenance: 350; Paper Supplies: 250; Non-Paper Supplies: 200

UNIT B

	1st	2nd	3rd	4th
Supplies:				
Paper	500	300	250	600
Non-Paper	450	300	250	300
Maintenance	450	400	350	400
Utilities:				
Electricity	200	150	250	250
Telephone	350	300	200	300
Expense Accounts	2,000	3,000	1,500	3,500
Postal	350	250	200	450

UNIT C

	Exp. Acct.	Main	P. Fees	Phone	Elec.	Paper	Non-Paper
1st Q.	4,100	800	300	800	600	300	400
2nd Q.	3,200	650	600	650	400	400	200
3rd Q.	3,000	850	300	450	450	250	350
4th Q.	3,600	750	550	700	500	350	350

7 (#1)

	1st Q.	2nd Q.	3rd Q.	4th Q.	TOTAL
EXPENSE ACCTS.					
MAINTENANCE					
POSTAL FEES					

SUPPLIES:
  PAPER
  NON-PAPER					

UTILITIES
  ELECTRICITY
  TELEPHONE					

TOTAL					

16. The only expense that decreased between the 3rd and 4th quarter was
    A. maintenance
    B. electricity
    C. telephone
    D. non-paper supplies

16.____

17. Between the 1st and 2nd quarter, the LARGEST percent decrease occurred in which category?
    A. Telephone
    B. Expense accounts
    C. Non-paper supplies
    D. Paper supplies

17.____

18. If the rate of increase for expense accounts were to be the same from the 4th quarter of 2019 to the 1st quarter of 2020, what amount would be spent for expense accounts in the 1st quarter of 2019?
    A. $1,538   B. $6,164   C. $15,389   D. $6,189

18.____

19. The category which had the MOST stable expenses throughout 2019 is
    A. electricity
    B. expense accounts
    C. postal fees
    D. maintenance

19.____

20. On the whole, all the units are LEAST expensive to maintain during which quarter?
    A. 1st   B. 2nd   C. 3rd   D. 4th

20.____

Questions 21-24.

DIRECTIONS: Questions 21 through 24 are to be answered on the basis of the following charts.

TYPES OF PUBLIC WAREHOUSES – 2019
(Hypothetical Data)

Category of Operation	Number	Total Revenue ($000)	Proportion of Total Revenue in 2019
Local trucking and storage (including household goods)	4687	823,959	?
General Merchandise Warehousing	?	610,566	28.74
Refrigerated Goods (including food lockers)	1534	?	16.55
Farm Products	744	155,085	7.30
Special Warehousing	?	136,861	6.44
Household Goods	423	46,698	?
TOTAL	10026	2,124,765	100.00

GENERAL MERCHANDISE WAREHOUSING
(Hypothetical Data)

Year	Number of Establishments	Public Floor Space (000 sq.ft.)	Number of Paid Employees	Revenue ($000)
1994	1,197	108,315	22,283	$171,542
1999	1,512	119,325	22,496	200,934
2004	1,483	129,170	22,880	248,282
2009	1,677	163,168	28,295	379,910
2019	2,170	296,067	32,495	620,566

21. Approximately how many square feet of public floor space were held by the average general merchandise warehousing establishment in 2019?
    A. 136   B. 973   C. 97,298   D. 136,440

21.____

22. If one-third as many new general merchandise warehouses opened between December of 2014 and December of 2016 as opened between January 2017 and December of 2019, approximately how many general merchandise warehousing establishments existed at the end of 2016? (Assume that the totals in the table are year-end figures and that no warehouse closed in that time.)
    A. 105   B. 1,302   C. 1,407   D. 1,276

22.____

23. What was the average amount of public space used for general merchandise warehousing from 2014 through 2019? _____ square feet.
    A. 103,995,000   B. 22,149,340   C. 129,995   D. 129,994,500

23.____

24. In which category of operation was the average revenue per establishment GREATEST?
    A. Local trucking and storage
    B. General merchandise warehousing
    C. Refrigerated goods
    D. Cannot be determined from information given

24.____

Questions 25-28.

DIRECTIONS: Questions 25 through 28 are to be answered on the basis of the following charts.

CUMMINGS EMPLOYMENT TRAINING
COMPARATIVE BUDGET DATA: 2017-2019
(Hypothetical Data)

Income	2017	2018	2019
Federal Funds:	57,900	64,070	?
Commodities Support Project	20,000	26,900	29,800
CSBG Grants	14,000	10,000	0
Training Contracts	?	27,170	54,840
County Funds	12,400	17,500	23,070
Grants:	0	?	16,000
Smith Foundation	0	8,000	12,000
Wealth-Rite Corp.	0	5,000	?
TOTAL	70,200	?	?

Expenses			
Personnel:	51,750	71,300	90,950
Salaries	45,000	?	?
Benefits	6,750	?	11,850
Office	10,120	13,540	17,505
Training Materials	6,800	8,500	9,540
Transportation	1,530	2,230	3,230
TOTAL	70,200	95,570	?

25. For each dollar spent on training materials in 2019, how many dollars were spent on salaries?
    A. 8.28   B. .12   C. 7.9   D. .79

25.____

26. By what percent did the program's spending increase from 2017 to 2018?
    A. 73%   B. 36%   C. 136%   D. 74%

26.____

27. It is MOST likely that which of the following amounts was spent in 2018?
    A. $45,000   B. $93,000   C. $62,000   D. $69,000

27.____

28. In 2019, 3,025 people were trained through the Cummings Program. Two women were trained for every five men.
How much did it cost to train men in the 2019 Cummings Program?
   A. $48,400   B. $72,600   C. $34,560   D. $86,429

28.____

Questions 29-32.

DIRECTIONS: Questions 29 through 32 are to be answered on the basis of the following chart.

State	Total Below Poverty: All Ages		High Risk Age Groups Below Poverty							
			Pregnant Women		Children 0-4		Children 5-17		Age 60+	
	Number	%*	Number	%**	Number	%**	Number	%**	Number	%**
Conn.	242,650	8.0	2,325	8.0	27,346	15	65,260	10	38,446	8
Maine	140,996	13.0	1,606	13.0	13,847	18	36,015	15	27,002	15
Mass.	532,458	9.6	5,227	9.6	52,535	16	140,277	12	83,599	9
N.H.	75,364	8.5	875	8.5	6,851	11	17,130	9	14,635	11
R.I.	93,959	10.3	940	10.3	9,321	12	23,195	13	18,756	11
Vt.	59,059	12.1	706	12.1	5,961	17	13,940	13	9,476	13
Total	1,144,486	9.3	11,679	9.6	115,861	15.5	295,817	11.9	192,314	9.6

* Percent of Total Population Within State
** Percent of Total Population Within Each High Risk Group

29. What proportion of the people in Massachusetts living below the poverty level are over 60 years of age?
   A. 9.6%   B. 16%   C. 8%   D. 53%

29.____

30. Approximately what percent of the total New England population is shown to be in high risk age groups?
   A. 54%   B. 46.6%   C. 9%   D. 5%

30.____

31. If among those individuals living below the poverty level the male to female ratio is 1:4, how many females were living below the poverty level in New England in 2019?
   A. 915,589   B. 286,122   C. 228,897   D. 968,542

31.____

32. In Massachusetts, 3,473 pregnant women living below the poverty level received federally-funded prenatal care.
If the participation rate is consistent for Connecticut and Rhode Island, how many pregnant women living below the poverty level received federally-funded prenatal health care in Connecticut?
   A. 1,545
   B. 3,499
   C. 2,949
   D. Cannot be determined from information given

32.____

Questions 33-36.

DIRECTIONS: Questions 33 through 36 are to be answered on the basis of the following chart.

HYPERTENSION SCREENING PROGRAM, 2015-2019
(Hypothetical Data)

	2015	2016	2017	2018	2019
Persons Screened: (thousands)	3,040	3,810	2,950	2,600	2,540
% Over 65	10%	12%	11%	13%	9%
% Under 35	12%	14%	15%	17%	17%
Expenditures: From local, state, and federal funding sources (millions)	15.55	23.05	24.00	24.50	25.65
% Local	7%	8%	6%	4%	7%
% State	20%	14%	19%	22.5%	25%

33. In which three years were the amounts from federal sources APPROXIMATELY the same:
    A. 2015, 2016, 2017
    B. 2016, 2017, 2018
    C. 2017, 2018, 2019
    D. 2015, 2017, 2018

34. Between 2015 and 2016, the amount spent to screen individuals in the 35-65 age bracket increased by
    A. $.93   B. $4,915   C. 40.5%   D. 45%

35. For every $10 provided by the federal government in 2018, how many dollars were spent by the state governments?
    A. $3.06   B. $1.25   C. $.33   D. $4.30

36. From this table, one could conclude that
    A. there are more people under 35 who have hypertension than there are people over 65 with hypertension
    B. the number of people under 35 screened for hypertension steadily increased between 2016 and 2019
    C. the amount of local funds used for hypertension screening has remained approximately the same from 2017 to 2019
    D. the amount of federal funds used for hypertension screening increased from 2015 to 2017

Questions 37-40.

DIRECTIONS: Questions 37 through 40 are to be answered on the basis of the following graph and information.

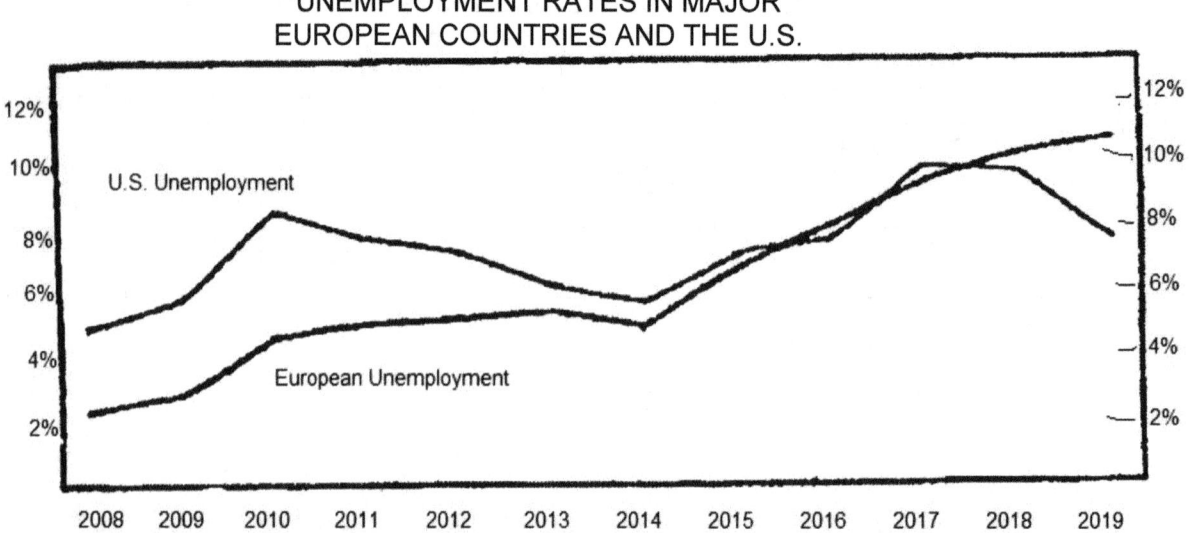

WHAT THE NUMBERS SAY: The economy is slowing down. GNP grew only by 1.3% in the first quarter.

MONTHLY DATA	3/2020	2/2020	1/2019	3/2019	2002
Employment (seasonally adjusted)					
Number of unemployed (millions)	8.396	8.399	8.484	8.793	2.975
Overall employment rate	7.3%	7.3%	7.4%	7.8%	3.8%
Black unemployment rate	15.2%	16.3%	14.%	16.6%	7.4%
Wages					
Average weekly earnings: current dollars	$297.70	$295.64	$295.80	$288.40	$101.84
Average weekly earnings: 2012 dollars	N/A	$170.99	$171.78	$172.59	$184.83
Prices					
All items Consumer Price Index	318.8	317.4	316.1	307.3	100.00
Increase from one year earlier	3.7%	3.5%	3.6%	4.7%	2.9%
Food increase from one year earlier	4.0%	2.4%	2.6%	4.0%	0.9%
Interest Rates					
Mortgage (effective, on new homes)	11.91%	12.21%	12.27%	12.02%	6.50%
Prime Interest Rate	10.5%	10.5%	10.61%	11.5%	5.61%

QUARTERLY DATA (billions of dollars at annual rates, seasonally adjusted)	2020 1st	2019 4th	2019 1st	2002
Gross National Product	3819.9	3758.7	3553.3	796.3
Balance of Trade (exports minus imports)	N/A	-91.5	-103.1	+3.8
Wages, Salaries, and Benefits	1447.8	1427.4	1354.0	471.9
Corporate Profits	N/A	291.6	277.4	79.3
Gross National Product in 2007 dollars	1668.0	1662.4	1610.9	1007.7

NOTES: N/A means not available. Wages are the average for private-sector nonfarm workers; no taxes have been subtracted.
SOURCES: Employment, wages, and prices are from the Department of Labor, Bureau of Labor Statistics. Mortgage interest rate is from the Federal Home Loan Bank Board. GNP and its components are from the Department of Commerce, Bureau of Economic Analysis.

37. Compare the average weekly earnings, in current dollars, for February of 2007 with the average weekly earnings, in current dollars, for March of 2019. 37.____
    A. $7.24 more   B. $1.60 less   C. $7.40 more   D. $9.30 more

38. The average weekly earnings in 2012 dollars, from March of 2019 to February of 2020 38.____
    A. increased .009%
    B. decreased .009%
    C. increased .25%
    D. decreased .9%

39. From 2002 to the last quarter of 2019, the Balance of Trade declined 39.____
    A. 4%   B. 25.1%   C. 23.1%   D. 25.8%

40. From this table, one could conclude that 40.____
    A. black unemployment will continue to decline throughout 2020
    B. buying power has increased since 2019
    C. the increase in buying power has not kept pace with the increase in wages since 2002
    D. from 2002 to the last quarter of 2019, corporate profits decreased more than 250%

Questions 41-44.

DIRECTIONS: Questions 41 through 44 are to be answered on the basis of the following chart.

14 (#1)

NEW YORK STOCK EXCHANGE
(Hypothetical Data)

	CLOSING			CHANGE		
	4/28/2019	10/27/2019	10/28/2019	Change	Percent	Pct. 6 mos.
PlanResearch	18	22³/₈	31	?	?	+72.2%
Unitrode	14	13	11¾	-1¼	-9.6%	-16.07%
Wurlitzer	3¼	2¾	2½	-¼	-9.1%	-23.08%
Dow Indus.	1825.37	1841.79	?	-3²/₃	-.2%	+.7%
IBM	159.25	119.44	120¾	+1.31	+1.1%	-24.2%
PogoProd.	4.33	?	?	?	?	-13.5%
Cullinet	9¹/₈	8⁷/₈	8³/₈	-½	-5.6%	-8.2%
CM	81	70 1/3	70	+1/3	+.5%	+13.6%
NYSE Composite	138.44	137.62	137.89	$.27	+.2%	-.4%

41. PanResearch, from 10/27 to 10/18, 41.____
    A. increased 28.6% B. decreased 8.6%
    C. increased 38.6% D. increased 34.6%

42. On 10/28, the value of Dow Industrials, compared to the NYSE Composite, was 42.____
    A. $1,704.17   B. $1,703.90   C. 13¹/₃ times   D. 130 times

43. If, on October 29, PogoProd increased 20% from the October 28 figure, its closing price on that day would have been 43.____
    A. 4%
    B. $4.49
    C. $5.90
    D. cannot be determined from information given

44. If Cullinet closed on 4/28/2019 at 35% less than it closed six months before, the closing price for Cullinet on 10/28/2018 would have been 44.____
    A. 10.125   B. 12.32   C. 14.04   D. 15.21

KEY (CORRECT ANSWERS)

1. A	11. C	21. D	31. A	41. C
2. C	12. A	22. D	32. A	42. C
3. C	13. B	23. D	33. B	43. B
4. B	14. B	24. B	34. C	44. C
5. D	15. D	25. A	35. A	
6. A	16. A	26. B	36. D	
7. A	17. C	27. C	37. A	
8. D	18. C	28. D	38. D	
9. B	19. D	29. B	39. D	
10. A	20. C	30. D	40. C	

PRINCIPLES AND PRACTICES, OF ADMINISTRATION, SUPERVISION AND MANAGEMENT

TABLE OF CONTENTS

	Page
GENERAL ADMINISTRATION	1
SEVEN BASIC FUNCTIONS OF THE SUPERVISOR	2
I. Planning	2
II. Organizing	3
III. Staffing	3
IV. Directing	3
V. Coordinating	3
VI. Reporting	3
VII. Budgeting	3
PLANNING TO MEET MANAGEMENT GOALS	4
I. What is Planning	4
II. Who Should Make Plans	4
III. What are the Results of Poor Planning	4
IV. Principles of Planning	4
MANAGEMENT PRINCIPLES	5
I. Management	5
II. Management Principles	5
III. Organization Structure	6
ORGANIZATION	8
I. Unity of Command	8
II. Span of Control	8
III. Uniformity of Assignment	9
IV. Assignment of Responsibility and Delegation of Authority	9
PRINCIPLES OF ORGANIZATION	9
I. Definition	9
II. Purpose of Organization	9
III. Basic Considerations in Organizational Planning	9
IV. Bases for Organization	10
V. Assignment of Functions	10
VI. Delegation of Authority and Responsibility	10
VII. Employee Relationships	11

DELEGATING		11
I.	WHAT IS DELEGATING:	11
II.	TO WHOM TO DELEGATE	11
REPORTS		12
I.	DEFINITION	12
II.	PURPOSE	12
III.	TYPES	12
IV.	FACTORS TO CONSIDER BEFORE WRITING REPORT	12
V.	PREPARATORY STEPS	12
VI.	OUTLINE FOR A RECOMMENDATION REPORT	12
MANAGEMENT CONTROLS		13
I.	Control	13
II.	Basis for Control	13
III.	Policy	13
IV.	Procedure	14
V.	Basis of Control	14
FRAMEWORK OF MANAGEMENT		14
I.	Elements	14
II.	Manager's Responsibility	15
III.	Control Techniques	16
IV.	Where Forecasts Fit	16
PROBLEM SOLVING		16
I.	Identify the Problem	16
II.	Gather Data	17
III.	List Possible Solutions	17
IV.	Test Possible Solutions	18
V.	Select the Best Solution	18
VI.	Put the Solution into Actual Practice	19
COMMUNICATION		19
I.	What is Communication?	19
II.	Why is Communication Needed?	19
III.	How is Communication Achieved?	20
IV.	Why Does Communication Fail?	21
V.	How to Improve Communication	21
VI.	How to Determine If You Are Getting Across	21
VII.	The Key Attitude	22
HOW ORDERS AND INSTRUCTIONS SHOULD BE GIVEN		22
I.	Characteristics of Good Orders and Instructions	22
FUNCTIONS OF A DEPARTMENT PERSONNEL OFFICE		23

SUPERVISION		23
I.	Leadership	23
	A. The Authoritarian Approach	23
	B. The Laissez-Faire Approach	24
	C. The Democratic Approach	24
II.	Nine Points of Contrast Between Boss and Leader	25
EMPLOYEE MORALE		25
I.	Some Ways to Develop and Maintain Good Employee Morale	25
II.	Some Indicators of Good Morale	26
MOTIVATION		26
EMPLOYEE PARTICIPATION		27
I.	WHAT IS PARTICIPATION	27
II.	WHY IS IT IMPORTANT?	27
III.	HOW MAY SUPERVISORS OBTAIN IT?	28
STEPS IN HANDLING A GRIEVANCE		28
DISCIPLINE		29
I.	THE DISCIPLINARY INTERVIEW	29
II.	PLANNING THE INTERVIEW	29
III.	CONDUCTING THE INTERVIEW	30

PRINCIPLES AND PRACTICES, OF
ADMINISTRATION, SUPERVISION AND MANAGEMENT

Most people are inclined to think of administration as something that only a few persons are responsible for in a large organization. Perhaps this is true if you are thinking of Administration with a capital A, but administration with a lower case a is a responsibility of supervisors at all levels each working day.

All of us feel we are pretty good supervisors and that we do a good job of administering the workings of our agency. By and large, this is true, but every so often it is good to check up on ourselves. Checklists appear from time to time in various publications which psychologists say tell whether or not a person will make a good wife, husband, doctor, lawyer, or supervisor.

The following questions are an excellent checklist to test yourself as a supervisor and administrator.

Remember, Administration gives direction and points the way but administration carries the ideas to fruition. Each is dependent on the other for its success. Remember, too, that no unit is too small for these departmental functions to be carried out. These statements apply equally as well to the Chief Librarian as to the Department Head with but one or two persons to supervise.

GENERAL ADMINISTRATION: General Responsibilities of Supervisors

1. Have I prepared written statements of functions, activities, and duties for my organizational unit?

2. Have I prepared procedural guides for operating activities?

3. Have I established clearly in writing, lines of authority and responsibility for my organizational unit?

4. Do I make recommendations for improvements in organization, policies, administrative and operating routines and procedures, including simplification of work and elimination of non-essential operations?

5. Have I designated and trained an understudy to function in my absence?

6. Do I supervise and train personnel within the unit to effectively perform their assignments?

7. Do I assign personnel and distribute work on such a basis as to carry out the organizational unit's assignment or mission in the most effective and efficient manner?

8. Have I established administrative controls by:

    a. Fixing responsibility and accountability on all supervisors under my direction for the proper performance of their functions and duties.

b. Preparations and submitting periodic work load and progress reports covering the operations of the unit to my immediate superior.

c. Analysis and evaluation of such reports received from subordinate units.

d. Submission of significant developments and problems arising within the organizational unit to my immediate superior.

e. Conducting conferences, inspections, etc., as to the status and efficiency of unit operations.

9. Do I maintain an adequate and competent working force?

10. Have I fostered good employee-department relations, seeing that established rules, regulations, and instructions are being carried out properly?

11. Do I collaborate and consult with other organizational units performing related functions to insure harmonious and efficient working relationships?

12. Do I maintain liaison through prescribed channels with city departments and other governmental agencies concerned with the activities of the unit?

13. Do I maintain contact with and keep abreast of the latest developments and techniques of administration (professional societies, groups, periodicals, etc.) as to their applicability to the activities of the unit?

14. Do I communicate with superiors and subordinates through prescribed organizational channels?

15. Do I notify superiors and subordinates in instances where bypassing is necessary as soon thereafter as practicable?

16. Do I keep my superior informed of significant developments and problems?

SEVEN BASIC FUNCTIONS OF THE SUPERVISOR

I. PLANNING
This means working out goals and means to obtain goals. <u>What</u> needs to be done, <u>who</u> will do it, <u>how</u>, <u>when</u>, and <u>where</u> it is to be done.

SEVEN STEPS IN PLANNING

A. Define job or problem clearly.
B. Consider priority of job.
C. Consider time-limit—starting and completing.
D. Consider minimum distraction to, or interference with, other activities.
E. Consider and provide for contingencies—possible emergencies.
F. Break job down into components.

G. Consider the 5 W's and H:
   WHY..........is it necessary to do the job? (Is the purpose clearly defined?)
   WHAT........needs to be done to accomplish the defined purpose?
   ....is needed to do the job? (Money, materials, etc.)
   WHO..........is needed to do the job?
   ....will have responsibilities?
   WHERE......is the work to be done?
   WHEN........is the job to begin and end? (Schedules, etc.)
   HOW..........is the job to bed done? (Methods, controls, records, etc.)

II. ORGANIZING

This means dividing up the work, establishing clear lines of responsibility and authority and coordinating efforts to get the job done.

III. STAFFING

The whole personnel function of bringing in and <u>training</u> staff, getting the right man and fitting him to the right job—the job to which he is best suited.

In the normal situation, the supervisor's responsibility regarding staffing normally includes providing accurate job descriptions, that is, duties of the jobs, requirements, education and experience, skills, physical, etc.; assigning the work for maximum use of skills; and proper utilization of the probationary period to weed out unsatisfactory employees.

IV. DIRECTING

Providing the necessary leadership to the group supervised. Important work gets done to the supervisor's satisfaction.

V. COORDINATING

The all-important duty of inter-relating the various parts of the work.
The supervisor is also responsible for controlling the coordinated activities. This means measuring performance according to a time schedule and setting quotas to see that the goals previously set are being reached. Reports from workers should be analyzed, evaluated, and made part of all future plans.

VI. REPORTING

This means proper and effective communication to your superiors, subordinates, and your peers (in definition of the job of the supervisor). Reports should be read and information contained therein should be used, not be filed away and forgotten. Reports should be written in such a way that the desired action recommended by the report is forthcoming.

VII. BUDGETING
This means controlling current costs and forecasting future costs. This forecast is based on past experience, future plans and programs, as well as current costs.

You will note that these seven functions can fall under three topics:

Planning) Make a plan Staffing) Reporting) Watch it work
Organizing) Directing) Get things done Budgeting)
 Controlling)

PLANNING TO MEET MANAGEMENT GOALS

I. WHAT IS PLANNING?

   A. Thinking a job through before new work is done to determine the best way to do it
   B. A method of doing something
   C. Ways and means for achieving set goals
   D. A means of enabling a supervisor to deliver with a minimum of effort, all details involved in coordinating his work

II. WHO SHOULD MAKE PLANS?

   Everybody!
   All levels of supervision must plan work. (Top management, heads of divisions or bureaus, first line supervisors, and individual employees.) The higher the level, the more planning required.

III. WHAT ARE THE RESULTS OF POOR PLANNING?

   A. Failure to meet deadline
   B. Low employee morale
   C. Lack of job coordination
   D. Overtime is frequently necessary
   E. Excessive cost, waste of material and manhours

IV. PRINCIPLES OF PLANNING

   A. Getting a clear picture of your objectives. What exactly are you trying to accomplish?
   B. Plan the whole job, then the parts, in proper sequence.
   C. Delegate the planning of details to those responsible for executing them.
   D. Make your plan flexible.
   E. Coordinate your plan with the plans of others so that the work may be processed with a minimum of delay.
   F. Sell your plan before you execute it.
   G. Sell your plan to your superior, subordinate, in order to gain maximum participation and coordination.
   H. Your plan should take precedence. Use knowledge and skills that others have brought to a similar job.
   I. Your plan should take account of future contingencies; allow for future expansion.
   J. Plans should include minor details. Leave nothing to chance that can be anticipated.
   K. Your plan should be simple and provide standards and controls. Establish quality and quantity standards and set a standard method of doing the job. The controls will indicate whether the job is proceeding according to plan.
   L. Consider possible bottlenecks, breakdowns, or other difficulties that are likely to arise.

V. Q. WHAT ARE THE YARDSTICKS BY WHICH PLANNING SHOULD BE MEASURED?
A. Any plan should:
— Clearly state a definite course of action to be followed and goal to be achieved, with consideration for emergencies.
— Be realistic and practical.
— State what's to be done, when it's to be done, where, how, and by whom.
— Establish the most efficient sequence of operating steps so that more is accomplished in less time, with the least effort, and with the best quality results.
— Assure meeting deliveries without delays.
— Establish the standard by which performance is to be judged.

Q. WHAT KINDS OF PLANS DOES EFFECTIVE SUPERVISION REQUIRE?
A. Plans should cover such factors as:
— Manpower: right number of properly trained employees on the job
— Materials: adequate supply of the right materials and supplies
— Machines: full utilization of machines and equipment, with proper maintenance
— Methods: most efficient handling of operations
— Deliveries: making deliveries on time
— Tools: sufficient well-conditioned tools
— Layout: most effective use of space
— Reports: maintaining proper records and reports
— Supervision: planning work for employees and organizing supervisor's own time

MANAGEMENT PRINCIPLES

I. MANAGEMENT
Q. What do we mean by management?
A. Getting work done through others.

Management could also be defined as planning, directing, and controlling the operations of a bureau or division so that all factors will function properly and all persons cooperate efficiently for a common objective.

II. MANAGEMENT PRINCIPLES

A. There should be a hierarchy—wherein authority and responsibility run upward and downward through several levels—with a broad base at the bottom and a single head at the top.

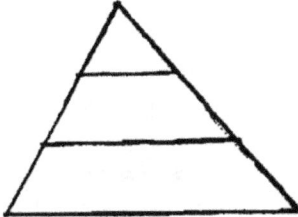

B. Each and every unit or person in the organization should be answerable ultimately to the manager at the apex. In other words, *The buck stops here!*

C. Every necessary function involved in the bureau's objectives is assigned to a unit in that bureau.

D. Responsibilities assigned to a unit are specifically clear-cut and understood.

E. Consistent methods of organizational structure should be applied at each level of the organization.

F. Each member of the bureau from top to bottom knows: to whom he reports and who reports to him.

G. No member of one bureau reports to more than one supervisor. No dual functions.

H. Responsibility for a function is matched by authority necessary to perform that function. Weight of authority.

I. Individuals or units reporting to a supervisor do not exceed the number which can be feasibly and effectively coordinated and directed. Concept of *span of control*.

J. Channels of command (management) are not violated by staff units, although there should be staff services to facilitate and coordinate management functions.

K. Authority and responsibility should be decentralized to units and individuals who are responsible for the actual performance of operations.
Welfare – down to Welfare Centers
Hospitals – down to local hospitals

L. Management should exercise control through attention to policy problems of exceptional performance, rather than through review of routine actions of subordinates.

M. Organizations should never be permitted to grow so elaborate as to hinder work accomplishments.

III. ORGANIZATION STRUCTURE

Types of Organizations
The purest form is a leader and a few followers, such as:

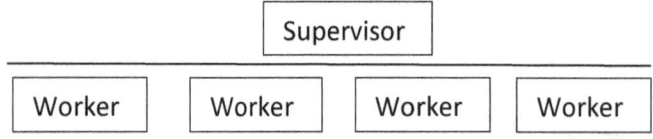

(Refer to organization chart) from supervisor to workers.

The line of authority is direct, The workers know exactly where they stand in relation to their boss, to whom they report for instructions and direction.

Unfortunately, in our present complex society, few organizations are similar to this example of a pure line organization. In this era of specialization, other people are often needed in the simplest of organizations. These specialists are known as staff. The sole purpose for their existence (staff) is to assist, advise, suggest, help or counsel line organizations. Staff has no authority to direct line people—nor do they give them direct instructions.

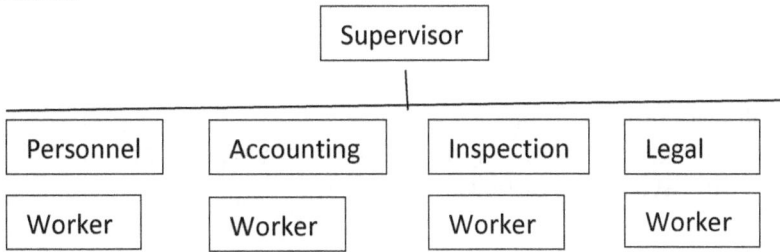

Line Functions
1. Directs
2. Orders
3. Responsibility for carrying out activities from beginning to end
4. Follows chain of command
5. Is identified with what it does
6. Decides when and how to use staff advice
7. Line executes

Staff Functions
1. Advises
2. Persuades and sells
3. Staff studies, reports, recommends but does not carry out
4. May advise across department lines
5. May find its ideas identified with others
6. Has to persuade line to want its advice
7. Staff: Conducts studies and research. Provides advice and instructions in technical matters. Serves as technical specialist to render specific services.

Types and Functions of Organization Charts
An organization chart is a picture of the arrangement and inter-relationship of the subdivisions of an organization.

A. Types of Charts:
   1. Structural: basic relationships only
   2. Functional: includes functions or duties
   3. Personnel: positions, salaries, status, etc.
   4. Process Chart: work performed
   5. Gantt Chart: actual performance against planned
   5. Flow Chart: flow and distribution of work

B. Functions of Charts:
   1. Assist in management planning and control
   2. Indicate duplication of functions
   3. Indicate incorrect stressing of functions
   4. Indicate neglect of important functions
   5. Correct unclear authority
   6. Establish proper span of control

C. Limitations of Charts:
   1. Seldom maintained on current basis
   2. Chart is oversimplified
   3. Human factors cannot adequately be charted

D. Organization Charts should be:
   1. Simple
   2. Symmetrical
   3. Indicate authority
   4. Line and staff relationship differentiated
   5. Chart should be dated and bear signature of approving officer
   6. Chart should be displayed, not hidden

ORGANIZATION

There are four basic principles of organization:
1. Unity of command
2. Span of control
3. Uniformity of assignment
4. Assignment of responsibility and delegation of authority

I. UNITY OF COMMAND

Unity of command means that each person in the organization should receive orders from one, and only one, supervisor. When a person has to take orders from two or more people, (a) the orders may be in conflict and the employee is upset because he does not know which he should obey, or (b) different orders may reach him at the same time and he does not know which he should carry out first.

Equally as bad as having two bosses is the situation where the supervisor is bypassed. Let us suppose you are a supervisor whose boss bypasses you (deals directly with people reporting to you). To the worker, it is the same as having two bosses; but to you, the supervisor, it is equally serious. Bypassing on the part of your boss will undermine your authority, and the people under you will begin looking to your boss for decisions and even for routine orders.

You can prevent bypassing by telling the people you supervise that if anyone tries to give them orders, they should direct that person to you.

II. SPAN OF CONTROL

Span of control on a given level involves:
A. The number of people being supervised
B. The distance
C The time involved in supervising the people. (One supervisor cannot supervise too many workers effectively.)

Span of control means that a supervisor has the right number (not too many and not too few) of subordinates that he can supervise well.

III. UNIFORMITY OF ASSIGNMENT

In assigning work, you as the supervisor should assign to each person jobs that are similar in nature. An employee who is assigned too many different types of jobs will waste time in going from one kind of work to another. It takes time for him to get to top production in one kind of task and, before he does so, he has to start on another.
When you assign work to people, remember that:

A. Job duties should be definite. Make it clear from the beginning <u>what</u> they are to do, <u>how</u> they are to do it, and <u>why</u> they are to do it. Let them know how much they are expected to do and how well they are expected to do it.
B. Check your assignments to be certain that there are no workers with too many unrelated duties, and that no two people have been given overlapping responsibilities. Your aim should be to have every task assigned to a specific person with the work fairly distributed and with each person doing his part.

IV. ASSIGNMENT OF RESPONSIBILITY AND DELEGATION OF AUTHORITY

A supervisor cannot delegate his final responsibility for the work of his department. The experienced supervisor knows that he gets his work done through people. He can't do it all himself. So he must assign the work and the responsibility for the work to his employees. Then they must be given the authority to carry out their responsibilities.

By assigning responsibility and delegating authority to carry out the responsibility, the supervisor builds in his workers initiative, resourcefulness, enthusiasm, and interest in their work. He is treating them as responsible adults. They can find satisfaction in their work, and they will respect the supervisor and be loyal to the supervisor.

PRINCIPLES OF ORGANIZATION

I. DEFINITION

Organization is the method of dividing up the work to provide the best channels for coordinated effort to get the agency's mission accomplished.

II. PURPOSE OF ORGANIZATION

A. To enable each employee within the organization to clearly know his responsibilities and relationships to his fellow employees and to organizational units
B. To avoid conflicts of authority and overlapping of jurisdiction.
C. To ensure teamwork.

III. BASIC CONSIDERATIONS IIN ORGANIZATIONAL PLANNING

A. The basic plans and objectives of the agency should be determined, and the organizational structure should be adapted to carry out effectively such plans and objectives.
B. The organization should be built around the major functions of the agency and not individuals or groups of individuals.

C. The organization should be sufficiently flexible to meet new and changing conditions which may be brought about from within or outside the department.
D. The organizational structure should be as simple as possible and the number of organizational units kept at a minimum.
E. The number of levels of authority should be kept at a minimum. Each additional management level lengthens the chain of authority and responsibility and increases the time for instructions to be distributed to operating levels and for decisions to be obtained from higher authority.
F. The form of organization should permit each executive to exercise maximum initiative within the limits of delegated authority.

IV. BASES FOR ORGANIZATION

A. Purpose (Examples: education, police, sanitation)
B. Process (Examples: accounting, legal, purchasing)
C. Clientele (Examples: welfare, parks, veteran)
D. Geographic (Examples: borough offices, precincts, libraries)

V. ASSIGNMENTS OF FUNCTIONS

A. Every function of the agency should be assigned to a specific organizational unit. Under normal circumstances, no single function should be assigned to more than one organizational unit.
B. There should be no overlapping, duplication, or conflict between organizational elements.
C. Line functions should be separated from staff functions, and proper emphasis should be placed on staff activities.
D. Functions which are closely related or similar should normally be assigned to a single organizational unit.
E. Functions should be properly distributed to promote balance, and to avoid overemphasis of less important functions and underemphasis of more essential functions.

VI. DELEGATION OF AUTHORITY AND RESPONSIBILITY

A. Responsibilities assigned to a specific individual or organizational unit should carry corresponding authority, and all statements of authority or limitations thereof should be as specific as possible.
B. Authority and responsibility for action should be decentralized to organizational units and individuals responsible for actual performance to the greatest extent possible, without relaxing necessary control over policy or the standardization of procedures. Delegation of authority will be consistent with decentralization of responsibility but such delegation will not divest an executive in higher authority of his overall responsibility.
C. The heads of organizational units should concern themselves with important matters and should delegate to the maximum extent details and routines performed in the ordinary course of business.
D. All responsibilities, authorities, and relationships should be stated in simple language to avoid misinterpretation.
E. Each individual or organizational unit charged with a specific responsibility will be held responsible for results.

VII. EMPLOYEE RELATIONSHIPS

   A. The employees reporting to one executive should not exceed the number which can be effectively directed and coordinated. The number will depend largely upon the scope and extent of the responsibilities of the subordinates.
   B. No person should report to more than one supervisor. Every supervisor should know who reports to him, and every employee should know to whom he reports. Channels of authority and responsibility should not be violated by staff units.
   C. Relationships between organizational units within the agency and with outside organizations and associations should be clearly stated and thoroughly understood to avoid misunderstanding.

DELEGATING

I. WHAT IS DELEGATING?
Delegating is assigning a job to an employee, giving him the authority to get that job done, and giving him the responsibility for seeing to it that the job is done.

   A. What To Delegate
      1. Routine details
      2. Jobs which may be necessary and take a lot of time, but do not have to be done by the supervisor personally (preparing reports, attending meetings, etc.)
      3. Routine decision-making (making decisions which do not require the supervisor's personal attention)

   B. What Not To Delegate
      1. Job details which are *executive functions* (setting goals, organizing employees into a good team, analyzing results so as to plan for the future)
      2. Disciplinary power (handling grievances, preparing service ratings, reprimands, etc.)
      3. Decision-making which involves large numbers of employees or other bureaus and departments
      4. Final and complete responsibility for the job done by the unit being supervised

   C. Why Delegate?
      1. To strengthen the organization by developing a greater number of skilled employees
      2. To improve the employee's performance by giving him the chance to learn more about the job, handle some responsibility, and become more interested in getting the job done
      3. To improve a supervisor's performance by relieving him of routine jobs and giving him more time for *executive functions* (planning, organizing, controlling, etc.) which cannot be delegated

II. TO WHOM TO DELEGATE
People with abilities not being used. Selection should be based on ability, not on favoritism.

REPORTS

I. **DEFINITION**
A report is an orderly presentation of factual information directed to a specific reader for a specific purpose

II. **PURPOSE**
The general purpose of a report is to bring to the reader useful and factual information about a condition or a problem. Some specific purposes of a report may be:

   A. To enable the reader to appraise the efficiency or effectiveness of a person or an operation
   B. To provide a basis for establishing standards
   C. To reflect the results of expenditures of time, effort, and money
   D. To provide a basis for developing or altering programs

III. **TYPES**

   A. Information Report: Contains facts arranged in sequence
   B. Summary (Examination) Report: Contains facts plus an analysis or discussion of the significance of the facts. Analysis may give advantages and disadvantages or give qualitative and quantitative comparisons
   C. Recommendation Report: Contains facts, analysis, and conclusion logically drawn from the facts and analysis, plus a recommendation based upon the facts, analysis, and conclusions

IV. **FACTORS TO CONSIDER BEFORE WRITING REPORT**

   A. <u>Why</u> write the report?: The purpose of the report should be clearly defined.
   B. <u>Who</u> will read the report?: What level of language should be used? Will the reader understand professional or technical language?
   C. <u>What</u> should be said?: What does the reader need or want to know about the subject?
   D. <u>How</u> should it be said?: Should the subject be presented tactfully? Convincingly? In a stimulating manner?

V. **PREPARATORY STEPS**

   A. Assemble the facts: Find out who, why, what, where, when, and how.
   B. Organize the facts: Eliminate unnecessary information
   C. Prepare an outline: Check for orderliness, logical sequence
   D. Prepare a draft: Check for correctness, clearness, completeness, conciseness, and tone
   E. Prepare it in final form: Check for grammar, punctuation, appearance

VI. **OUTLINE FOR A RECOMMENDATION REPORT**

   Is the report:
   A. Correct in information, grammar, and tone?
   B. Clear?
   C. Complete?

D. Concise?
E. Timely?
F. Worth its cost?

Will the report accomplish its purpose?

MANAGEMENT CONTROLS

I. CONTROL

What is control? What is controlled? Who controls?

The essence of control is action which adjusts operations to predetermined standards, and its basis is information in the hands of managers. Control is checking to determine whether plans are being observed and suitable progress toward stated objectives is being made, and action is taken, if necessary, to correct deviations.

We have a ready-made model for this concept of control in the automatic systems which are widely used for process control in the chemical land petroleum industries. A process control system works this way. Suppose, for example, it is desired to maintain a constant rate of flow of oil through a pipe at a predetermined or set-point value. A signal, whose strength represents the rate of flow, can be produced in a measuring device and transmitted to a control mechanism. The control mechanism, when it detects any deviation of the actual from the set-point signal, will reposition the value regulating flow rate.

II. BASIS FOR CONTROL

A process control mechanism thus acts to adjust operations to predetermined standards and does so on the basis of information it receives. In a parallel way, information reaching a manager gives him the opportunity for corrective action and is his basis for control. He cannot exercise control without such information, and he cannot do a complete job of managing without controlling.

III. POLICY

What is policy?

Policy is simply a statement of an organization's intention to act in certain ways when specified types of circumstances arise. It represents a general decision, predetermined and expressed as a principle or rule, establishing a normal pattern of conduct for dealing with given types of business events—usually recurrent. A statement is therefore useful in economizing the time of managers and in assisting them to discharge their responsibilities equitably and consistently.

Policy is not a means of control, but policy does generate the need for control.

Adherence to policies is not guaranteed nor can it be taken on faith. It has to be verified. Without verification, there is no basis for control. Policy and procedures, although closely related and interdependent to a certain extent, are not synonymous. A policy may be adopted, for example, to maintain a materials inventory not to exceed one million dollars.

A procedure for inventory control could interpret that policy and convert it into methods for keeping within that limit, with consideration, too, of possible but foreseeable expedient deviation.

IV. PROCEDURE

What is procedure?

A procedure specifically prescribes:
A. What work is to be performed by the various participants
B. Who are the respective participants
C. When and where the various steps in the different processes are to be performed
D. The sequence of operations that will insure uniform handling of recurring transactions
E. The paper that is involved, its origin, transition, and disposition

Necessary appurtenances to a procedure are:
A. Detailed organizational chart
B. Flow charts
C. Exhibits of forms, all presented in close proximity to the text of the procedure

V. BASIS OF CONTROL – INFORMATION IN THE HANDS OF MANAGERS

If the basis of control is information in the hands of managers, then reporting is elevated to a level of very considerable importance.

Types of reporting may include:
A. Special reports and routine reports
B. Written, oral, and graphic reports
C. Staff meetings
D. Conferences
E. Television screens
F. Non-receipt of information, as where management is by exception
G. Any other means whereby information is transmitted to a manager as a basis for control action

FRAMEWORK OF MANAGEMENT

I. ELEMENTS

A. Policy: It has to be verified, controlled.

B. Organization is part of the giving of an assignment. The organizational chart gives to each individual in his title, a first approximation of the nature of his assignment and orients him as being accountable to a certain individual. Organization is not in a true sense a means of control. Control is checking to ascertain whether the assignment is executed as intended and acting on the basis of that information.

C. Budgets perform three functions:
1. They present the objectives, plans, and programs of the organization in financial terms.

2. They report the progress of actual performance against these predetermined objectives, plans, and programs.
3. Like organizational charts, delegations of authority, procedures, and job descriptions, they define the assignments which have flowed from the Chief Executive. Budgets are a means of control in the respect that they report progress of actual performance against the program. They provide information which enables managers to take action directed toward bringing actual results into conformity with the program.

D. Internal Check provides in practice for the principle that the same person should not have responsibility for all phases of a transaction. This makes it clearly an aspect of organization rather than of control. Internal Check is static, or built-in.

E. Plans, Programs, Objectives
People must know what they are trying to do. Objectives fulfill this need. Without them, people may work industriously and yet, working aimlessly, accomplish little. Plans and Programs complement Objectives, since they propose how and according to what time schedule the objectives are to be reached.

F. Delegations of Authority
Among the ways we have for supplementing the titles and lines of authority of an organizational chart are delegations of authority. Delegations of authority clarify the extent of authority of individuals and in that way serve to define assignments. That they are not means of control is apparent from the very fact that wherever there has been a delegation of authority, the need for control increases. This could hardly be expected to happen if delegations of authority were themselves means of control.

II. MANAGER'S RESPONSIBILITY

Control becomes necessary whenever a manager delegates authority to a subordinate because he cannot delegate and then simply sit back and forget4 about it. A manager's accountability to his own superior has not diminished one whit as a result of delegating part of his authority to a subordinate. The manager must exercise control over actions taken under the authority so delegated. That means checking serves as a basis for possible corrective action.

Objectives, plans, programs, organizational charts, and other elements of the managerial system are not fruitfully regarded as either controls or means of control. They are pre-established standards or models of performance to which operations are adjusted by the exercise of management control. These standards or models of performance are dynamic in character for they are constantly altered, modified, or revised. Policies, organizational set-up, procedures, delegations, etc. are constantly altered but, like objectives and plans, they remain in force until they are either abandoned or revised. All of the elements (or standards or models of performance), objectives, plans, and programs, policies, organization, etc. can be regarded as a *framework of management*.

III. CONTROL TECHNIQUES

Examples of control techniques:
A. Compare against established standards
B. Compare with a similar operation
C. Compare with past operations
D. Compare with predictions of accomplishment

IV. WHERE FORECASTS FIT

Control is after-the-fact while forecasts are before. Forecasts and projections are important for setting objectives and formulating plans.

Information for aiming and planning does not have to be before-the-fact. It may be an after-the-fact analysis proving that a certain policy has been impolitic in its effect on the relation of the company or department with customer, employee, taxpayer, or stockholder; or that a certain plan is no longer practical, or that a certain procedure is unworkable.

The prescription here certainly would not be in control (in these cases, control would simply bring operations into conformity with obsolete standards) but the establishment of new standards, a new policy, a new plan, and a new procedure to be controlled too.

Information is, of course, the basis for all communication in addition to furnishing evidence to management of the need for reconstructing the framework of management.

PROBLEM SOLVING

The accepted concept in modern management for problem solving is the utilization of the following steps:

A. Identify the problem
B. Gather data
C. List possible solutions
D. Test possible solutions
E. Select the best solution
F. Put the solution into actual practice

Occasions might arise where you would have to apply the second step of gathering data before completing the first step.

You might also find that it will be necessary to work on several steps at the same time.

I. IDENTIFY THE PROBLEM

Your first step is to define as precisely as possible the problem to be solved. While this may sound easy, it is often the most difficult part of the process.

It has been said of problem solving that you are halfway to the solution when you can write out a clear statement of the problem itself.

Our job now is to get below the surface manifestations of the trouble and pinpoint the problem. This is usually accomplished by a logical analysis, by going from the general to the particular; from the obvious to the not-so-obvious cause.

Let us say that production is behind schedule. WHY? Absenteeism is high. Now, is absenteeism the basic problem to be tackled, or is it merely a symptom of low morale among the workforce? Under these circumstances, you may decide that production is not the problem; the problem is *employee morale*.

In trying to define the problem, remember there is seldom one simple reason why production is lagging, or reports are late, etc.

Analysis usually leads to the discovery that an apparent problem is really made up of several subproblems which must be attacked separately.

Another way is to limit the problem, and thereby ease the task of finding a solution, and concentrate on the elements which are within the scope of your control.

When you have gone this far, write out a tentative statement of the problem to be solved.

II. GATHER DATA

In the second step, you must set out to collect all the information that might have a bearing on the problem. Do not settle for an assumption when reasonable fact and figures are available.

If you merely go through the motions of problem-solving, you will probably shortcut the information-gathering step. Therefore, do not stack the evidence by confining your research to your own preconceived ideas.

As you collect facts, organize them in some form that helps you make sense of them and spot possible relationships between them. For example, plotting cost per unit figures on a graph can be more meaningful than a long column of figures.

Evaluate each item as you go along. Is the source material absolutely, reliable, probably reliable, or not to be trusted.

One of the best methods for gathering data is to go out and look the situation over carefully. Talk to the people on the job who are most affected by this problem.

Always keep in mind that a primary source is usually better than a secondary source of information.

III. LIST POSSIBLE SOLUTIONS

This is the creative thinking step of problem solving. This is a good time to bring into play whatever techniques of group dynamics the agency or bureau might have developed for a joint attack on problems.

Now the important thing for you to do is: Keep an open mind. Let your imagination roam freely over the facts you have collected. Jot down every possible solution that occurs to you. Resist the temptation to evaluate various proposals as you go along. List seemingly absurd ideas along with more plausible ones. The more possibilities you list during this step, the less risk you will run of settling for merely a workable, rather than the best, solution.

Keep studying the data as long as there seems to be any chance of deriving additional ideas, solutions, explanations, or patterns from it.

IV. TEST POSSIBLE SOLUTIONS

Now you begin to evaluate the possible solutions. Take pains to be objective. Up to this point, you have suspended judgment but you might be tempted to select a solution you secretly favored all along and proclaim it as the best of the lot.

The secret of objectivity in this phase is to test the possible solutions separately, measuring each against a common yardstick. To make this yardstick try to enumerate as many specific criteria as you can think of. Criteria are best phrased as questions which you ask of each possible solution. They can be drawn from these general categories:

- Suitability – Will this solution do the job?
  Will it solve the problem completely or partially?
  Is it a permanent or a stopgap solution?

- Feasibility - Will this plan work in actual practice?
  Can we afford this approach?
  How much will it cost?

- Acceptability - Will the boss go along with the changes required in the plan?
  Are we trying to drive a tack with a sledge hammer?

V. SELECT THE BEST SOLUTION

This is the area of executive decision.

Occasionally, one clearly superior solution will stand out at the conclusion of the testing process. But often it is not that simple. You may find that no one solution has come through all the tests with flying colors.

You may also find that a proposal, which flunked miserably on one of the essential tests, racked up a very high score on others.

The best solution frequently will turn out to be a combination.

Try to arrange a marriage that will bring together the strong points of one possible solution with the particular virtues of another. The more skill and imagination that you apply, the greater is the likelihood that you will come out with a solution that is not merely adequate and workable, but is the best possible under the circumstances.

VI. PUT THE SOLUTION INTO ACTUAL PRACTICE

As every executive knows, a plan which works perfectly on paper may develop all sorts of bugs when put into actual practice.

Problem-solving does not stop with selecting the solution which looks best in theory. The next step is to put the chosen solution into action and watch the results. The results may point towards modifications.

If the problem disappears when you put your solution into effect, you know you have the right solution.

If it does not disappear, even after you have adjusted your plan to cover unforeseen difficulties that turned up in practice, work your way back through the problem-solving solutions.

> Would one of them have worked better?
> Did you overlook some vital piece of data which would have given you a different slant on the whole situation? Did you apply all necessary criteria in testing solutions? If no light dawns after this much rechecking, it is a pretty good bet that you defined the problem incorrectly in the first place.

You came up with the wrong solution because you tackled the wrong problem.

Thus, step six may become step one of a new problem-solving cycle.

COMMUNICATION

I. WHAT IS COMMUNICATION?
We communicate through writing, speaking, action, or inaction. In speaking to people face-to-face, there is opportunity to judge reactions and to adjust the message. This makes the supervisory chain one of the most, and in many instances the most, important channels of communication.

In an organization, communication means keeping employees informed about the organization's objectives, policies, problems, and progress. Communication is the free interchange of information, ideas, and desirable attitudes between and among employees and between employees and management.

II. WHY IS COMMUNICATION NEEDED?

   A. People have certain social needs
   B. Good communication is essential in meeting those social needs
   C. While people have similar basic needs, at the same time they differ from each other
   D. Communication must be adapted to these individual differences

An employee cannot do his best work unless he knows why he is doing it. If he has the feeling that he is being kept in the dark about what is going on, his enthusiasm and productivity suffer.

Effective communication is needed in an organization so that employees will understand what the organization is trying to accomplish; and how the work of one unit contributes to or affects the work of other units in the organization and other organizations.

III. HOW IS COMMUNICATION ACHIEVED?

Communication flows downward, upward, sideways.

A. Communication may come from top management down to employees. This is downward communication.

   Some means of downward communication are:
   1. Training (orientation, job instruction, supervision, public relations, etc.)
   2. Conferences
   3. Staff meetings
   4. Policy statements
   5. Bulletins
   6. Newsletters
   7. Memoranda
   8. Circulation of important letters

   In downward communication, it is important that employees be informed in advance of changes that will affect them.

B. Communications should also be developed so that the ideas, suggestions, and knowledge of employees will flow upward to top management.

   Some means of upward communication are:
   1. Personal discussion conferences
   2. Committees
   3. Memoranda
   4. Employees suggestion program
   5. Questionnaires to be filled in giving comments and suggestions about proposed actions that will affect field operations.

   Upward communication requires that management be willing to listen, to accept, and to make changes when good ideas are present. Upward communication succeeds when there is no fear of punishment for speaking out or lack of interest at the top. Employees will share their knowledge and ideas with management when interest is shown and recognition is given.

C. The advantages of downward communication:
   1. It enables the passing down of orders, policies, and plans necessary to the continued operation of the station.
   2. By making information available, it diminishes the fears and suspicions which result from misinformation and misunderstanding.
   3. It fosters the pride people want to have in their work when they are told of good work.
   4. It improves the morale and stature of the individual to be *in the know*.

21

5. It helps employees to understand, accept, and cooperate with changes when they know about them in advance.

D. The advantages of upward communication:
1. It enables the passing upward of information, attitudes, and feelings.
2. It makes it easier to find out how ready people are to receive downward communication.
3. It reveals the degree to which the downward communication is understood and accepted.
4. It helps to satisfy the basic social needs.
5. It stimulates employees to participate in the operation of their organization.
6. It encourage employees to contribute ideas for improving the efficiency and economy of operations.
7. It helps to solve problem situations before they reach the explosion point.

IV. WHY DOES COMMUNICATION FAIL?

A. The technical difficulties of conveying information clearly
B. The emotional content of communication which prevents complete transmission
C. The fact that there is a difference between what management needs to say, what it wants to day, and what it does say
D. The fact that there is a difference between what employees would like to say, what they think is profitable or safe to say, and what they do say

V. HOW TO IMPROVE COMMUNICATION

As a supervisor, you are a key figure in communication. To improve as a communicator, you should:
A. Know: Knowing your subordinates will help you to recognize and work with individual differences.
B. Like: If you like those who work for you and those for whom you work, this will foster the kind of friendly, warm, work atmosphere that will facilitate communication.
C. Trust: Showing a sincere desire to communicate will help to develop the mutual trust and confidence which are essential to the free flow of communication.
D. Tell: Tell your subordinates and superiors *what's doing*. Tell your subordinates *why* as well as *how*.
E. Listen: By listening, you help others to talk and you create good listeners. Don't forget that listening implies action.
F. Stimulate: Communication has to be stimulated and encouraged. Be receptive to ideas and suggestions and motivate your people so that each member of the team identifies himself with the job at hand.
G. Consult: The most effective way of consulting is to let your people participate, insofar as possible, in developing determinations which affect them or their work.

VI. HOW TO DETERMINE WHETHER YOU ARE GETTING ACROSS

A. Check to see that communication is received and understood
B. Judge this understanding by actions rather than words
C. Adapt or vary communication, when necessary
D. Remember that good communication cannot cure all problems

VII. THE KEY ATTITUDE

Try to see things from the other person's point of view. By doing this, you help to develop the permissive atmosphere and the shared confidence and understanding which are essential to effective two-way communication.

Communication is a two-way process:
A. The basic purpose of any communication is to get action.
B. The only way to get action is through acceptance.
C. In order to get acceptance, communication must be humanly satisfying as well as technically efficient.

HOW ORDERS AND INSTRUCTIONS SHOULD BE GIVEN

I. CHARACTERISTICS OF GOOD ORDERS AND INSTRUCTIONS

  A. Clear
  Orders should be definite as to
  —What is to be done
  —Who is to do it
  —When it is to be done
  —Where it is to be done
  —How it is to be done

  B. Concise
  Avoid wordiness. Orders should be brief and to the point.

  C. Timely
  Instructions and orders should be sent out at the proper time and not too long in advance of expected performance.

  D. Possibility of Performance
  Orders should be feasible:
  1. Investigate before giving orders
  2. Consult those who are to carry out instructions before formulating and issuing them

  E. Properly Directed
  Give the orders to the people concerned. Do not send orders to people who are not concerned. People who continually receive instructions that are not applicable to them get in the habit of neglecting instructions generally.

  F. Reviewed Before Issuance
  Orders should be reviewed before issuance:
  1. Test them by putting yourself in the position of the recipient
  2. If they involve new procedures, have the persons who are to do the work review them for suggestions.

  G. Reviewed After Issuance
  Persons who receive orders should be allowed to raise questions and to point out unforeseen consequences of orders.

23

   H. Coordinated
   Orders should be coordinated so that work runs smoothly.

   I. Courteous
   Make a request rather than a demand. There is no need to continually call attention to the fact that you are the boss.

   J. Recognizable as an Order
   Be sure that the order is recognizable as such.

   K. Complete
   Be sure recipient has knowledge and experience sufficient to carry out order. Give illustrations and examples.

A DEPARTMENTAL PERSONNEL OFFICE IS RESPONSIBLE FOR THE FOLLOWING FUNCTIONS

1. Policy
2. Personnel Programs
3. Recruitment and Placement
4. Position Classification
5. Salary and Wage Administration
6. Employee performance Standards and Evaluation
7. Employee Relations
8. Disciplinary Actions and Separations
9. Health and Safety
10. Staff Training and Development
11. Personnel Records, Procedures, and Reports
12. Employee Services
13. Personnel Research

SUPERVISION

I. LEADERSHIP

All leadership is based essentially on authority. This comes from two sources: It is received from higher management or it is earned by the supervisor through his methods of supervision. Although effective leadership has always depended upon the leader's using his authority in such a way as to appeal successfully to the motives of the people supervised, the conditions for making this appeal are continually changing. The key to today's problem of leadership is flexibility and resourcefulness on the part of the leader in meeting changes in conditions as they occur.

Three basic approaches to leadership are generally recognized:

A. The Authoritarian Approach
   1. The methods and techniques used in this approach emphasize the / in leadership and depend primarily on the formal authority of the leader. This authority is sometimes exercised in a hardboiled manner and sometimes in a benevolent

manner, but in either case the dominating role of the leader is reflected in the thinking, planning, and decisions of the group.
2. Group results are to a large degree dependent on close supervision by the leader. Usually, the individuals in the group will not show a high degree of initiative or acceptance of responsibility and their capacity to grow and develop probably will not be fully utilized. The group may react with resentment or submission, depending upon the manner and skill of the leader in using his authority.
3. This approach develops as a natural outgrowth of the authority that goes with the leader's job and his feeling of sole responsibility for getting the job done. It is relatively easy to use and does not require must resourcefulness.
4. The use of this approach is effective in times of emergencies, in meeting close deadline as a final resort, in settling some issues, in disciplinary matters, and with dependent individuals and groups.

B. The Laissez-Faire or Let 'em Alone Approach
1. This approach generally is characterized by an avoidance of leadership responsibility by the leader. The activities of the group depend largely on the choice of its members rather than the leader.
2. Group results probably will be poor. Generally, there will be disagreements over petty things, bickering, and confusion. Except for a few aggressive people, individuals will not show much initiative and growth and development will be retarded. There may be a tendency for informal leaders to take over leadership of the group.
3. This approach frequently results from the leader's dislike of responsibility, from his lack of confidence, from failure of other methods to work, from disappointment or criticism. It is usually the easiest of the three to use and requires both understanding and resourcefulness on the part of the leader.
4. This approach is occasionally useful and effective, particularly in forcing dependent individuals or groups to rely on themselves, to give someone a chance to save face by clearing his own difficulties, or when action should be delayed temporarily for good cause.

C. The Democratic Approach
1. The methods and techniques used in this approach emphasize the *we* in leadership and build up the responsibility of the group to attain its objectives. Reliance is placed largely on the earned authority of the leader.
2. Group results are likely to be good because most of the job motives of the people will be satisfied. Cooperation and teamwork, initiative, acceptance of responsibility, and the individual's capacity for growth probably will show a high degree of development.
3. This approach grows out of a desire or necessity of the leader to find ways to appeal effectively to the motivation of his group. It is the best approach to build up inside the person a strong desire to cooperate and apply himself to the job. It is the most difficult to develop, and requires both understanding and resourcefulness on the part of the leader.
4. The value of this approach increases over a long period where sustained efficiency and development of people are important. It may not be fully effective in all situations, however, particularly when there is not sufficient time to use it properly or where quick decisions must be made.

All three approaches are used by most leaders and have a place in supervising people. The extent of their use varies with individual leaders, with some using one approach predominantly. The leader who uses these three approaches, and varies their use with time and circumstance, is probably the most effective. Leadership which is used predominantly with a democratic approach requires more resourcefulness on the part of the leader but offers the greatest possibilities in terms of teamwork and cooperation.

The one best way of developing democratic leadership is to provide a real sense of participation on the part of the group, since this satisfies most of the chief job motives. Although there are many ways of providing participation, consulting as frequently as possible with individuals and groups on things that affect them seems to offer the most in building cooperation and responsibility. Consultation takes different forms, but it is most constructive when people feel they are actually helping in finding the answers to the problems on the job.

There are some requirements of leaders in respect to human relations which should be considered in their selection and development. Generally, the leader should be interested in working with other people, emotionally stable, self-confident, and sensitive to the reactions of others. In addition, his viewpoint should be one of getting the job done through people who work cooperatively in response to his leadership. He should have a knowledge of individual and group behavior, but, most important of all, he should work to combine all of these requirements into a definite, practical skill in leadership.

II. NINE POINTS OF CONTRAST BETWEEN *BOSS* AND *LEADER*

   A. The boss drives his men; the leader coaches them.
   B. The boss depends on authority; the leader on good will.
   C. The boss inspires fear; the leader inspires enthusiasm.
   D. The boss says I; the leader says *We*.
   E. The boss says *Get here on time*; the leader gets there ahead of time.
   F. The boss fixes the blame for the breakdown; the leader fixes the breakdown.
   G. The boss knows how it is done; the leader shows how.
   H. The boss makes work a drudgery; the leader makes work a game.
   I. The boss says *Go*; the leader says *Let's go*.

EMPLOYEE MORALE

Employee morale is the way employees feel about each other, the organization or unit in which they work, and the work they perform.

I. SOME WAYS TO DEVELOP AND MAINTAIN GOOD EMPLYEE MORALE

   A. Give adequate credit and praise when due.
   B. Recognize importance of all jobs and equalize load with proper assignments, always giving consideration to personality differences and abilities.
   C. Welcome suggestions and do not have an *all-wise* attitude. Request employees' assistance in solving problems and use assistants when conducting group meetings on certain subjects.
   D. Properly assign responsibilities and give adequate authority for fulfillment of such assignments.

E. Keep employees informed about matters that affect them.
F. Criticize and reprimand employees privately.
G. Be accessible and willing to listen.
H. Be fair.
I. Be alert to detect training possibilities so that you will not miss an opportunity to help each employee do a better job, and if possible with less effort on his part.
J. Set a good example.
K. Apply the golden rule.

II. SOME INDICATIONS OF GOOD MORALE

A. Good quality of work
B. Good quantity
C. Good attitude of employees
D. Good discipline
E. Teamwork
F. Good attendance
G. Employee participation

MOTIVATION

DRIVES

A drive, stated simply, is a desire or force which causes a person to do or say certain things. These are some of the most usual drives and some of their identifying characteristics recognizable in people motivated by such drives:

A. Security (desire to provide for the future)
   Always on time for work
   Works for the same employer for many years
   Never takes unnecessary chances
   Seldom resists doing what he is told

B. Recognition (desire to be rewarded for accomplishment)
   Likes to be asked for his opinion
   Becomes very disturbed when he makes a mistake
   Does things to attract attention
   Likes to see his name in print

C. Position (desire to hold certain status in relation to others)
   Boasts about important people he knows
   Wants to be known as a key man
   Likes titles
   Demands respect
   Belongs to clubs, for prestige

D. Accomplishment (desire to get things done)
   Complains when things are held up
   Likes to do things that have tangible results
   Never lies down on the job
   Is proud of turning out good work

E. Companionship (desire to associate with other people)
   Likes to work with others
   Tells stories and jokes
   Indulges in horseplay
   Finds excuses to talk to others on the job

F. Possession (desire to collect and hoard objects)
   Likes to collect things
   Puts his name on things belonging to him
   Insists on the same location

Supervisors may find that identifying the drives of employees is a helpful step toward motivating them to self-improvement and better job performance. For example: An employee's job performance is below average. His supervisor, having previously determined that the employee is motivated by a drive for security, suggests that taking training courses will help the employee to improve, advance, and earn more money. Since earning more money can be a step toward greater security, the employee's drive for security would motivate him to take the training suggested by the supervisor. In essence, this is the process of charting an employee's future course by using his motivating drives to positive advantage.

EMPLOYEE PARTICIPATION

I. WHAT IS PARTICIPATION

Employee participation is the employee's giving freely of his time, skill, and knowledge to an extent which cannot be obtained by demand.

II. WHY IS IT IMPORTANT?

The supervisor's responsibility is to get the job done through people. A good supervisor gets the job done through people who work willingly and well. The participation of employees is important because:

A. Employees develop a greater sense of responsibility when they share in working out operating plans and goals.
B. Participation provides greater opportunity and stimulation for employees to learn, and to develop their ability.
C. Participation sometimes provides better solutions to problems because such solutions may combine the experience and knowledge of interested employees who want the solutions to work.
D. An employee or group may offer a solution which the supervisor might hesitate to make for fear of demanding too much.

E. Since the group wants to make the solution work, they exert pressure in a constructive way on each other.
F. Participation usually results in reducing the need for close supervision.

II. HOW MAY SUPERVISORS OBTAIN IT?

Participation is encouraged when employees feel that they share some responsibility for the work and that their ideas are sincerely wanted and valued. Some ways of obtaining employee participation are:

A. Conduct orientation programs for new employees to inform them about the organization and their rights and responsibilities as employees.
B. Explain the aims and objectives of the agency. On a continuing basis, be sure that the employees know what these aims and objectives are.
C. Share job successes and responsibilities and give credit for success.
D. Consult with employees, both as individuals and in groups, about things that affect them.
E. Encourage suggestions for job improvements. Help employees to develop good suggestions. The suggestions can bring them recognition. The city's suggestion program offers additional encouragement through cash awards.

The supervisor who encourages employee participation is not surrendering his authority. He must still make decisions and initiate action, and he must continue to be ultimately responsible for the work of those he supervises. But, through employee participation, he is helping his group to develop greater ability and a sense of responsibility while getting the job done faster and better.

STEPS IN HANDLING A GRIEVANCE

1. Get the Facts
    a. Listen sympathetically
    b. Let him talk himself out
    c. Get his story straight
    d. Get his point of view
    e. Don't argue with him
    f. Give him plenty of time
    g. Conduct the interview privately
    h. Don't try to shift the blame or pass the buck

2. Consider the Facts
    a. Consider the employee's viewpoint
    b. How will the decision affect similar cases
    c. Consider each decision as a possible precedent
    d. Avoid snap judgments—don't jump to conclusions

3. Make or Get a Decision
    a. Frame an effective counter-proposal
    b. Make sure it is fair to all
    c. Have confidence in your judgment
    d. Be sure you can substantiate your decision

4. Notify the Employee of Your Decision
   Be sure he is told; try to convince him that the decision is fair and just.

5. Take Action When Needed and If Within Your Authority
   Otherwise, tell employee that the matter will be called to the attention of the proper person or that nothing can be done, and why it cannot.

6. Follow through to see that the desired result is achieved.

7. Record key facts concerning the complaint and the action taken.

8. Leave the way open to him to appeal your decision to a higher authority.

9. Report all grievances to your superior, whether they are appealed or not.

DISCIPLINE

Discipline is training that develops self-control, orderly conduct, and efficiency.

To discipline does not necessarily mean to punish.

To discipline does mean to train, to regulate, and to govern conduct.

I. THE DISCIPLINARY INTERVIEW

Most employees sincerely want to do what is expected of them. In other words, they are self-disciplined. Some employees, however, fail to observe established rules and standards, and disciplinary action by the supervisor is required.

The primary purpose of disciplinary action is to improve conduct without creating dissatisfaction, bitterness, or resentment in the process.

Constructive disciplinary action is more concerned with causes and explanations of breaches of conduct than with punishment. The disciplinary interview is held to get at the causes of apparent misbehavior and to motivate better performance in the future.

It is important that the interview be kept on an impersonal a basis as possible. If the supervisor lets the interview descend to the plane of an argument, it loses its effectiveness.

II. PLANNING THE INTERVIEW

Get all pertinent facts concerning the situation so that you can talk in specific terms to the employee.

Review the employee's record, appraisal ratings, etc.

Consider what you know about the temperament of the employee. Consider your attitude toward the employee. Remember that the primary requisite of disciplinary action is fairness.

Don't enter upon the interview when angry.

Schedule the interview for a place which is private and out of hearing of others.

III. CONDUCTING THE INTERVIEW

A. Make an effort to establish accord.
B. Question the employee about the apparent breach of discipline. Be sure that the question is not so worded as to be itself an accusation.
C. Give the employee a chance to tell his side of the story. Give him ample opportunity to talk.
D. Use understanding—listening except where it is necessary to ask a question or to point out some details of which the employee may not be aware. If the employee misrepresents facts, make a plain, accurate statement of the facts, but don't argue and don't engage in personal controversy.
E. Listen and try to understand the reasons for the employee's (mis)conduct. First of all, don't assume that there has been a breach of discipline. Evaluate the employee's reasons for his conduct in the light of his opinions and feelings concerning the consistency and reasonableness of the standards which he was expected to follow. Has the supervisor done his part in explaining the reasons for the rule? Was the employee's behavior unintentional or deliberate? Does he think he had real reasons for his actions? What new facts is he telling? Do the facts justify his actions? What causes, other than those mentioned, could have stimulated the behavior?
F. After listening to the employee's version of the situation, and if censure of his actions is warranted, the supervisor should proceed with whatever criticism is justified. Emphasis should be placed on future improvement rather than exclusively on the employee's failure to measure up to expected standards of job conduct.
G. Fit the criticism to the individual. With one employee, a word of correction may be all that is required.
H. Attempt to distinguish between unintentional error and deliberate misbehavior. An error due to ignorance requires training and not censure.
I. Administer criticism in a controlled, even tone of voice, never in anger. Make it clear that you are acting as an agent of the department. In general, criticism should refer to the job or the employee's actions and not to the person. Criticism of the employee's work is not an attack on the individual.
J. Be sure the interview does not destroy the employee's self-confidence. Mention his good qualities and assure him that you feel confident that he can improve his performance.
K. Wherever possible, before the employee leaves the interview, satisfy him that the incident is closed, that nothing more will be said on the subject unless the offense is repeated.

www.ingramcontent.com/pod-product-compliance
Lightning Source LLC
Chambersburg PA
CBHW081800300426
44116CB00014B/2186